MUSSOLINI

An Intimate Biography
by His Widow

MUSSOLINI

An Intimate Biography
by His Widow

Rachele Mussolini

as told to
ALBERT ZARCA

1974
WILLIAM MORROW & COMPANY, INC., NEW YORK

Published in the United States in 1974.

English translation copyright © 1973 by
Rachele Mussolini.

French edition published by Librairie Artheme Fayard under
the title Mussolini Sans Masque © 1973 by Librairie Artheme
Fayard.

Published in Great Britain in 1973 under the title *The Real
Mussolini.*

Printed in the United States of America.

1 2 3 4 5   78 77 76 75 74

Design by Helen Roberts

Library of Congress Cataloging in Publication Data

Mussolini, Rachele (Guidi) 1892-
    Mussolini: an intimate biography by his widow,
Rachele Mussolini.

    French ed. has title: Mussolini sans masque.
    1. Mussolini, Benito, 1883-1945. I. Zarca, Albert.
II. Title.
DG575.M8M8352   945.091′092′4 [B]   74-1129
ISBN 0-688-00266-8

Contents

PUBLISHER'S NOTE

A chronology of the events in
Mussolini's life and career will
be found following the main text.

1/ Mussolini and Destiny

"Remember Napoleon, Benito, since you admire him so much. True, he was powerful; he mastered Europe and even ruled countries farther afield. But what did he really do? As soon as he won one victory, he looked for more. After each conquest, he still wanted a bigger empire. And what happened to him, Benito? He lost the lot! Everything crumbled under his feet. Don't be like him. Remember that song we sang when we were children: 'Napoleon with all his superb . . . wound up on Elba.' "

"What do you want me to do? Resign? Raise chickens in Romagna? You must be joking, Rachele."

"No, I don't want you to raise chickens in Romagna. I want you to stop in time, to become part of history while you're still alive, to devote ten or fifteen years of your life to your wife and children after giving thirty to politics. Political life is too dirty to be good all the time. So far you've been lucky, you've known only the good times, but watch out from now on."

This conversation occurred in May, 1936, when my husband, Benito Mussolini, and I were staying at Rocca delle Caminate, our home in Romagna. A few days earlier, Benito had stood on the balcony of the Palazzo Venezia, announcing

1

to an ecstatic crowd the creation of the Empire after the Ethiopian conquest. Now we were alone, and nobody heard me entreating him to abandon power.

On the surface, there was nothing to warrant such a step. At the time Benito, who was not yet fifty-three (he was born on July 29, 1883), was in perfect health. And in a political sense he had never been so strong either in Italy or abroad. Our armies had crushed the Ethiopians completely. The lira flourished as one of Europe's most stable currencies, and the League of Nations' sanctions—imposed on Italy after the Ethiopian adventure—had failed. With patriotic fervor, the Italian people had themselves helped thwart the sanctions by giving their gold to the government. In Rome, for instance, the Queen and I had been among 250,000 women who had cast their wedding rings into a brazier on the marble base of the Tomb of the Unknown Soldier. And in 1935, numerous Italians living in the United States had ingeniously sent the tons of copper that Italy so badly needed—inventing a special copper postcard engraved with Christmas greetings.

Even such prominent opponents of Benito as the philosopher Benedetto Croce and the former prime minister Vittorio Emmanuele Orlando had recently acted with my husband, whom foreign powers were hailing as "a realist," "influential," and "wise."

There were no black clouds to darken the horizon, yet I could not resist the urge to persuade my husband to quit the political scene, my desire doubtless fostered by the marvelous weather that enhanced our family holiday at Rocca delle Caminate. Two of our children, Vittorio and Bruno, who were pilots, had just returned safely from combat in Ethiopia, and we were especially happy to have them with us again.

I seized my chance one afternoon after a long drive through the Romagnole countryside. Soon after lunch, unescorted by secretary, prefect, or security police, we'd gone out alone in our Alfa Romeo Spider. Benito was wearing a beret pulled low over his forehead, and I had a scarf knotted under my chin, and we were enjoying ourselves like twenty-year-olds.

We'd stopped several times at peasant houses—as was Benito's habit in Romagna—and, as always happened, after the first few moments of surprise and emotion, Benito and the locals began chatting about the crop, the cows, the house, and the children. To the people of Romagna he was still "Muslen," the son of Alessandro the *fabbroferraio*, or blacksmith. I'd had to tug at his sleeve to remind him of the time.

So for the moment, he was alone with me in the garden, splitting logs with his sleeves rolled up, while I poked about in a bed of roses. Occasionally I glanced at him, and seeing him with his tanned skin, a hint of gentleness in his mature expression, I could almost understand why women fell on his neck, at his feet, or into the sea when he went bathing.

Once he had chopped the logs, Benito called, "You know what the King suggested the other day? He wanted to make me a prince."

"I hope you didn't accept."

"Are you joking? Can you see me arriving somewhere with the usher announcing 'His Excellency Prince Mussolini'?"

"And I'd be Princess Rachele Mussolini! Lord, what an idea!"

"Don't worry. I kept a straight face, though the thought of my head beneath a crown made me want to laugh out loud, and I answered: 'Majesty, I'm touched by this gesture, but I cannot accept. I was born Mussolini and I'll die Mussolini, without title.'"

"And what did the King say?"

"'You could at least take a dukedom.' Again I refused." Then, pretending to look upset, Benito added, "You won't be Princess Mussolini or the Duchess of Rocca delle Caminate. You'll stay Rachele Mussolini."

And we began to laugh. I could scarcely believe this story and had to make Benito swear it was true. Then he went on,

"I know someone who'd dearly have liked to be made a duke
—your 'cousin,' the Marquis of Sabotino."

"Badoglio? He already has the Collar of the Annunziata
and a marquisate. Isn't that enough?"

"Apparently not. We are happy with the Collar of the
Annunziata, but some people still want more."

Perhaps I should mention that the Collar of the Annunziata was the highest distinction the King could confer. My
husband had received the honor some years before, and it made
us honorary "cousins" to the King—just as we were "cousins"
of Marshal Pietro Badoglio, another holder of the decoration.

These relaxed moments offered too good an opportunity
to let slip. "Tell me, Benito. Suppose you went further. Suppose you said to the King, 'Your Majesty, you summoned me
to govern when the country was in chaos. I have restored
peace and prosperity at home and made Italy great and powerful abroad. Now the Italians aren't all 'ice-cream sellers' any-
more. They're proud of their country. Before me, you were
King of Italy. Now you are Emperor. Everything is going
well, so I am putting Italy back into your hands and I'm
resigning.' "

"In fact, you want to pension me off, do you?"

"No, Benito. You'll write articles, your memoirs. You've
your newspaper in Milan. It's going so well, we're even living
off it. I'm not asking you to retire completely. But think of all
you've done already for Italy. What more do you want to do?
Our country has never been so great or well respected. Look
back fifteen years. There was civil war then. And what have
we now?"

My husband stayed silent for a while. He listened, frowning slightly, more surprised than annoyed by my outburst. I
had stopped because I was scared I'd already gone too far.
But etched in my mind was the warning I'd been given by a
gypsy woman when I was sixteen. She'd predicted: "You will
receive the highest honors. In fact, you'll be the equal of a
queen. Then everything will crumble away, and there'll be a
time of mourning." I was aware that the first part of this

prediction had already come true. I'd been loaded with honors and was by now "cousin" to the Queen. But what about the other part of the prophecy? Suddenly I felt frightened.

"Think, Benito," I said. "Our children have grown up. We're happy, but we could be even happier. I know I'm selfish, but I'm also thinking of you. When you left for the royal palace in 1922 and later telephoned to tell me everything that had happened, what did I say to you? I told you that you were now the people's servant even though you were your own master. Now you can be what you were before, with the added weight of your success. You could be the arbiter, the man the people consult when there's a national problem. You could become part of history while you are still alive.

"No more decisions to be ratified, no more pitfalls to avoid, no more tensions or fears for yourself and the children. There are men waiting for you to make your first mistake so that they can scoff and say, 'Mussolini has fallen.' Cut the ground from under their feet."

I stopped, breathless. I'd put everything into my plea, for the first time in twenty-six years of anxiety, tears, joys—and love. For once I'd spoken my true feelings.

Benito took me tenderly by the arm, as if to protect me, his expression a trifle vague. Perhaps he was looking back over what he'd already achieved. I began to feel that I might succeed, that my dream might conceivably become reality. I put my hand on his and murmured, "Try, Benito, please."

"I'll see," he replied, his voice faint with emotion, as it was to be nine years later, during the final tragedy, when he called to ask me to take care of the children. "I'll think about it. Don't upset yourself over it, Rachele."

We went back to the house. On the steps I turned my head. The smell of burning wood was mingling with the scent of pine and flowers; the countryside was settling down for the night. The sunset over the misty hills of our Romagna had never seemed so lovely.

Some days later my husband left for Rome. We had not discussed his retirement again. I was waiting for the summer holidays at Riccione to do so. Besides, I knew that he was extremely busy and that it would be a tactical error to press him for a decision.

But on this occasion, time was against me, and the success of my own initiative was my undoing. As soon as he arrived in Rome, Benito told Achille Starace, the secretary of the National Fascist Party, about my suggestion, and even asked Starace to look into the practical aspects of his leaving.

Starace, frantic at the idea of Mussolini's resigning, alerted various officials of the regime. He and several others were loyal and decent. In their eyes the Duce's work was not over; he had to continue in government. There were also opportunists, whom Mussolini had brought out of obscurity, who confused Italy's interests with their own financial gain, and who were the first to desert him at times of trouble. This time, even they agreed that Mussolini must be prevented from resigning, whatever the cost. They'd plenty of arguments in their favor—among them Communist penetration in Spain, which had been behind the Duce's recent decision to send help to General Franco.

Finally, my husband agreed to stay in power. Apart from political reasons, there were several factors working against me. First, Benito had disclosed the proposal too soon, when I was not there to balance the scales with my own side of the argument. And then I'd forgotten how difficult it is for a man to give up what he has fought so hard to win. After years of hardship, Benito Mussolini was savoring the delights of triumph and the heady wine of glory.

Some days earlier, on the balcony of the Palazzo Venezia, he had watched the frenzied crowds yelling "Du-ce! Du-ce!" to show the Italian people's total support of his regime. It seems amazing that I had not remembered it, for I'd been there too—an anonymous face lost in the crowd, holding Romano and Anna-Maria, our two youngest children, and listening to his speech amplified through loudspeakers. With a lump in my throat, I'd been carried away by my own thoughts:

Suppose all these people knew that you were the wife of the man who is speaking, the man they are cheering—knew that this evening, at home, he'd ask: "Well, what did you think of my speech?"

A year later, in October, 1937, my husband had another opportunity to change the destiny of both himself and his country.

My son Vittorio, then a film producer, thought the American market—the most important in the world—would provide a profitable outlet for Italian films. At that time, the box-office revenue from American films shown on Italian screens was frozen in the banks. He planned, therefore, to use this capital to make films in Italy on, say, poetic subjects, and then to distribute these films in the United States. His exports of Italian culture would allow the Americans to make good their losses and would also bring work to our own industry. After preliminary approaches to the Americans, he planned a trip to the United States.

Vittorio feared his father would oppose the idea, since relations between the two countries were somewhat cool. Italy was helping General Franco to fight the Communists in Spain, a policy that the American government, if not the American people, freely criticized.

But Benito enthusiastically endorsed his son's idea, and Vittorio left for America. There he had talks and visited studios, and in general did what he had gone to do. Shortly before his return, he was told that the President and Mrs. Roosevelt wished to entertain him at the White House. This in itself came as no surprise, for Benito had welcomed the Roosevelts' son John at the Palazzo Venezia on a visit to Rome. Vittorio therefore thought that Roosevelt was merely being polite.

The invitation was for October 13, 1937. Also present were Fulvio Sulvich, the Italian ambassador in Washington, and William Phillips, his American counterpart in Rome. My son was received in the room from which Roosevelt broadcast his famous fireside chats to the American people. Eleanor

Roosevelt served tea during a dull formal chat about Vittorio's journey to the United States and John's to Italy. When the President joined them, he welcomed Vittorio warmly, asking him to prolong his stay and making flattering remarks about Italy.

Then, suddenly casting pleasantries aside, he said, "Will you please give my regards to the Italian Premier and tell him that I would dearly like to meet him? I would like to have a personal conversation with him so that we can get better acquainted with the problems of our two countries. Italy is the only non-Allied country with which the United States can maintain close relations without compromising its democratic traditions. This is because of Italy's history and geographical position, and because the seat of the Catholic Church is within her borders. Signor Mussolini is the only man who can keep a balance in Europe. Germany and Russia are at opposite poles from America, and we can do nothing with them.

"I know that Signor Mussolini cannot leave his country for long. I'm in the same position. So could you tell him that I suggest we meet in neutral waters—say, on a ship on the high seas? And I would be glad if we could meet next spring at the latest."

On his first evening back with us at the Villa Torlonia, Vittorio described his amazing conversation in Washington. Roosevelt had told Vittorio that he'd chosen less conventional channels to seek the meeting with my husband because he thought them better. The diplomats could deal with the details later.

Benito would have considered the proposal, even if he found the novelty of it American in flavor, but he doubted Roosevelt's sincerity; he would have preferred talks with a different President. He believed that, under his democratic exterior, Roosevelt was in fact running a dictatorship. Besides, he believed Roosevelt was making the same mistakes in regard to Europe as Wilson had. I remember how, in 1919, when Benito returned from the banquet given for Wilson in Milan, which he'd attended as editor of the *Popolo d'Italia,* he told me he'd been disappointed in the President and his self-centered politics.

In any case, Roosevelt's invitation came a month too late. At the end of September, 1937, Benito had returned from his triumphant five-day visit to Germany, and his relations with the Führer were by then too close for a change of sides.

And yet, if Roosevelt hadn't attacked Italy so fiercely for aiding Franco, had not linked fascism with communism and Nazism as the three scourges—thus dismissing Mussolini's restraining influence—something might have come of a meeting between them, especially as Benito was on excellent terms with the American press and was respected in the United States.

Indeed, in 1910 a Socialist newspaper had invited him to settle in the United States and edit the paper's daily edition. We had almost gone, but Benito gave up the idea because I was expecting our first child, Edda; he was afraid the trip would be too difficult for me.

When I was in a concentration camp at the end of the war, I told an American officer that my husband had been offered the chance to live in the United States. He replied, "You realize we could have had Benito Mussolini as president."

In fact, Benito Mussolini had other chances to change the course of events—perhaps even of history. Later his fate was often linked to the vagaries of war—to luck—but in the years before the outbreak of World War II, Mussolini held all the cards. He was in a position to make momentous decisions, totally independent of others. And each time, the head of government gave way to the man; the qualities and defects of the man took precedence over political considerations. Whether he was wrong or right it is not for me to judge, but I think these episodes merit a mention.

Even at the most crucial time in his life, Benito was true to himself by thinking first of others. This was on April 25,

1945, three days before his death, when he could have saved himself by taking refuge in Spain and perhaps meeting a different fate.

Years after the war, Vittorio told me that he'd worked out a plan that was complete save for one detail—his father's consent. On April 25, Vittorio outlined a plan to Air Marshal Bonomi that involved flying my husband to Spain. Bonomi confirmed that some three-engine planes were ready to leave Ghedi Aerodrome, near Brescia, and guaranteed to get Benito to Spain provided he left quickly.

That same day, Benito was in Milan. Now in control of the Prefecture, he had convened a succession of meetings to decide on future action. When Vittorio arrived at my husband's office in the morning, he found his father alone. Outside, the yard and corridors seethed with nervous activity; everybody searched madly for some solution to the insoluble problem of Italy's confusion at the end of the World War. Benito asked Vittorio what he wanted, and my son, fearing a sudden interruption, quickly described his plan. He said that, once safe in Spain, Benito could negotiate with the Allies and thus help Italy in her terrible dilemma. In fact, Vittorio tried every means to persuade my husband, as I had done when I appealed to him to resign in his hour of glory.

Benito listened, not reacting at all until Vittorio had finished. Then, smiling and pointing to the door through which came excited chatter, he asked: "You think that's the right solution? Fine. And have you a plane for all those Fascists outside and the Fascists in the north?"

To serve Italy, he had remained in office nine years earlier. Now, true to himself, he thought it his duty to stay with his followers in that fateful hour. I think he considered his attitude not heroic but simply logical.

2/ Mussolini's Stormy Courtship

In Italy and elsewhere, reactions varied strikingly when it was learned that I proposed to write my memories of Mussolini. Some people claimed that I'd portray him in a false light, trying to excuse his mistakes and persuade the world to forgive him.

Such people don't know me well. Intimates consider me objective and untainted by politics—a reputation that must have some basis, for in 1945, when my husband was dead and I in prison, a partisan secretly told me, "Donna Rachele, do not worry. We have received official orders from Moscow not to touch a hair of your head."

When Benito was at the height of power, I once even threatened to shout "Down with Mussolini" under his window in the Palazzo Venezia—in a public demonstration seeking to open his eyes to the treachery of followers whom he blindly trusted.

I have never looked for forgiveness for Mussolini, because I do not recognize that he did anything wrong. He made war, but was he the only head of government who ever did this? His crime was to have lost. True, he entered into an alliance with Hitler, but somewhere there are secret archives proving how strenuously he tried to safeguard peace. As for the other military and political leaders of his time, they hardly dare examine their consciences.

I want neither forgiveness for Mussolini nor pity for myself. Despite the tales that I was an abandoned wife, submissive to Benito and resigned to his infidelities, I can look back over eighty years and say that I have lived the life I wanted. At one time my private intelligence network, backed by police officials, made me the best-informed woman in Italy. My husband's liaisons were a problem for me. I admit that three women caused me great unhappiness—but where is the man who does not deceive his wife at some time or another? Anyone in the Duce's position was bound to attract attention.

If I were a boastful person I would say that of all the women Benito held in his arms I'm the only one qualified to write about the real Mussolini. I was the only one who really knew him. I'd known him since I was seven years old. We first met in 1900, when Benito was seventeen, ten years older than I.

He was the eldest of three children. His mother, Rosa Maltoni, who taught me at school, was as gentle and retiring as his father, Alessandro, was well-known in Romagna and even outside Italy. The Mussolinis lived in Dovia, a little village in the Predappio district deep in Romagna, where Alessandro eked out a living as a blacksmith. But his fame sprang from his activities as a Socialist revolutionary; many evenings in Romagna passed in his recounting his exploits. Alessandro's notoriety rested on his skill at smashing ballot boxes and terrorizing the royalist police—not that they ever missed a chance to march him off to prison under armed escort.

From his earliest years Benito gave his mother cause for concern. As a child, for instance, he was very slow in learning to talk. Finally his mother had him examined by a doctor, who immediately put her mind at rest. "Don't let it worry you," he assured her. "He will talk. He may even talk too much."

Later, his father imposed strong discipline, never hesitating to add blows to words when he wanted to make his point. In fact, Benito learned as much about life at the forge as he did from his father's conversations, which he scarcely understood. From the earliest moment, Alessandro was keen to instill the rudiments of socialism in his son. He even christened this first-born child Benito Amilcare Andrea in memory of three revolutionary heroes—Benito Juarez the Mexican and the Italians Amilcare Cipriani and Andrea Costa. He wanted his son to be properly educated. So Benito was sent to the primary school in Predappio, where he left scars on the heads of any school-fellows who disagreed with him.

Then, when he was nine, his parents sent him to Faenza, to a boarding school run by the Salesian fathers. Benito told me later that his record there was deplorable. He objected to the seating arrangements in the dining hall, where there was one table for the lower classes at thirty lire, another for the middle classes at forty-five lire, and a top table for the nobility at sixty lire. He never accepted his place at the lowest table. He fought more than ever and inflicted two blows for every one he received. In the end the principal was compelled to send him home.

In October, 1895, Benito attended the Royal Normal School in Forlimpopoli. Although he was involved in various escapades, he did well there. During his later years at the school, he began to hold political meetings with some success. At the age of seventeen he even wrote some articles for Forlì and Ravenna newspapers. As he had a good voice, the head-master once arranged for him to speak at a commemoration of Verdi in the municipal theater. To the surprise of his audience, Benito delivered a speech about the prevailing social conditions. *Avanti!*, the Socialist daily paper to which he was appointed editor some twelve years later, mentioned the incident briefly.

Meanwhile, I was in the second class at the primary school in Dovia. Although their land was sunny and fertile, the peasants of Romagna were continually in revolt against the establishment as embodied by the monarchy and the Church. It was not unusual for the driver to hold up a whole train if he saw a priest stepping on board. Generally speaking, the peasants were poor. My parents worked on one of the vast estates stretching along the slopes from Salto, where we lived, to the outskirts of Predappio-on-the-Hill. My family consisted of five sisters. We were all fairly lively, though I suspect I was the sharpest. Nicknamed "Fearless," I was slim, with blond hair and small, mischievous blue eyes. No one was better at climbing trees or catching birds than I.

When the time came for school, I was the only sister who decided to attend classes. I wanted to learn everything. My parents would rather have kept me at home, but I persevered and stormed until they agreed. I was even prepared to walk the five miles to school every day.

Because his mother was ill, Benito had returned home to take over her job teaching in the primary school in Dovia. He noticed me on the first day, not for the reasons that drove him to threaten suicide ten years later, but because I was wild in class—never still for a moment. I was so intent on tomfoolery that I didn't even notice the ruler descending on my knuckles. Half hurt and half angry, I put my hand to my mouth. Then I found myself staring into huge black eyes that expressed such willpower that, without really listening to the teacher's remarks, I immediately calmed down.

After this show of strength, I didn't see Benito again for nine years. However, I still heard talk of Mussolini—Alessandro Mussolini, that is—and a kind of aura seemed to surround the name.

When my father died suddenly, in 1901, leaving us destitute, we were forced to move to Forlì, where the family broke up. My mother went into service, and we were all put out to work.

And so at the age of eight I earned my first wages, of three lire a month. But it was purgatory; the vegetable sellers who employed me were hateful people, giving me an old sack full of crushed straw to sleep on in a small hut so cold it was used as a wine store. A young woman with tuberculosis had slept on the sack before me. But the worst torture was seeing the children of the house laughing around the table at mealtimes, while I was made to sit on the terrace with a cracked plate and an iron spoon. Blinking back my tears, I discovered the meaning of social inequality at a tender age.

I was only too glad to leave and work for a fencing master. His daughter and I used to enjoy watching his lessons and playing "musketeers" with sticks of wood. I did not stay there long, however, as his wife was scarcely a good influence.

My next employers, the Chiedini family, were the best. Although they were rich "conservatives"—the name we give the wealthy in Romagna—they were kind and affectionate to me. The future began to look brighter. My mother had finally found a permanent post at the little inn for which Alessandro Mussolini had left his blacksmith's trade after his wife's death, in 1905. Besides, I was sixteen by then, and at that age life always looks rosy, especially if one is pretty. I had too much good sense to lose my head over the compliments that came my way, but I enjoyed them.

The handsome young son of the Chiedinis' neighbors even proposed to me while we were walking through the vineyards one day. He swore to make me happy if I accepted him, adding persuasively that I was too beautiful to be a servant; I ought to be a princess, he said. But because he never lifted me onto his horse, I refused him.

Some days later, a gypsy woman told me my fortune, astonishing me by predicting that great things were in store for me. She gave me a small stone, saying, "Keep this, but give me a bag of flour." I could hardly refuse, and though my employers scolded me for it, with such promises for the future I didn't care. One day, the gypsy had said, I would be the equal of the Queen.

One Sunday in 1908, when I was leaving the church at Forlì with my employers' little girl, someone called my name. It was Benito Mussolini. He'd grown a moustache and a small beard, and he wore a loose necktie, a big black hat, and a threadbare suit with newspapers sticking out of the pockets. But what struck me the most of all was the gleam in his eyes, which now seemed larger than ever. Considering his skill as an orator later on, his opening gambit was scarcely original: "Hello, Chiletta [a diminutive of Rachele], you've grown. You're a young lady now." I should have replied in the same vein, but the expression in his eyes disturbed me.

As we walked on together, that sun-drenched day, I proudly noted how deferentially the passersby greeted Benito, and felt that some of their respect was reflected on me. Although we walked all the way back to the Chiedinis' house, I was careful not to tell them of our meeting, for I remembered the delight Signor Chiedini had taken in describing all the details of Benito's arrest a few days earlier.

Before he left, Benito asked, "Why don't you ever come and see your mother at my father's inn?"

"Because the Chiedinis have forbidden me to visit the house of a revolutionary," I replied. "But I'll ask the signora's permission."

Each time we met on subsequent Sundays, our affection for each other grew. Not that Benito ever played the great lover, but his very presence told me much. We went for long walks through the countryside, hardly speaking. Now and again, Benito would kick a stone out of the way as if he were dismissing an idea or an opponent, then turn to me and say, "We'll get rid of them in the end. We'll chase out the bourgeoisie, the rich landowners who get a good living from their estates without even bothering to cultivate them."

I had my own revolutionary ideas, but his forcefulness made me uneasy. I said, "They'll put you in prison, Benito, as they did before."

"So? I'm not ashamed to go to prison for reasons like that. I'd be proud. I'm not a murderer or a thief."

One Sunday Signora Chiedini gave me permission to visit

the Mussolinis' inn. I went in the morning and helped to wait at table; then, after lunch, Benito and I went dancing. He was a fine dancer. As we said good-bye, he asked, "Why do you stay with the Chiedinis? You ought to be at the inn with your mother and my father. Listen, in a week's time I'm going to Trent to work on Cesare Battisti's newspaper. I'd like you to be settled at the inn before I leave."

"I'll see," I replied. But everything had already been decided. Three days later I knocked at the door of the inn, and Alessandro Mussolini had a new servant. He didn't regret it, for within days his customers were clamoring to be served by the "little blonde."

To celebrate the occasion, the evening before Benito's departure his father opened several bottles of wine. Benito played the violin and we danced. I discovered then what a fine musician he was. After the guests had gone, Benito took me to one side, telling me that we'd be married on his return. There was no proposal, no question of seeking my agreement; he simply told me that he'd decided for both of us. Under the circumstances, I saw no need to reply. Silently, I determined that I would not even think about his proposal in his absence, and by the time I retired to bed I'd forgotten all about matrimony.

Suitors showered attention on me again while, more carefree than ever, I devoted myself to my work at the inn. I was particularly skillful, so they said, at serving a local dish consisting of fish from the Adriatic. For a third time my hand was sought in marriage—this time by a young surveyor from Ravenna named Olivieri, I think. I refused him, much to my mother's disappointment and even more to Alessandro's. He realized that I was fond of Benito, but was familiar enough with his son's politics to know that our marriage would breed unhappiness for me.

Two months later, a postcard arrived from Trent. Beneath his signature Benito had written, "Give my best wishes to

Rachele and remind her not to forget what I told her." Clearly, he still had his own ideas, but Alessandro advised me not to wait, however much his son persisted.

"My wife was a victim of politics," he confided. "Benito won't make you happy, Rachele. You mustn't wait for him. If you find what you're looking for, then grab it with both hands."

Stark in my memory were Rosa Maltoni's tears as her husband was dragged off to prison. I had no desire to follow in her footsteps, but I was still undecided.

Eight months elapsed before Benito returned to Forlì—expelled by the Austrian authorities in Trent, he told us, for having inflamed Italian nationalism with a provocative article in the *Popolo*, in which he had argued that the frontier did not stop at Ala, a small town on the existing Austrian-Italian border. He proudly explained that the Trent Socialists had called a strike in protest against his expulsion.

He'd shaved his little beard, but otherwise he returned looking much the same, his pockets still stuffed with newspapers, his violin tucked under his arm. The reputation he'd acquired in Trent followed him to Forlì, where he was promptly appointed secretary of the local Socialist branch.

Politics engrossed him, but Benito now put his private life in order. Having learned about a particular male companion of mine, he made me burn the young man's letters. Then, in a brief encounter, he tersely ordered my friend not to meet me again. He, Benito Mussolini, was back on the scene. His meaning was all too clear, and the Mussolini reputation did the rest; never again did I see the young man.

I was extremely put out by this behavior. I might have been fond of Benito, but solitary confinement was quite another matter. I fought back, emphasizing that the reason I could never marry him was his politics, that a man who spent all his time at political demonstrations or in prison was no husband for me. His father rallied to my support, advising Benito to leave me alone. "You're not short of girls," he said.

Protesting, I was confined to the inn. Not only was I forbidden to go out dancing, I was not even allowed to serve the customers. Benito had rented a room in Forlì but came each day, taking over my job as waitress and washer-up. Though the customers didn't take to this at first—a little blonde has more appeal than a moustache—they soon became reconciled when Benito played the violin. But his father was distraught.

"What a dreadful state of affairs," he lamented. "A trained teacher serving in a restaurant!"

But Benito shrugged it off, replying that he considered no job degrading. He was so jealous he would have done anything to keep me away from others.

Matters came to a head one evening in the autumn of 1909. Benito had organized a Socialist meeting, and Alessandro asked, "Would you care to come with me? You can hear Benito speak, then stay on for the dance." Much as I wanted to go, I was scared of offending Benito, for he'd forbidden me to go dancing and attend political meetings. My presence, he told me, paralyzed him when he got up to speak.

Nevertheless, I accepted the invitation and managed to hear Benito without being seen. I felt proud when the enthusiastic cries of "Viva Benito! Viva Muslen!" greeted his speech.

Now came the dance—alas, a catastrophe. I remember the band's playing "The Red Flag" before the opening waltz. No sooner was I partnered than the trouble began. Suddenly I came face to face with an enraged Benito. Angrily snatching me from my partner's arms, he finished the dance with me, his great eyes glaring. Then, hauling me outside, he called for a taxi. Benito sat in silence during the drive home, refusing to be calmed by a friend, the lawyer Gino Giommi, who was sharply rebuked. But once we reached the inn, the scene was terrible.

My mother and Benito's father had caught up with us by then. At once Benito attacked them, bitterly reproaching them for allowing me to go to the dance, boorishly ignoring their explanations. His tactics to change my mind had varied over the weeks, alternating from gentle persuasion to threats of suicide. "If you don't want me, I'll throw myself under a streetcar," he would say. Indeed, he threatened to take me with him if I refused him.

By now my mother, who was normally patient and gentle, decided that it was time to intervene. We were sitting in the kitchen, I remember, my mother and I on one side of the table, facing Benito on the other.

"I warn you," she protested, "Rachele is still under age. She won't be eighteen for another year. If you won't leave her alone, I shall lodge an official complaint against you, and you'll be sent to jail."

"Right," said Benito, and left the room. But he was back within moments, pointing his father's revolver at my mother's face. "Now it's my turn to warn you," he shouted. "You see this revolver, Signora Guidi? It holds six bullets. If Rachele turns me down, there will be one bullet for her and five for me. It's for you to choose."

Within two minutes it was all decided. I was engaged to Benito. I was glad, really, for I suspect I'd been in love with him since I was seven. I just needed a final nudge to send me over the brink.

Benito returned to his lodgings in the center of Forlì, but by morning he was back to announce his plans. I was to go to the home of Pina, my sister, at Villa Carpena, some five miles from Forlì, and there I was to stay.

Benito came to see me each evening, sometimes on foot, sometimes on a bicycle. He said the journey gave him time to think. When he arrived, he would take from his pocket a bundle of newspapers and sheets of paper covered with his precise handwriting. After he read his article for the following day's paper to Chinchin, my sister's father-in-law, we would walk in the countryside. Naturally, we held hands and kissed, but we did none of the gazing into each other's eyes and rolling in the grass that so many lovers do. Even if we'd been inclined that way, it was December, and too cold and wet for such pleasures.

Practical by nature, Benito soon realized that the situation could not last. So one afternoon in January, 1910, he came earlier than usual. To my sister he calmly remarked, "Pina, I have found an apartment for Rachele. I want her to come and live with me and be the mother of my children. Tell her to hurry because I have other things to do."

While Pina tearfully broke the disquieting news to me, Benito sat confidently downstairs reading his article as usual to Chinchin. It took me five minutes to reach a decision. "We'll be going then," I said.

My humble trousseau consisted of a pair of shoes then three years old, two handkerchiefs, a blouse, an apron, and a few lire. We walked the five miles to Forlì in torrential rain, with an escort of dogs barking as if they were outraged by what we were doing.

I was pleasantly surprised to find that Benito had reserved two communicating rooms at Forlì's best hotel. Grandly, he ordered the porter to run a bath for the signora. "I believe that's already been attended to," the porter replied, wiping up the puddles from our dripping clothes.

The next morning, Benito took me to an old building in the Via Merenda. It had been beautiful once. "That's it," he said. This was our home, a top-floor apartment at the end of a corridor that was rife with gloom. To reach it, we had to climb a stairway so narrow that when I was expecting our first child, Edda, a few months later, I could hardly pass. Benito had already installed some furniture—a bed, a table, two chairs, and a charcoal stove. My mother supplied us with our other needs, and our thirty-five-year union began.

I should point out that, legally, we were not married. The Socialist doctrine forbade it. In those days the Socialists took such exception to bourgeois practices that any member who contracted a civil or religious marriage was promptly expelled. So Benito and I had not appeared before a registrar or a priest, though events impelled us to do so some years later.

3/ The Birth of Our Children

Throughout his time in office, Benito rarely drank a glass of wine. Now and again he might wet his lips, since it was inconceivable that the head of the government of a wine-producing country did not appreciate the national drink, but he never drank heartily, even with friends. From this was born the legend of the Duce's temperance. True, he was abstemious, but few people are aware that this now worthy virtue originated in something many a family has experienced at least once: an unforgettable night on the town.

It happened in 1911. We had been living together for a year and were not at all rich. Indeed, our income totaled no more than 120 lire a month, Benito's earnings as secretary of the local branch of the Socialist Party and then as editor of the party weekly, *Lotta di Classe*, which he had founded in January, 1910. From his wages he gave twenty lire to the party and the rest to me. Obviously, after we had spent fifteen on the rent, not much remained for us to live on.

All we owned were the few items of furniture that Benito had bought, and his wardrobe—a black suit that I'd seen him wearing for two years, a wide-brimmed Romagnole hat, a threadbare necktie, two shirts graying with age, and a pair of shoes. My belongings consisted of what I had brought in my bundle.

From the beginning, Benito's day fell into an almost fixed routine. Rising early, he washed, shaved, ate a breakfast of bread and coffee, and left the house—the whole operation taking twenty minutes at the most. Stopping at a kiosk on the Piazza Aurelio Saffi, he scanned all the newspapers at breakneck speed. Not once was he made to pay, for the owner not only knew him but stood entranced by this daily marathon. Next Benito carried on to the tiny office where he edited his journal or held long conferences, which were accompanied by wild gesticulations.

Around midday he came home for lunch, gulping it down within minutes and reading a newspaper propped against a bottle as he ate. He didn't even notice what was on his plate—usually tagliatelle, fresh vegetables (which he loved), and fruit. When I urged him to eat more, he replied that as a child he'd never been accustomed to eating big meals. He once said, "On weekdays we had soup at midday and chicory in the evening. Then on Sunday my mother would make broth from a pound of mutton for the five of us—Father, Mother, my brother, Arnaldo, my sister, Edvige, and me."

Sometimes he spent the afternoon at home writing his articles. He would cover sheet after sheet of paper in his small, rapid handwriting, crumpling up a page and throwing it on the floor when the words refused to flow, or getting up to stride about the room seeking inspiration.

In the evening his headquarters moved to the Macaron, Forli's main café, at the corner of the Serrughi Building on the Piazza Aurelio Saffi. This was a focal point for the Socialists, Benito's friends, and on occasion the police came to search or make arrests. Young people often enlisted Benito's help with their homework, for both young and old still looked on him as the teacher he was trained to be. Benito would sit at a table, working out the problems in pencil on the marble itself, then would move to another table as soon as one was covered with notes and calculations.

These Socialist gatherings sometimes went on far into the night, usually on market days—Mondays and Fridays—when the tense atmosphere was so charged with political frenzy that mounted Carabiniere, their truncheons drawn, occasionally scattered the crowd. Strategically, Benito made political capital at such times by inciting the peasants from the neighboring countryside with his inflammatory speeches. Then he returned home with his clothes torn and muddy, his body bruised—but quite happy. Triumphantly he used to say, "What a fight, Rachele."

When he was not battling with the forces of the law, it was with the Republicans or even with fellow Socialists. Local branches outside Forlì held more moderate views and strongly rejected Benito's commitment to overthrow the monarchy, the Church, and the existing regime.

So eventful were our two years in Forlì that I didn't notice the time passing. It was only at night that I counted the hours, straining my ears for the sound of Benito's footsteps or his voice. I was sure that sooner or later he would be brought home bleeding and critically hurt, or that I would never see him alive again.

Such were my fears and sentiments one night after I'd waited up for him till dawn. My head in my hands, I was sobbing my heart out, utterly convinced that Benito was either in prison or dead in the morgue, when I heard shuffling on the stairs. Trembling, I cautiously opened the door to see two strange men supporting my husband, whose face was ashen and wild-eyed.

"Don't worry, it's nothing," the men said. "He talked a lot tonight and didn't realize he drank an incredible amount of coffee laced with cognac." Then they left him to me to deal with as best I could, and went away.

As I struggled to undress him, he stared at me with a curiously blank expression. Then, without warning, he burst into life, shouting and raving like a lunatic obsessed with the madman's craving to smash. He began to break up the apartment—furniture, our few pieces of china, even the mirror. Desperately I woke a neighbor, and we called Dr. Bofandi (whose son became prefect of Forlì in 1940 and was still in office when my husband was arrested in 1943). Between us we tied Benito to the bed, and to my relief he gradually calmed down.

On waking the following afternoon, Benito was quite bewildered, refusing to believe my account of what had happened. "Look," I shouted, pushing a pile of rubbish toward him, "you've broken everything. It'll cost a fortune to replace it." He said nothing but just stared at the fragments of glass, china, and wood. "Get this into your head," I said. "I'll never agree to be married to an alcoholic. When I was little I had an aunt who drank, and that was enough trouble. I admit you have your good qualities—and I'm even ready to forget about the other women—but if ever you come home again in that state, I'll kill you."

Benito heard me out without saying a word. Then, taking my hand, he led me to the bed where one-year-old Edda lay sleeping. "I swear to you, on her head, that I'll never do it again," he said.

I knew he'd keep his promise, because Benito was devoted to his daughter. He would rock her, spend hours watching her sleep, and to wake her would sometimes play the violin over her bed. Indeed, apart from the times when he could not avoid sipping a little wine, Benito never again drank alcohol. That memorable night was the start of the Duce's legendary temperance.

My husband's undoubted affection for his children amazed even his own father, who had never thought his son capable of such feelings. The birth of Edda, on September 1, 1910, put him in a fluster. He insisted on buying the cot for this first child himself, though usually he was uninterested in domestic matters, and actually carried it home on his shoulders. Like all babies, Edda would sometimes wake and cry in the night. Whatever the time, he would play his violin until she went back to sleep.

Later, when she was just three, he took her everywhere

—even to his newspaper office. So by the age of four she already knew the alphabet and used to write it proudly with chalk on the kitchen floor. And Benito, who was equally proud, did not want me to wipe it away.

It was at about this time that Benito got hold of the idea that if hair was cut short it would later grow more beautiful. He cut Edda's. The first evening there were tears, because the lock of hair Edda had wound around her finger as she went to sleep was gone. Even the violin failed to help. But the next day the ever practical Benito bought a ball of linen, unraveled the ends, and hung them on the bed behind her head. When she was sleepy, Edda had merely to catch hold of the ball.

After Vittorio was born, in September, 1916, we had the same routine in Milan. The neighbors were treated to a concert every time he woke in the night.

When they were grown up, my children derived great delight from comparing their birth dates. Apart from Bruno, who was born on April 22, all—Edda, Vittorio, Romano, and Anna-Maria—arrived in September. And every time they talked about it, they asked the same sly question (which infuriated me): "Mummy, are we really Christmas babies?"

When Edda and Vittorio were born we had celebrations, but at Bruno's birth it was different. We were then living in Milan, where Benito edited the *Popolo d'Italia*, the flourishing daily paper that he himself had launched. On April 22, 1918, Benito, finding it imperative to go to Genoa, looked sternly at me with his great eyes before catching the train. "I hope you're not going to take advantage of my absence by giving birth to our son," he said (he had already assumed it would be a boy). "I don't want to be the last to be told again, as I was with Vittorio."

"Don't worry, you can go," I replied as I cleaned the floors. "You'll be there when he's born."

That same evening Manlio Morgagni, the manager of the *Popolo d'Italia*, greeted Benito at the station with a broad grin and the words "It's a boy. Rachele's doing well."

Benito leaped into a taxi, dashed up the stairs, and before even looking at the baby, said severely, "I told you to wait for me. Why didn't you?"

Men are like that. They want to be in charge all the time. So that he could be involved, he determined to take my mother's place and cook for me during the following days. From the bedroom, which adjoined the kitchen, I gave him instructions, but I soon realized it was useless. Benito had burned all the saucepans, and now I could not even boil an egg. Moreover, he'd spent the month's housekeeping money in two days. As a result, after twenty-four hours I got up to prevent even worse havoc.

Romano's birth, just over nine years later—on September 26, 1927—was almost disastrous. Endless precautions were taken, because by then I was the wife of the head of government and had the services of a midwife and a well-known gynecologist. The latter annoyed me so much with his new techniques—and reminders that I was the Duce's wife—that one day I burst out, "You know, when a woman's in labor, the pains don't change with her social status. A peasant and a queen both feel the same way."

But the crisis came with the actual birth, because my husband, who was in Rome, heard that the baby was about to be born. Once again, so confident was he that it would be a boy, he announced through the Stefani News Agency that I had delivered a son, adding that the child had been named Romano in honor of Rome. After driving madly to the Villa Carpena, where I was confined, Benito was horrified to discover that the baby had still to be born. The time was five in the afternoon.

"Well, what are we going to do?" he asked me. "Stefani's office has already announced the birth and all the details."

"What can I do? You go and sleep. I'll send someone to tell you what is happening."

He was a simple man at heart. At about midnight, Cina, our maid, knocked at his door. "Duce, it's arrived. It's a boy," she told him.

My husband threw on his shirt inside out, and rushing into my room, took the baby in his arms, kissed me, and began to shout, though he usually spoke so quietly, "It's marvelous, Rachele, really marvelous. You've made me very happy." I never knew whether he was more pleased to have a boy or confirmation of the news he had broadcast too early.

When our last child, Anna-Maria, was born, on September 3, 1929, Benito and I were both taken by surprise. Learning from my experience with Romano, I had told him that the baby was due on a date later than was really expected. So dispensing with the gynecologist (who had begged to be mentioned in the press report) and with the midwife (who had asked for the same publicity because she reckoned she had taken part in the proceedings), I went through the confinement on my own and called Benito in Rome.

"She's been born," I said calmly.

"Who?"

"The baby."

"What baby?"

"Ours. Now you can find a name."

I hung up, delighted at having played such a trick on him. I fully expected him to call back, telling me what he wanted us to call her, but no call came. The following day I read in the papers that I'd given birth to a baby, Anna-Maria. Benito had outwitted me, but even so I was glad, for Anna-Maria was my mother's name.

When we became grandparents, Benito enjoyed playing with the little ones. He asked them not to make much noise because it gave him a headache, but they had such fun. Duce or no Duce, my husband was down on the carpet playing horses and racing about like any other parent or grandparent. One day, when Edda and her husband, Galeazzo Ciano, had invited us to lunch, Benito vanished with their children before the meal. Suddenly a maid, hearing shouts from behind the drawing-room door, opened it and was horrified to see the Duce on the floor. She thought he was ill or hurt, but he was just playing a game with Edda's children, Fabrizio and Raimonda, nicknamed Cicino and Dindinna.

Benito always worried about the children's shoes. They had to be one size larger than necessary. He used to say to me, "I suffered so much as a child. I had to wear my shoes even when they didn't fit any longer, because my parents couldn't afford others. And later I couldn't even pay for them myself. So now I don't want my children to suffer the same tortures. Their shoes must be comfortable."

I remember another story about the children. On the back of his head, near the neck, Benito had a wart. Count Pulle, a doctor friend, wanted him to have it removed. "It's nothing, Duce," he told him. "It'll only take a few minutes. Have it removed. It's not nice to look at."

"Nice or not, I don't care," replied Benito. "This wart is a great delight to my children and grandchildren. My great-grandchildren will find it too, if it stays where it is."

In fact, the children—especially Guido, Vittorio's eldest —made a game of climbing on my husband's shoulders. When they pressed on the wart with an index finger, he would go, *"Dring-Dring,"* in a shrill voice and join in the children's laughter.

4 / Mussolini Becomes a Fascist

In December, 1912, when Mussolini was appointed editor of *Avanti!*, the daily newspaper of the Italian Socialist Party, we went to live in Milan. One evening in October, 1914—the 20th, I think—Benito returned from Bologna bitter and depressed.

"We'll have to start all over again, Rachele," he said. "They've fired me from the paper."

"What happened?"

"The Socialist Party is totally opposed to my campaign for Italian intervention on the Allied side against Germany and Austria-Hungary. The executive committee considers the paper's attitude contrary to party policy, so they've dismissed me."

"What are we going to do now?"

"First, we shall need enough money to live. Then we must think about starting another paper. I'm lost without an outlet for my ideas. I must have a paper of my own."

"Surely they're going to pay you some kind of compensation. They owe it to you."

"I know, but I refused to take anything. I don't want anything more to do with them. I told them I'd work on a building site if I had to, but I wouldn't touch their money."

I was extremely upset—especially for Benito's sake, for

he had driven himself hard during the past two years. When he had taken over as editor of *Avanti!*, the daily circulation had been only 20,000. In less than two years he had built that figure to 100,000. I had watched him writing his articles and editorials until far into the night. Sometimes, while waiting to check the proof, he would take me to the theater, then spend several hours in the office.

I was all the more unhappy because, with his usual unselfishness, he had refused to accept the full salary as editor. While certain colleagues earned a thousand lire a month, he preferred to take half that sum to pare down *Avanti!*'s expenses. It had incensed me when he came to tell me of his decision in Forlì. I had asked, "Why should others get what's due to you? How do you know if we can live on five hundred lire? Who does the shopping and who knows the cost?" Benito had trouble pacifying me.

When we'd left Forlì for Milan, we'd had to sell our belongings to pay for the fares and our lodgings in the first few days. But as the months passed, it had looked as if everything was working out. We'd found an apartment in a working-class area, at 19 via Castel Morrone, and made it fairly comfortable. I'd begun to think we had left the dark days behind forever. Now, suddenly, it was different. I didn't wish to add to my husband's worries, but I wondered how we were going to pay our monthly rent of eighty lire. And what were we going to eat when our money ran out? Fortunately, Benito's first impulse was always to consider his family. He understood what I was thinking and borrowed money so that we would at least subsist.

The next task was to find enough capital to start a newspaper. At our home Benito convened a "council of war," bringing together political friends and others interested in the idea of a new paper edited by Mussolini. Among them were Filippo Naldi, the editor of the *Resto del Carlino* of Bologna; Manlio Morgagni, who later ran the *Popolo d'Italia*; Nicola Bonservizi; Sandro Giuliani; Lido Caiani; Gino Rocca; and Giacomo di

Belsito. The two hundred lire Naldi had in his pocket formed the basis of the paper's assets.

Luckily, Morgagni secured an advertising contract, for which four thousand lire were to be paid in advance. Then a subscription scheme was launched, and I became treasurer, recording payments and issuing receipts. Benito and his friends combed Italy for funds and with Naldi's help formed a team consisting of a printing technican and two subeditors, who gave signed agreements in exchange for advance payments. The *Messageria Italiana* was to deal with the launching and with sales, and a new advertising agency willingly agreed to take over publicity.

My husband at last published the first edition of the *Popolo d'Italia*. He had won a great victory over the reformist Socialists (then in the majority), over everyone who had tried to ruin him, and over his own lack of confidence. November 15, 1914, was a momentous day. I didn't see Benito at all the night before. He had stayed at the presses checking the whole paper, line by line and word by word, and had subtitled the paper a "Socialist daily"—indicating that, even though the Socialist Party's executive committee had opposed him, he was still a Socialist at heart.

Pale, unshaven, exhausted, he was jubilant all the same. But he knew that the hardest task might still lie ahead, defending the *Popolo d'Italia* against Socialist Party opposition. So he rallied us all—my mother, myself, our women friends—to make a daily tour of the news vendors, making sure that the paper was well displayed and checking how it was selling.

Our home was in a state of permanent chaos, and people I had never seen wandered endlessly in and out. Subscriptions arrived from all over Italy. Sometimes there would be only four or five lire at a time, since people paid what they could afford. But there were also larger sums, of five hundred or a thousand lire. As soon as Morgagni took over the advertising, the number of contracts increased.

One Sunday, Benito and I were out walking with Edda.

We stopped by a news kiosk and Benito, questioning the man in charge, asked casually, "Does this paper sell well?"

"Not bad," came the reply, "but if that brain Mussolini wrote an article every day it'd sell a hundred times better."

Benito remained inscrutable.

The creation of the *Popolo d'Italia* spawned many rumors about Benito: that he had received money from abroad, that he had been paid to persuade the Italian government to enter the war against Germany and Austria on the Allied side. Mussolini always told me that at the outset of World War I he'd thought Italy should remain neutral; but that after the Battle of the Marne he believed neutrality would bring Italy nothing, that she would not benefit by any postwar settlement.

He had never forgotten the reason for his expulsion from Trent in 1909—Austria's intolerance of his militant Italian nationalism. Any opportunity to revise the Austrian-Italian border should be grasped with both hands, he thought. He was convinced, furthermore, that the Italian people would not see the need for a great social upheaval until after they had fought a war. In Benito's mind, war was halfway to social revolution, as proved to be the case.

At a Socialist meeting in Milan soon afterward, he explained why he had changed his attitude toward the war. He had not made his decision lightly, but after lengthy consideration and after realizing that there was no alternative. I remember being struck by what he said when he came home. "They hate me because they still love me," he claimed. "But they won't take away my Socialist beliefs or keep me from fighting for the revolutionary cause by tearing up my card."

As to the accusations that Mussolini accepted money from abroad, I was unaware of any such dealings while I was in charge of the finances. Indeed, if there had been financial backing he could have paid his colleagues and the printing bills slightly more often. Later, in 1915, Marcel Cachin, a French Communist, did in fact come to our house. I remember him well, because he neither spoke nor understood Italian and we had difficulty communicating when Benito was not there. Cachin had several conversations with my husband, but as far as I know he never brought the money he is supposed to have brought. Besides, Mussolini was in contact with other Socialists and Communists apart from Cachin, and he saw Lenin himself in Milan soon after he founded the *Popolo d'Italia.*

Lenin had journeyed from Switzerland to try to induce Mussolini to rejoin the Socialist Party, but Benito would have none of it, despite his liking for Lenin. They had met in Switzerland early in the century, when Mussolini was working and studying there. I found Lenin a kind, likable man with his little beard and academic spectacles. Much later Benito commented, "Lenin's great good fortune was to have died before Stalin could have him killed."

After the excitement of creating the paper, I had to bear the agonies of Benito's "dueling period," when he defended the honor of his political philosophy—his interventionist policy—with the sword. Indeed, life with Mussolini held many surprises. The night before his first combat, I couldn't sleep for fright, and when he and his seconds left at dawn, I was convinced he would never return alive. Everything else apart, there was the stark fact that his opponent was an officer. Colonel Cristoforo had deviated from the party, but this departure did not detract from his skill as a swordsman. As for Benito, he was full of quiet self-confidence, trying his best to comfort me with the remark, "Don't worry, Rachele. I've had good coaching from Camillo Ridolfi." But I was sure that, however brilliant an instructor Benito's friend Ridolfi was, the worst was bound to befall.

The day before, I'd bought Benito the new shirt he'd asked for, and now I lay awake all night listening to low voices, as he discussed tactics with his fencing master and seconds in the adjoining room. The clashing of swords sounded so ominous that I blocked my ears, certain that Benito was about to die. I saw them leave at dawn, decked out in black like undertaker's men, top hats in their hands.

Mussolini in 1904—a revolutionary syndicalist in Switzerland.
Syndication International

Despite my fears, Benito returned without a scratch, carrying in his arms a little cat. "I found him on the way there," he told me. "He brought me luck, we'd better keep him." That cat must have had an endless supply of luck for all the duels that followed. Each time Benito disagreed with anyone—a political opponent or even a friend—the argument had to be settled on the dueling field, strictly following the correct code of conduct. My husband must have fought a dozen times, against all types of people, including a Socialist, an anarchist, and even Claudio Treves, Benito's predecessor as editor of *Avanti!* That was one of the fiercest fights, for Benito came home without the bottom of one ear and with his shirt soaked in blood. Treves, however, was in much worse shape, with a deep wound in the armpit.

That particular duel stirred me to action. So often had Benito returned unscathed that I no longer worried for his life. But the cost of his dueling had begun to irritate me. He had to pay the fencing master and the doctor and find something for his seconds—only a gift, perhaps, but it still cost money. They also had to engage lookouts to warn them if the police were coming, for dueling carried severe penalties, by royal decree. Indeed, my husband was brought to trial several times for this reason.

That a new shirt should be ruined in a couple of hours infuriated me. I tried to wash off the blood, but in vain. So I told Benito, "I've had enough of this. Your shirt can stay as it is and I'll keep it for the next time. You don't imagine I'm going to throw money down the drain every time you disagree with someone. Either you stop fighting duels or you can go in this shirt."

My husband kept the shirt and carried on fighting. Eventually the duels became so much a part of our lives that we worked out a code in which to discuss them, so as not to alarm my mother, who couldn't bear them. First thing in the morning, Benito would say, "Today we're making spaghetti." Immediately I'd pack a little bag for him with everything that he needed. After the fight he'd call me. If everything had gone well, he would bellow, "You can throw out the spaghetti." We used to celebrate in the evening by going to a puppet show, one of his favorite forms of entertainment.

I must confess I enjoyed my husband's tales about his duels, for he had a great sense of humor and a fine eye for the twists of fortune that add spice to an adventure. One day, for instance, Benito and his opponent were earnestly crossing swords in a field when they heard loud weeping. A group of women coming to wash their laundry in the river had accidentally stumbled across the fight. They took to their heels in a mad rush, shrieking, "Help, help, they're killing each other!" The duelists had to stop and finish the fight elsewhere—under a bridge, I think.

One other time Benito and his opponent rented a room, locking the door to avoid being disturbed. Having pushed the furniture to one side, they were in the thick of the fight when the lookout warned that the police were coming. Grabbing their top hats in one hand, they ran out still brandishing their swords. With the police in hot pursuit, they leapt into a car in true gangster-film style and drove off to the station. There they boarded a freight train, and the fight that had started in a room ended in a little village.

Much later, after Benito's arrest on July 25, 1943, I remembered the code language we'd used for the duels and thought I might be able to apply a similar system. I was allowed to write to him, though I had no idea where he was, and so my letters had to go to the Carabiniere. I knew that my mail would be censored. Consequently, to let him know that everyone in Romagna keenly awaited his return, I wrote: "Everyone here is waiting for the water to flow in the river again." When Benito replied that he was sorry to hear there was a drought in Romagna, I gave up all attempts to use symbols.

Our life in Milan also had its amusing side—our visits to the theater, for example. One evening, possessing complimentary tickets sent to the newspaper, Benito suggested that we should go to the theater before he visited the printers to check copy. Within minutes of reaching the theater I was sorry he'd persuaded me to go. Every time he disapproved of something, Benito broke into peals of laughter and volubly criticized both the play and the actors. When angry eyes turned in our direction, I shrank back into my seat in embarrassment, but Benito so disliked the show that he felt entitled to poke fun at it. In 1909, he had himself written a novel called *The Cardinal's Mistress*, which, published in the *Popolo* of Trent, had boosted the paper's circulation considerably.

I pointed out how inconsiderate he was being, but Benito thought that no management had the right to bore the public with such appalling plays.

"Write about it in the paper, then," I admonished him, "but don't draw attention to yourself like that."

"You think I care if I'm attracting attention? I go to the theater to be entertained. If I'm not entertained, I say so. That's all."

Our next theater visit was to see an opera—*Parsifal*, I think. To my great relief, Benito slept from start to finish. From then on he tended to doze off during theatrical performances, he was so tired. When he was obliged to attend a theater as head of government, or even if he had gone simply because he liked the show, he began to feel sleepy as soon as he sat down. He would then push his chair to the back of the box and sleep steadily to the end.

That habit wasn't peculiar to Benito. Indeed, many eminent people take similar discreet catnaps. At least they fulfill their obligation to be seen by the public when the performance is over. Not that my husband really fell into this category, for I know that he genuinely enjoyed plays and concerts. When he first came to power he often went to the theater. But people's hysterical reaction soon forced him to minimize these visits. He therefore organized recitals for the family at the Villa

Torlonia. The children, above all, still remember them, for no excuse to absent themselves was tolerated. Their father made them attend, even though they found it a torture.

If Benito was not the ideal theatergoer, he had an almost naïve enthusiasm for vaudeville and variety acts. As he watched, he became totally oblivious to his surroundings. This was typical of him to the end of his life. When we watched a film at the Villa Torlonia or at our vacation home at Gargnano, I knew in a flash when the titles appeared whether Benito would stay till the end. If it was a sad, poetic, or romantic film, he was bound to get up and go. But if it was a Laurel and Hardy comedy or if it had a historical basis, Benito would then be almost childlike, showing unsuppressed pleasure and applauding every custard pie that hit its target.

Once I'd established which plays provoked him, I decided not to accompany Benito to see them. My mother agreed to accompany him, instead, but after just one evening she swore she'd never go again. I must admit that the experience was traumatic. That evening, to express his annoyance, Benito had taken off his shoe and thrown it at the actors. My mother was still stammering with fright when she came home, whereas Benito laughed gleefully.

After that, understandably, she thought up any conceivable excuse not to go to the theater with him. Because he never wanted to go alone, I engaged a young lady for the ticklish mission as his female companion. That didn't last long, for I'd taken the precaution of picking someone too plain for Benito's taste. He decided he would rather go on his own—and we were all happy.

5/ How Mussolini Came to Power

One day, in Edda's history textbook I read some fine words supposedly spoken by my husband when King Victor Emmanuel III first received him as the prime minister, on October 30, 1922. "Majesty, I bring you the Italy of Vittorio Veneto."

The authors must have meant that Mussolini was bringing a victorious Italy. At the beginning of 1922, the country was in the shocking state that had begun with the defeat at Caporetto during World War I. But by the end of October the riots and chaos that were the prelude to Mussolini's triumphant March on Rome had been subdued, and Italy enjoyed unity in victory.

When I told my husband that his words rang like a clarion call and were appropriate to the occasion, he answered, to my astonishment, that he had never uttered them. Though history may have to be rewritten, I must reveal that Mussolini never spoke these words. But disclosure in no way diminishes the importance of the occasion, for if there had been no March on Rome, our fate might have been strikingly different.

Whatever his position in 1919, my husband never imagined that he would be the head of government three years later. For us, 1919 was a black year. If I'd made a New Year wish for 1920—perhaps I actually did—it would have been that the coming year be completely unlike the last.

We'd experienced all kinds of difficulties in 1919, both on the political front and within the family. While still nursing Bruno, I succumbed to Spanish flu, the epidemic that killed over 500,000 people in Italy, more than the total of our victims of World War I. In that same year Bruno caught diphtheria, his illness affecting Benito far more than any political success or defeat, though perhaps *defeat* would be more accurate, since he'd recently suffered grave political setbacks. My husband and I spent whole days at Bruno's bedside, watching his breathing, his slightest movement—indeed, the faintest sign that he was getting better or worse. Benito hardly ate a thing and left the house just long enough to see the newspaper to press. Even then he phoned from the office for reports on Bruno's condition. We didn't think Bruno would ever recover, and for hours on end I held him in my arms, weeping silently. The doctors finally pronounced him out of danger, and my husband's eyes filled with tears of joy when I told him. But one-year-old Bruno had no sooner recovered from this illness than he suffered a bronchial complaint, and by the time he'd got over that his weight had dropped to about fifteen pounds.

These sharp fluctuations between hope and despair left us exhausted. Benito was affected the most, for he hated sickness in others as much as in himself, and seeing the children ill depressed him. He felt so helpless that he would have summoned doctors from the four corners of the earth if he'd thought it would help his children's recovery.

The political scene was equally gloomy. On March 23, 1919, Benito founded the Fasci di Combattimento—the Fascist movement of citizens pledged to the principle of militant nationalism—but when he came home that evening, he wasn't particularly elated. He'd announced in the *Popolo d'Italia* that sympathizers could join his new party by enrolling at a meeting at the Dal Verma, a theater in Milan, but depressingly, in spite of the public notice, only 147 people responded—a meager turnout that caused Benito to transfer the meeting to a small hall in the Piazza San Sepulcro so that it wouldn't look too ridiculous. It now seems odd, but when appointing the executive committee of his new Fascist party, Benito merely chose at random from the first row of enthusiasts.

Despite the lack of popular support, some months later, at a general election in November, 1919, my husband stood as a Fascist candidate opposing the Socialists. He had other men of importance under his banner, including two well-known figures—Filippo Tommaso Marinetti, the founder of the Futurist movement, and Arturo Toscanini, the orchestra conductor. The evening after the election, at about eleven, Benito phoned me. "It's a total fiasco," he said. "We haven't a single seat. In the Galeria [the central district of Milan] the people are rioting against us, the Socialists most of all. I'm afraid some of them may come to the house. Don't worry about it, but to be on the same side, you'd better find shelter for the children."

Desperately, my mother and I looked around for a hiding place. Finally we decided that the attic, under the roof, which we could reach by an inside stairway, offered the only safety. I wrapped Edda, Vittorio, and Bruno in blankets and settled them up there as best I could. Vittorio, who was nearly three, asked, "What's the matter, Mamma, is the house on fire?"

And Edda, who was just nine, answered, "Be quiet. If they hear you they'll cut your throat."

Then I went down into our apartment and mounted guard behind the shutters. Since the summer we'd been living in new quarters on the top floor of 38 Foro Bonaparte. It was a pleasant building, not far from a park but equally close to the offices of the Socialist Party. It was from there that I feared the greatest danger—more so because an uproar rose from the street below and from the areas held by our opponents.

After an hour or two, I saw a curious sight—a strange procession in which men bore coffins. At first I thought it was a trick of the eyes, for at night the streetlamps barely pierced the mist, and torches carried in the cortège made the macabre scene look even more eerie. By the time the crowd had reached our house, the coffins were clearly defined and sinister, as were the faces of men brandishing their fists and shouting, "Mussolini is dead! Mussolini is dead! Here is his corpse and the bodies of his friends."

By now I was totally engulfed by panic, even doubting the state of my mind. Half of me was convinced that my husband was dead, while the other half wanted to rush at the men in the street and snatch his body from them. But I couldn't leave my mother and the three children. (Much later, in 1945, I was to endure the same terror when, hearing gunfire, I saw from my window young Italians, both Fascists and non-Fascists, falling under the fire of the pursuing partisans.)

This unbearable agony lasted until morning. Contrary to his practice, my husband hadn't called me once, and his silence seemed to confirm the piece of playacting I had witnessed. Worse still, the caretaker came to me in great distress in the morning. According to *Avanti!*, he said, a corpse identified as Benito Mussolini's had been pulled from the river. The news left me almost demented, until a compassionate policeman, putting an end to my torment, asked the caretaker to tell me that Benito was safe. He'd been arrested during the demonstrations in the night, the man explained, and was now in the San Vittore prison. Rather strangely, Benito was freed during the course of the day. Toscanini and Luigi Albertini, the editor of *Corriere della Sera*—the most important paper in Italy and one fiercely opposed to my husband—had obtained his release. This gesture of Albertini's would save his paper from extinction three years later.

From the opposition he encountered after the election in 1919, Benito learned his lesson about the family's safety. The next morning he reminded me of the hand grenades he'd brought back from the front in World War I and explained to me how they worked; relieved, I put them on top of a wardrobe. "This way," I said, "they'll get one in the teeth before they hurt us." I completed my arsenal with a revolver that Benito brought me. During the day I kept it in my handbag, and at night I put it under Vittorio's bed, since he slept in our room. Benito never liked weapons, but I was determined to defend the family to the death. I'd always enjoyed shooting and hunting, and I think that, of the two of us, I would have been the first to fire had it proved imperative.

Luckily for everyone, there was no need to use the revolver, and 1919 came to an end with a few, less serious accidents—though one of them might have cost Benito his life. Driving my husband home from a Fascist congress, Leandro Arpinati, a supporter, crashed into a roadside barrier that suddenly came down. Though hurled for some yards, Benito escaped with only bruises and shock. The injury to Arpinati was much more serious.

It would be misleading to say that 1919 ended without any further incident, for in September of that year the flamboyant poet and militant patriot Gabriele d'Annunzio embarked on a critical adventure in Fiume, a town on the Adriatic which, following the agreements signed at the end of World War I, wasn't part of the Italian-occupied zone. D'Annunzio's venture had important consequences for the emerging Fascist movement.

Fiume's independence had led to skirmishes with the French, which had excited public opinion in Italy and reawakened Italian nationalism. An international commission was probing the situation when D'Annunzio decided to act on his own. One evening—September 11, I think—my husband and I were leaving a theater when a man handed Benito a note. It was a message from D'Annunzio. "The die is cast," he wrote. "I am leaving now. Tomorrow morning I shall arm myself and take Fiume. May the God of Italy come to my aid." With a group of loyal supporters, he seized Fiume without further ado.

This operation, which by its impulsiveness was in character for the famous poet and World War I hero, was an open insult to the Italian authorities. Though my husband thought Fiume should be Italian, he found himself in an embarrassing position, thinking D'Annunzio's behavior rash and premature. Still, he helped D'Annunzio, never dreaming for one moment that the venture would succeed. In fact that is what happened, though the success was short-lived. After a surfeit of parades and ceremonies in Fiume, D'Annunzio's friends took him less and less seriously, and on Christmas Eve, 1920, Italian marines stormed Fiume. D'Annunzio quit four days later.

Even then my husband didn't desert D'Annunzio. He realized that, by occupying Fiume, the impetuous poet had fired the spirit of Italian nationalism. He had proved that the basic feeling was waiting to be inflamed. All the men the poet had gathered round him, the Arditi, or legionnaires, whom D'Annunzio had armed, now turned to my husband, injecting new blood into the Fascist movement. Ceremony, which appealed so much to D'Annunzio, in its less exaggerated aspects suggested many ideas to the organizers of Fascist demonstrations.

All this earned Benito's gratitude, and he never forgot D'Annunzio, even when he was leading the government. Apart from D'Annunzio's qualities as a leader of men—for which some people even thought to make him Duce of Italy rather than Mussolini—Benito admired D'Annunzio as a poet. They remained close friends.

I did not, however, always share these sentiments, particularly after 1922, when I saw how D'Annunzio was exploiting Mussolini's friendship and admiration. His whole way of life irritated me. For example, he never sent letters by post. If he was writing to someone in another town, he would send his correspondence by messenger. If he wanted to communicate with someone abroad, he would send a telegram. And as the telegrams were lengthy as letters, they cost a ludicrous amount of money, which he never paid. Indeed, my husband finally had to instruct the minister of posts and telecommunications to stop charging D'Annunzio for his telegrams. That method was cheaper for the state than increasing D'Annunzio's pension.

More than once I asked Benito, "How can you admire someone like that? You've always paid your debts, aren't you shocked by his offhandedness?"

Benito tried to placate me. "Come now," he smiled, "you don't measure talent in terms of debts."

I remember that when Edda was married, D'Annunzio did something we found very amusing. He sent a "winged messenger" with a present from the commandant at Lake Garda to the Duce's daughter. Such a ceremony was made of the whole affair that Edda and I were sure the parcel must contain some treasure. Instead, we were surprised to find red pajamas beautifully embroidered with dragons and lotus flowers, like the ones peddled to tourists as "made in China." I made an outfit of shirt and trousers from them to go cycling in.

Benito began to weary of the eccentricities of his brilliant friend after he spent a short holiday at D'Annunzio's house on Lake Garda. He had hoped to rest, but returned more exhausted than before and, moreover, astounded by what he had seen. All the servants, he told me, bore names taken from mythology, novels, and D'Annunzio's poetry. And every time they encountered their master they had to bow deeply and fold their arms. Whatever they were carrying was allowed to drop, and there were frequent breakages.

Benito could never get used to being awakened at five every morning by cannon shot from the little warship *Redipuglia*, which D'Annunzio had installed in his garden. "Mind you," Benito explained, "I was almost glad to get out of that bed. There were two stone archangels guarding the foot of it, life-size, too." To his amazement, my husband discovered that D'Annunzio himself slept in a coffin—to get used to it, so he said, as a foretaste of his approaching death. In fact, D'Annunzio died soon after and managed to shock us even from beyond the grave.

D'Annunzio died on March 1, 1938. Benito went to the

poet's house to pay his last respects and had a strange adventure there which he described to me on his return. After meditating for a while before D'Annunzio's remains, Benito was retiring to bed when he learned that, because of a clause in the deceased's will, he was expected to fulfill an unusual ceremony. Furthermore, it must be carried out at once.

To Benito's amazement, a surgeon solemnly presented him with a sharpened sword on a velvet cushion, explaining that he was to cut off one of the poet's ears—"the loveliest and purest part of the body"—which D'Annunzio had left him as a token of their friendship. And Benito was to bring this legacy home with him. He had never been in such an embarrassing situation.

We were sitting at dinner with our youngest children, Romano and Anna-Maria, as he told this story. (Bruno, an officer in the air force, was at Guidonia Aerodrome, and Vittorio and Edda were already married and no longer living at the Villa Torlonia.) Romano and Anna-Marie, looking slightly queasy, put down their forks and stopped eating, and Romano, who was eleven, asked his father, "Did you cut it off, Papa?"

The boy looked so scared that I dreaded his father's reply. But Benito said nothing. Instead, he put his hand in his pocket and, with deliberate slowness, brought out his large handkerchief.

When he opened it, Romano gave a strangled cry and Anna-Marie covered her eyes with her hands. I was choking. None of us could relax. Then all at once Benito blew his nose noisily, as if he had a cold. "You think I'm a cannibal?" he grunted. "I was in a real predicament, but I managed to make them see that I couldn't accept my legacy." He smiled. "I must have caught a cold at Gardona."

Compared to 1919 and 1921, 1920 was a rather uneventful year. We led an ordinary life and politically luck began to turn in my husband's favor.

There was also an important family event. Benito bought our first car, a Bianchi Torpedo, a four-seater with folding seats. It was white or gray, I don't remember which, but I do remember how glad we were to have it. On Sundays we went out driving, the children in the back and Benito and I in the front. At that time we made a handsome couple. Benito had become very elegant after his return from the front in 1917, and he wore a black or gray suit (he always wore dark colors) with a stiff-collared shirt and a fine necktie. I was a follower of fashion and had lovely dresses with wide hems and pinched-in waists. I loved the buttoned boots, which gave me an elegant nineteenth-century look. Later we had a chauffeur and looked like any other middle-class family in Milan.

In the evening we often went to the operetta at the nearby Fossati Theater. I had even reached an agreement with Benito that he should cause less disturbance when he disliked the performance. It was then that I began to grow really fond of Milan. We were happy. The children had their own friends, and Edda was attending school. Like every father who feels he has missed his vocation, Benito decided she must study the violin. But both Edda and I were against it—she because the idea had no appeal, and I because the lessons cost me ten lire a time.

Journalism and politics consumed much of Benito's time. This meant that I saw far less of him. As a newspaper editor and a politician he was extremely active. He traveled a great deal, but when he was in Milan his headquarters were the "cellar," a room he'd furnished in the offices of the *Popolo d'Italia* on the Via Paolo de Cannobio. During the next two years there was much telephoning to and from our house—as during the royal investiture, when Mussolini became the official head of government, in 1922—but the nerve center of what became the March on Rome was Benito's cellar.

The Galeria, or central district, of Milan, near La Scala (where well-known establishments like Biffi's and the Savini Restaurant still stand), was a recognized hub of political activity. Benito used to drink coffee there and have long discussions with his friends. Altogether he led the same sort of life

but on a loftier plane as he had led at Forlì when he ran the
Lotta di Classe. Now, however, he owned an influential daily
paper and led a party that he'd founded and that was growing
in power.

In 1920, Fascism seemed to gather momentum. In the
autumn municipal elections the Fascists won four seats in the
Socialist stronghold of Bologna, and the Socialists held Milan
with only a tiny majority. A grave and highly significant incident marked the inaugural session of the municipal council
of Bologna, on November 21, 1920. On that date, Giulio Gior-
dani, a Fascist councillor, was shot dead in a riot, and suddenly
all the hostility between the Fascists and the Left became
explicit.

When Benito arrived home that afternoon, bad-tempered
and angry, he related what had happened, then immediately
after dinner left the house. I had a confused feeling that we
were about to go through yet another harassing time. From
that day there was a pitiless struggle between the Fascists and
the "Reds," who outnumbered them; for all divisions of the
Left wing—into Socialists, republicans, popularists, and so on
—had broken down. Now there were only the Reds opposing
the Fascists. Benito agreed to organize reprisals against these
Reds, but before that he wrote a stern article in the *Popolo
d'Italia* warning his opponents that, although he hated all forms
of war, especially civil war, he intended to answer extremist
violence with force.

The small landowners and industrialists, haunted by the
specter of the Russian Revolution of 1917 and disturbed by
the unrest erupting all over Italy as a result of the Socialists'
haphazard incitement of the workers, began to join with the
war veterans and other Fascist sympathizers in support of
Mussolini. It was a time of political change in Italy—a time,
too, when a change came over Benito.

Suddenly, the would-be social revolutionary of 1908,
1912, and even 1920 became the defender of law and order.
Or rather, the Reds and Communists, whose infiltration into

The prime minister at the London Conference of Premiers, 1922, with (l. to r.) Poincaré, Bonar Law, and Theunis. *Syndication International*

Inspecting experimental grain fields with the King, 1926. *Radio Times Hulton Picture Library*

With German ministers Brüning and Curtius, during their visit to Rome, 1931.
Syndication International

With Cardinal Gasparri at the formal signing of the Lateran Treaties.
Keystone

Europe had made Mussolini increasingly apprehensive, became the creators of disorder. And the Mussolini who'd incited the masses to revolt now looked for social revolution within the legal structure. He was fighting on two fronts—against the Reds and against government weakness.

As I'd expected, 1921 was more eventful both at home and on the political front. In March, I had a premonition in a dream. For some time Benito had been taking flying lessons with Cesare Redaelli, an excellent instructor. One night I dreamt that my husband was trapped in the aircraft's cockpit by a wall of flames. When I woke up, I told him about the dream and begged him not to fly.

"Don't worry," he said. "I promise."

As further assurance, he left his leather flying coat at home. But soon my peace of mind was shattered. The telephone rang, and before I'd even answered it I told my mother: "I'm sure it's Benito. He's had an accident. He's refused to take my advice."

I was right. During a takeoff from Bresso, there had been engine failure, and his plane had crashed. When eventually I saw a car approaching our home, I dashed down the stairs. Benito, supported by a doctor, came hobbling toward me with a broken knee. I didn't bother to ask if he was in pain, but burst out angrily, "Well done. I'm very glad."

Then I broke down, sobbing, while he murmured kindly, "Calm down, Rachele, it's nothing. I shall even have to stay quietly at home."

Quiet he was not, for he had a very high fever, but at least he stayed at home for three weeks.

From the general election of May 15, 1921, Mussolini emerged the *onorevole,* or deputy, of Parliament, having been elected in Bologna-Ferrara-Ravenna-Forlì and in Milan-Pavia. The Milan results pleased him most of all, because he'd received 124,918 votes there this time, as opposed to 4,064 in 1919. It was then that he forged links with the men who later

became the quadrumvirs of the March on Rome—Italo Balbo,
Michele Bianchi, Cesare Maria de Vecchi, and Emilio de Bono.

Throughout this period Benito strove to avoid violence
and to achieve better—calmer—relations with the Reds. In
July, 1921, at a meeting of the National Fascist Council, he
won approval, despite some internal opposition, of a plan by
Ivanoe Bonomi, the prime minister, who was seeking a truce
between the Socialists and Fascists. Totally against the wishes
of his own party members, Benito went ahead and signed such
an agreement, in Rome on August 2, 1921. The matter didn't
rest there. A motion opposing his action was carried on August
16 at a congress of Fascists from Emilia, Romagna, Mantua,
Cremona, and Venice. Some of those who later helped Benito
—men like Italo Balbo and Roberto Farinacci—voted against
him on this issue.

Benito the man gained the upper hand over Benito the
politician. As he had done in 1914—and was to do in 1943,
when he accepted a decision made at a higher level—Benito
agreed to resign from his seat on the Fascist executive committee. I remember what he said that day, because I'd wondered if we were going to have to start again from nothing.
"The matter is settled. The man who has been defeated must
go. I'm leaving the top rank. I remain, and hope I shall be
allowed to remain, an ordinary soldier in the Milan *fasci*."

Fortunately, everything was put to rights on November 21,
1921, when four thousand Fascist delegates from all over Italy
assembled in Rome to join with Benito in founding the Partito
Nazionale Fascista. It's worth noting at this juncture that Benito's
status had changed since the Socialist Party had expelled him,
in 1914. Now he owned a thriving newspaper and was independent. And although he'd been a member of both the Socialist and Fascist executive committees, he didn't leave the
Fascist Party in 1921. Moreover, a number of Fascist leaders
—including Cesare Mossi, the associate secretary—continued
to support him. This meant that Benito hadn't committed an

irreparable act in resigning; fascism was, after all, Benito's "son"—to quote his own words.

In the midst of these political anxieties, I was confronted with a further disturbing prospect—another duel. Benito's opponent in that October of 1921 was a onetime Socialist friend, Francesco Cicotti, editor of the *Paese*, who challenged my husband after he'd been criticized in the *Popolo d'Italia*. Because of relentless police surveillance, Benito had to use the cunning of a fox to arrange the fight in a villa at Leghorn. Swords clashed until the fourteenth bout, when the doctors, who were worried about Cicotti's heart, ordered him to stop.

From my own experience I can say that we did not have time to fritter away at home. Benito was traveling all over Italy, for he was anxious to keep political clashes from getting out of hand. In order to reach trouble spots more quickly, he used a fighter plane of World War I which only added to my worries. I believe he was the first politician to travel by private plane.

Italo Balbo, the architect of the first major operation to threaten state authority, was behind many of the clashes Benito kept careful watch over. In one instance, in April, 1922, Balbo planned to kidnap the minister of agriculture during the latter's visit to Ferrara with the prefect of Bologna. Having asked the minister for a report on the condition of local agriculture, Balbo took the prefect of Ferrara aside and coolly told him that he would kidnap the minister unless Fascists who'd recently been arrested in Bologna were released at once. The prefect assured Balbo that the arrests had been purely a precautionary measure; the Fascists would be set free within two days. The prefect of Ferrara obtained a promise to this effect from his colleague in Bologna.

In August, 1922, the Fascists managed for the first time to compel government forces to obey their orders—in another incident that starred Italo Balbo. When party leaders in Parma asked Balbo to push out the Reds who were entrenched in the town, he summoned Fascist detachments, known as *squadre*, from several towns. Then, the following day, he saw the prefect of Parma, who received him in the presence of General Lodomez, the commander of the local garrison. Balbo fiercely attacked the prefect for his complacency toward the Reds and gave him twelve hours to allow government troops to tear down the barricades and disarm the Socialists. If the prefect failed, Balbo said, he and his forces would seize authority from the state.

The prefect asked for two hours' grace, after which the troops of General Lodomez destroyed the Reds' barricades. Because the troops did not also disarm the Reds, Balbo told the prefect that he'd have to use force. Intervening, Michele Bianchi, the party secretary, pleaded with Balbo to avoid a clash. Balbo therefore returned to the prefect and asked that the army take over. The bishop of Parma made an offer to mediate between the Socialists and Fascists—an offer that was flatly rejected, though he was treated with respect and given a guard of honor. The impasse was finally resolved at midnight on August 5. Visiting the hotel in which Balbo had set up his headquarters, General Lodomez announced that a state of siege had been declared and that the power invested in the prefect was now in army hands.

In September, 1922, two months before the famous March on Rome, to which all these incidents were leading, a similar operation took place in Bolzano. The Fascists thought the situation there ridiculous, for in effect this northern province was a state within the state. Signs of Italian authority there were so slight as to make one wonder whether the power of the state was not merely provisional. The uniforms of the militia dated from the Austrian Empire, and the Alto Adige had its own laws. Ivanoe Bonomi, a former prime minister, had even allowed the mayor of Bolzano to make a speech in German when the King visited the town.

Backed by the Fascist Party hierarchy, Alberto de Stefani, Flotille Starace, and Francesco Giunta soon settled matters in

Bolzano. Leading the *squadre* from Trentino, Venetia, and Lombardy, they occupied the town hall and the German schools (which were much more handsome and comfortable than the Italian) before setting out their conditions. The mayor was to be dismissed immediately, they proclaimed; the civil guards in Austrian uniforms were to be disbanded; and the Italian schools were to be transferred to the German buildings. After some hesitation, the Rome government finally approved these measures, even agreeing to the mayor's dismissal.

After Bolzano came Trent, where the Fascists sought to dismiss the commissioner for Venetia and Trentino because of poor administration. The government hung fire but once again agreed to Fascist demands, and the commissioner was dismissed.

All these operations, which Benito's supporters carried out so skillfully, led Italians to believe that at last there was an organized force in the country to deal with irregularities. And as the months passed, it became clear that Italy now possessed two authorities: the official one—the government in Rome; and the other exercised by the Fascists in the provinces.

This peculiar situation could not last indefinitely, because as one authority became weaker the other grew stronger. Mussolini could have taken power on August 22, 1922. The garrisons were rallying to his side; the generals were openly lending their support. He had the means, and one forceful maneuver would have tipped the scales. But although Mussolini had ambitions to lead Italy, he wanted to do so legally, with the army's support, which he thought was vital for a successful revolution.

The support that proved fascism was truly representative of the people's wishes had expressed itself by the autumn of that year; and in October Benito was ready to begin planning the famous March on Rome, which was to effect official transfer of the Italian government to the Fascist leaders.

On October 16, the whole business got under way. With Benito presiding, the Fascist leaders met in Milan, at the Via

San Marco, reviewing the political situation and setting up a quadrumvirate composed of Emilio de Bono, Cesare Maria de Vecchi, Italo Balbo, and Michele Bianchi. I remember we'd nicknamed De Vecchi the "Little Drum" and that De Bono already had a white beard. Later I valued the honesty of Bianchi.

People came to the house in what seemed an endless stream: men of all ages, some with a semblance of uniform, others quite simply in civilian clothes—all carrying bundles on their backs, with bread, ham, salami, cheese, and potatoes, and wood and kerosine for the campfires—for to avoid arrest by the police they were to sleep in the open countryside.

Some slept under our roof, to guard my husband whenever he returned for a few hours' rest. We expected trouble any moment—as much from the police as from the Reds. To reduce the danger to our home, the Fascists even rented the apartment opposite ours so that nobody dangerous could take it over. That way they could also maintain a better watch on the street from its windows. Each time an emergency seemed imminent, they gave the alarm by singing a song (which I still find myself humming sometimes): *"L'ardito è bello, L'ardito è forte, piace alle donne, paura non ha"* (The ardito is handsome, the ardito is strong, women like him, he knows no fear). From our apartment we kept a constant vigil on a palm tree growing in the courtyard. We were afraid that someone might climb its trunk and hurl something into our house.

On October 22, Benito left for Rome. He feared that certain Fascist extremists, obsessed by their desire for total revolution, might themselves seize power. Under the circumstances, he wanted to be on the spot to take the necessary precautions. I had seldom seen him so strained, for once more he was trying to stem the tide, to stay as close to the law as he possibly could.

From Rome, where he spent some hours, Benito went to a party congress in Naples—and nearly began the March on Rome. Indeed, some marchers could have started from Naples,

Il Duce with his daughter Edda when she was seventeen.
Syndication International

Morning ride at the Villa Torlonia.
Radio Times Hulton Picture Library

Mussolini and his violin, in the 1930's.
Radio Times Hulton Picture Library

and my husband very nearly gave the go-ahead to the forty thousand Fascist enthusiasts who awaited his signal. Instead, he merely finalized the plans for the March: there would be secret mobilization on October 27, and when the three Fascist columns converged on Rome during the morning of October 28, the prefectures and other big buildings would be occupied to signify Fascist takeover. The marches were to avoid any confrontation with the army, and the towns were to display the national flag.

Back in Milan, Benito continued to follow by telephone the negotiations his representatives were conducting with possible heads of government. Right up to the last minute, he assumed that the only purpose of the March was Fascist participation in the government; he was not possessed by any vision of a government led by himself.

In the evening of October 27, Benito suggested, to my annoyance, that we should see *The Merry Widow* at the Manzoni Theater. "How can you go and see *The Merry Widow* with so much on your mind?" I asked.

He did not answer right away, but fastening his shirt collar, he began to whistle. This was even more surprising, since he hated whistling, and woe betide the children or the maid if he caught them at it. Not until we were on our way did he explain his reasons for going. "Everything," he revealed, "is ready for the March on Rome. My presence at the theater will mislead the police. They'll think that there can't be anything in the offing if I'm going to a show."

Actually, once we'd made certain that he, Edda, and I had been noticed as a little family group, we discreetly left the Manzoni after some twenty minutes.

The next day Benito confided that he feared that Luigi Facta, the prime minister, who had resigned rather than fight the Fascists but had proclaimed a state of siege before stepping down, would try force if he thought Mussolini was about to take action. Clashes between the Fascists and those sections of the army that had stayed loyal to the government would have been inevitable. That's why Benito wanted to appear so relaxed in the theater the evening before—to put the police on the wrong track.

On the day of the March, October 28, the first round went to the Fascists. The King, a skillful politician, refused to sign Facta's proclamation of a state of siege. Throughout that day Benito was phenomenally calm, a characteristic of his after he'd made a decision. Both at the cellar and at home, the telephone calls from his supporters in Rome were unceasing. Antonio Salandra, a former prime minister, offered Benito five ministries in the government Salandra was trying to form in the wake of Facta's resignation. But Benito dryly refused, conscious that power was now within his reach—and only a matter of hours away.

Naturally, excitement mounted at home, but my husband ate lunch and dinner ostensibly indifferent to dramatic events. He even glanced at Edda's homework, and after dinner returned to his office, preparing the edition that contained his last article as a journalist. I remember some phrases that I reread recently: "A tremendous victory is in sight, with the almost unanimous approval of the nation. The government must be clearly Fascist. Fascism will not abuse its victory but is determined that it shall not be diminished. Fascism wants power and will have it."

A furor greeted the paper's publication on October 29. At home, while Benito was still asleep, his chauffeur Cirillo waited for him, playing the piano and singing "We have taken power" as if he'd achieved it all himself. Edda and Vittorio took the opportunity to miss school.

As soon as he rose, Benito, closeting himself in a room with me, told me to instruct the Milan *fasci* that they must on no account set fire to the opposition newspaper, *Corriere della Sera.* When the editor called some moments later, I set his mind at rest. Then Mussolini left for the *Popolo d'Italia.*

At about ten o'clock on that morning of October 29, I received a call from Rome. A man's voice said, "We wish to speak to Mussolini in person."

"He's not here," I replied. "You'll find him at the *Popolo d'Italia*."

"He's not there. We've already tried."

About half an hour later, there was another call from Rome, and this time I learned from where it came. "It is very urgent. We want to know where to find him. This is the palace speaking."

In fact, I had the King's aide-de-camp on the line, telling me that the King had decided to entrust the formation of the new government to Benito Mussolini. Provided they manage to find him, I thought.

Some minutes later Benito called.

"Benito, the palace is looking for you everywhere," I said. "Where have you been?"

"I know, I know. I've been in contact with the Quirinal. I must leave for Rome. Pack a bag with a suit and the usual things. But don't say anything to anybody."

Stubbornly, Benito had declined to leave Milan until he'd received a telegram officially confirming the King's desire that he should form a new government. Shortly before midday a first telegram had arrived, signed by General Cittadini, asking my husband to go to Rome for consultations with the King. But Benito had refused to leave, insisting on a telegram that asked him specifically to form the government. This arrived at midday, again signed by Cittadini. Then Benito uttered words that may have become legendary but were certainly true. "If only our father were still alive," he said, showing the telegram to his brother, Arnaldo.

As there was no train to Rome, Benito went to his newspaper office in the afternoon. He settled his affairs, prepared a special edition of the *Popolo d'Italia*, and made arrangements for the editorship to pass to his brother. He then met Cesare Rossi, thus ensuring that the news was passed on to the Fascist militia and to the general headquarters at Perugia, with a warning to the latter that they should not forget discipline in their enthusiasm.

In the evening he came home to an atmosphere of intense excitement. He took his case, said a brief good-bye (we had never been very demonstrative in the family), kissed the children, and left for the station—reminding me once again to make sure that the rival paper *Corriere della Sera* was not burned down.

There was a crowd of people on the station platform, and I heard from Cirillo, who was carrying his case, that Benito said to the stationmaster, "I wish to leave exactly on time. From now on everything must work perfectly."

At home calm was gradually restored. I went out for a little while and astonished myself by entering a church. I knelt down and said a prayer (which I kept to myself for a long time): "Lord, do not let us change. May my husband stay as he is and may I never give way to pride or vanity."

I was not in the capital to see the effects of the March on Rome, and so I never saw my husband arrive at the station at five-thirty on the evening of October 30, 1922. On the telephone later, he jubilantly explained how wonderful it had been to stand with the King on the balcony of the Quirinal and watch the procession of Black Shirts. It was not until he had closed his eyes for some seconds and then opened them that he knew it was not a dream. He, Benito Mussolini, was really head of the Italian government, the prime minister, the Duce.

6 / The First Steps of Mussolini the Dictator

When my husband became head of the Italian government, we suddenly discovered an incredible number of friends, people who at some time had rendered us some service and who with varying degrees of tact now reminded us of the fact.

One day in Milan, I was accosted by a man who told me that he'd lent my father-in-law, Alessandro, a wheelbarrow wheel that Alessandro had never returned. When I expressed my amazement (Alessandro had been dead for twelve years), I learned that the incident dated back nearly twenty-seven years. Without further question, I paid the man for the wheel.

From another man I received an enormous bouquet of flowers with a message begging for an interview. When I agreed to see him, he simply said that he was an ardent Fascist upon whom Mussolini could count for liberal support. I remembered having met this visitor two years before on a train between Forlì and Milan. During a discussion about politics, he'd explained at length to fellow passengers that Mussolini was a nobody. Much to his annoyance, I'd contradicted all his arguments and ended by saying, "You must know Mussolini personally to talk about him this way."

"Certainly, not only do I know him very well, but I also know his wife."

"I'm glad to hear it," I remarked sarcastically, "because I am Signora Mussolini."

The young man had been struck dumb. He did not find his tongue again until two years later, when my husband had come to power.

In Rome, Benito also became acquainted with a mass of people to whom, he now discovered, he was indebted for something. We were separated for long stretches of time at this point, because I was staying in Milan with the children, but Benito kept me informed of his activities during the daily telephone calls we arranged before he left for the capital.

"You know," he said one evening, "you'd be amazed how many veterans of the last war I keep meeting. Today, for example, I had a visit from someone who helped take me to the hospital when I was wounded in 1917."

"I hope you told him how grateful you were," I said.

"Of course I did. But there's just one problem. He's the sixth or eighth man with the same story. When I was wounded, there must have been a dozen people carrying me."

Another day he told me that during the afternoon he had received two visitors. The first was a man who insisted on seeing him, only to mutter once he was in his office, "I wanted to see you, I wanted to see you," before fainting. The second was a sergeant of the Carabiniere, who had brought a truncheon. He wanted to beg the Duce's forgiveness for having arrested him during a demonstration in Forlì and to offer him the truncheon he'd whacked him with.

"I forgave him and took the truncheon," said my husband philosophically.

After forty days we saw each other again. Benito had come back to Milan, incognito, but the news of his arrival soon spread. We managed nevertheless to have one week of family life from December 16 to 22.

As we could speak more freely and at greater length at home than we did on the telephone, I took the chance to ask him about his new life, his job as head of government, and his impressions of it all. It was then that he described his first conversation with King Victor Emmanuel III. He told me that he found the sovereign's bearing and edginess rather disappointing. "I got the impression," he added, "that the whole court had packed and was ready to leave at the first sign of insurrection. But I think Victor Emmanuel relaxed as soon as I told him what my objectives are. I think he'll trust me now and that I can rely on his support."

I digress here to say that I heard a report of the King's reactions soon after he saw my husband, and that it coincided with Benito's impressions. The King had said, "There's a fellow who'll go a long way. I had imagined he'd be different before I saw him."

I gathered from Benito that, as soon as his position was secure, he had had to contend with the demands of the more ambitious Fascists, who now came to claim their rewards and titles. For instance, one of the men chiefly responsible for the March on Rome had insisted on being made a marshal forthwith. And because of their overbearing manner, Benito had been forced to arrest some party members who ignored paying bills in restaurants and cafés.

"Victory," he commented, "has gone to their heads, and they're reeling with it. They're getting arrogant and pretentious. They'll exaggerate the slightest difference of opinion into a rift. They even fight among themselves. If only they would realize that now we have power we must restore the rule of law, if necessary to protect the losing side. But they won't, and I seem to spend an inordinate amount of time sorting out the petty quarrels of the people who should be helping me, instead of dealing with important national and international problems."

To avoid further disturbances, he hastened to send home everyone who had taken part in the March on Rome and, later, to create several new departments in the Ministry of the Interior so that all veterans and Fascists could be assimilated into such bodies as the border police, the forest guards, and the customs offices. Fortunately, it didn't take long to unravel all the knotty claims and put the would-be dictators in their places.

The most important task still remained—to set the faulty machinery of the state in motion again. To start with, my husband put his office as prime minister in the building housing the Ministry of the Interior, at the Palazzo Viminale. He then transferred it to the Palazzo Chigi, which was little more than a shell with no working amenities. "I've inherited a leaky vessel and a bunch of amazingly unbusinesslike civil servants, especially among the higher ranks," he confided. "They're the ones who come to work at ten in the morning. One day I was going up the stairs in the Ministry when I met someone coming down. It was just after eight. 'Is there anyone up there?' I asked. 'That madman Mussolini must be there. He's always in at eight,' he answered. Then he recognized me and was very embarrassed."

An Italian diplomat once remarked that no one outside the diplomatic corps could have the least idea of Italy's international standing, adding that, unified, Italy commanded less respect than she had divided. So as soon as he took office, my husband was concerned to restore his country to what he considered her rightful place on the international scene.

I lack the historian's authority to comment on the Lausanne conference on Turkey of November 18, 1922, or the London conference on German reparations, held a month later; all I know is that Benito made good use of both occasions to improve the status of Italy in the international context. I can report with a wife's authority, though, that Benito was as disappointed by his trip to London as he had been delighted by his journey to Lausanne.

"It's a dreadful town," he claimed. "There's a grayish dust that gets into everything—the rooms, the clothes, even the suitcases. It's worse than desert sand. I won't be going back in a hurry. The English don't understand our problems, or don't want to. Italy's just a trifle to them. But we'll change all that, you'll see."

Some people wonder why, over the next twenty years,

Mussolini left Italy only to go to Germany. I think it was because he felt uneasy abroad, and his impressions of London did nothing to make the idea of traveling more attractive to him.

On a personal level, his position of power doubtless had an effect on my husband. He had left Milan with a pair of black trousers and a blue jacket. He came back boasting well-cut suits—some of them in tweed—stiff-collared shirts, and dark but lovely neckties. His new hats greatly amused the children, especially a straw hat and a bowler from which he refused to be parted. Even if it was no longer fashionable, the bowler recalled happy associations for him. "There may be only three of us in the world wearing it—Stan Laurel, Oliver Hardy, and me. But this hat has protected my head from truncheons more than once."

Benito's particular penchant for hats was responsible for an incident that caused much laughter in the family, even if our chauffeur, Cirillo, found it less amusing. Cirillo had stayed in Milan and was still unused to fancy hats with odd names. One day Benito, who had just arrived from Rome, sent the chauffeur to fetch his gibus, or opera hat, from the car downstairs.

Cirillo disappeared. When he failed to reappear after some fifteen minutes, Benito grew impatient. Finally he sent me to see what was going on. I found Cirillo leaning against the car, and asked him what he was doing.

"I'm waiting, Donna Rachele."

"But what are you waiting for?"

"Signor Gibus. The prime minister told me to go down and fetch him. Perhaps he's late."

On another occasion, Benito laughingly told me over the telephone that one of his old friends, a journalist on the *Popolo d'Italia*, had phoned to ask how he should address him in the future, whether he should give Benito his full title of prime minister or carry on using the familiar second person.

"Can you imagine it?" my husband joked. "Who does he take me for? I'm still called Benito Mussolini and, as far as

I know, I haven't changed. Do you think I've changed, Rachele?"

"Not since last week perhaps. But you're more stylish now. You look more 'middle-class.' "

"But I have to be like this in Rome. I am the head of government, after all. I have to set an example and behave correctly toward foreign visitors. And they take their deportment lessons seriously at court, I can tell you."

"I'll have to take some so that I can come to Rome."

"That's all you'd need."

"And what about me, Benito, what should I call you?"

"Idiot, you're not going to start that Forlì business again!" And we burst out laughing.

The "Forlì business" was well known in the family, because Benito liked to tease me about it. It dated from 1910, when we had decided to live together. Benito was a qualified teacher, and like everyone else in Forlì, I addressed him according to his profession. That is the custom in Italy, even today. When we settled down together, I went on calling him "teacher" whenever I spoke to him. In fact I found it somewhat hard to use familiar speech. So eventually he asked me if I was waiting until we had four children before I could bring myself to call him Benito.

I did not manage to do so until the night he went out on his unforgettable spree, when I was so angry I overcame my shyness. But the question of how to address Benito remained, if not for me, at least for others like Cirillo. In 1912 he had become editor of the paper, which meant he was entitled to be called a *direttore*. In 1921 he was elected deputy or *onorevole*, and a year later he was prime minister, or *presidente*.

"I'll call him Duce," Cirillo told me, "because he is the Duce and that's the only title that doesn't seem to change."

He was quite right, for the Socialists, amazingly enough, had christened him Duce in 1912. Admittedly, he had been one of the best-known members of the party at the time. It happened during a banquet held to celebrate his release from prison, when Olindo Vernocchi, one of the veterans, said to him, "From today, Benito, you are not only the representative of the Romagna Socialists; you are the Duce of all revolutionary Socialists in Italy."

And so Benito Mussolini, the Fascist leader, went down in history with a title the Socialists had given him. It is true that he always remained a Socialist at heart, but I shall return to that later.

Whoever else may have regretted Mussolini's rise to power, a priest, Don Cirio Damiani, certainly did. A long-standing friend of the Mussolini family, he was also an inventor, having perfected first an ingenious draft system for domestic chimneys and then a kind of multibarreled gun, which, incidentally, the Russians later produced and called the "Katioushka."

In 1922, Don Cirio and my husband were exchanging letters about a new form of luminous mudguards for automobiles. On January 26, Benito wrote that in March he would personally deal with this invention, because, as he wrote, "Everything new is exciting to me, and in this case I have just helped to set up a workshop for making mudguards. I have also helped a young man to perfect a new spark plug, and your scheme looks very interesting to me."

Unfortunately, when my husband left for Rome, all Don Cirio's plans seemed to evaporate.

Anything new invariably looks good, and as soon as my husband had settled in Rome, the invitations came flooding in. I was asked to be godmother to various children and to sponsor a number of organizations. I declined politely but firmly, but I could not refuse to accompany my husband at certain public appearances, particularly in our native Romagna.

It would take too long to describe all the meetings I attended or chaired, for these were quite numerous. Yet I remember distinctly my first official appearance, during the summer of 1923. I took my place on the platform for the first time in the very towns where I had known poverty, in Forlì and Predappio, where I had spent my childhood and early youth. Of course, both Benito and I were proud and moved to be back there as important people now. As we sat in our special compartment waiting for the train to reach Forlì, Benito said with a smile, "Do you realize, Rachele, that some of the policemen there to salute me will be the same officers who once put handcuffs on me, dragged me off to prison, insulted and beat me? What shall I do to them?"

"Give them a good kick," I answered, for I had my own ideas on the subject.

"No, I can't do that. They were only doing their duty. They'll do even better now, because they'll be afraid I remember. Besides, there's no point in being vindictive. I've even forbidden the castor-oil treatment."

"You're wrong, you'll see how wrong you are."

Probably I should explain that the castor-oil treatment was a form of Fascist punishment used during reprisal operations, but only on important people—men of a certain social standing. If a lawyer, for instance, had paraded his anti-Fascist opinions or helped their opponents, the Fascist *squadre* would go to his house and force him to swallow the oil—not enough to make him seriously ill, but enough to confine him to his home for several days. Later the Fascists were accused of inhuman practices. I don't condone what they did—but surely the lavatory is preferable to a hospital bed and wounds inflicted by the present-day chains, stones, and Molotov cocktails.

One of the first measures that Mussolini took as prime minister was to forbid this use of castor oil, with harsh punishment for offenders. So obviously it was no treatment for the Forlì police.

As the train pulled into the station, an astonishing sight met my eyes—a great, surging mass of people. Never before had I experienced anything like this demonstration, and I found it extraordinarily impressive. All formality was swept aside, and we were carried to the car. There I discovered another drawback to success—the pretty flowered hat that I'd brought was reduced to rags. Benito, more accustomed to these occasions, spoke to the people in Romagnole dialect as the car crept slowly forward.

During a ceremony at the prefecture, I noticed Countess Merenda, who had been our landlady in 1910, when we first lived in Forlì. The moment was ripe to settle accounts with her, for I'd never forgotten her remark about us thirteen years before, when my husband was not distinguished. She was visiting the building one day, and when she reached our floor I overheard her ask her manager, "Can there really be such squalid people living in my house?"

I'd repeated her words to Benito the next morning when he was shaving. Before I had even finished what I was saying, he'd run to find a sheet of writing paper, his face still covered with soap. "Remember, Countess," he wrote, "my wife is a nobler woman than you."

Nothing further was done at the time, but her comment had lingered in my memory, and now I was determined that the "squalid people" should have their say—and in public. At some point of the ceremony someone asked me to speak. I accepted gladly and attacked from the start.

"When you become an important person," I began, "everybody wants to know you, to put out the red carpet for you. But when you are poor, well . . . I have never forgotten certain titled ladies who are, moreover, here today. . . ."

My speech was quickly interrupted. Sensing a storm, Benito made excuses, called me over to him, and asked for the ceremony to continue. Since then, I must admit, Countess Merenda has been extremely kind to me. Her friendliness has compensated for her rudeness in 1910.

Unfortunately, not every year was a happy one; nor, for that matter, was every month. After the initial shock of the March on Rome, his political rivals attacked Benito more fiercely than they had before he had come to power. There were violent interparty quarrels. In June of 1922, the Socialist party deputy, Giacomo Matteotti, was assassinated, and the uproar that followed shook fascism to its very roots. Not even Benito could escape stricture, for it was proved that some

Fascists had taken a hand in the crime. I think this was one of the few occasions when I saw my husband disgusted, offended, and demoralized all at once. He did all he could to trace the criminals, and once they had been apprehended, he made sure that harsh sentences were pronounced for all—Fascist members or not. But the Duce went further. He personally ensured that the Matteotti family were provided for, and even took a close interest in the children's education.

Benito had come to realize that danger lurked even in friends, that he could no longer trust anybody. He said so more than once. He observed, "I don't believe I could trust even my mother if she came back to life." He didn't mean it, for Benito Mussolini's trustfulness bordered on naïveté, as the future was to prove.

I felt that the previous ten years had taught me all there was to know about life. I had experienced anxiety about duels, arrests, and war, uncertainty about the future, the thrill of success—and I had discovered another Mussolini.

I shall not catalog all the attempts on Benito's life. There were not many. But together with the murder of Matteotti, they went far toward establishing the dictatorship. The parliamentary opposition tipped the scales by withdrawing to their ivory tower on the Aventine. Two attempts on his life affected me deeply. Not that I was insensible to the others, for no woman could ignore the risk of her husband's returning home dead or badly wounded. But these two incidents I could never forget.

The first, in April, 1926—which was in fact the second bid to destroy him—occurred the day he presided over a medical congress at the Capitol in Rome. As he was leaving, an Englishwoman named Violet Gibson fired five shots at him with a revolver. Yet in that instant, as if by a miracle, Benito turned his head, looking up toward a balcony, so that only one bullet found its mark, and that in the nose. He is reputed to have said at the time, "And it was really a woman!"

When he told me about it, he made the incident sound

almost funny. "You know, Rachele," he explained, "it wasn't the Englishwoman who nearly killed me, but the doctors. I was unlucky. It was a medical congress, and a score of them jumped on me, all hoping for the honor of saving Mussolini. I was afraid I'd never survive in the crush and had to fight my way out with fists."

On October 31 of that same year, 1926, when I myself witnessed an attempt to kill him, I realized that my husband had not exaggerated the Gibson episode. This time we were attending the opening of a new sports complex in Bologna. There were thirteen women at table, and Benito exclaimed, "It's a bad omen." In the afternoon, while I was waiting for my husband at the station, Marquis Paolucci arrived. He looked dreadful, and it was all he could do to say to me, "Be brave, Excellency, be brave." Momentarily I felt numb, but before I could panic Benito came from behind him in a surge of the crowd. He told me that while he was still in his car a young man had fired at him and missed. In that moment Benito had caught a glimpse of the young man's pale, tormented face, but before the police could intervene, the crowd had summarily lynched him.

"It's insane to make such a young boy the instrument of a crime," Benito said, more shaken by the fate of his would-be murderer than by thoughts of what might have been his own gruesome end. His escape from death had been slender. Not until we were traveling home did he notice the scorch marks on his jacket, and at the Villa Carpena I noticed blood on both vest and shirt. A bullet, grazing the skin above his heart, had been deflected by a notebook.

Some minutes after our arrival, while the rest of us were still recovering from shock, Benito was alone in his room playing his violin. He stopped only to say, "It's sickening to do such a thing, to give a weapon to a lad like that. He may have a mother waiting for him this evening."

7/ Mussolini and Women

There was a man who liked his women plump. He didn't mind if they were blond, brunette, or redheaded, just as long as they wore no perfume. And that man was Benito Mussolini.

My husband's liaisons with women were at one time among the favorite topics of the world's press. But putting everything into its true perspective, I can say that Mussolini's tally as a lover was no greater than that of any attractive Italian male. I have no desire out of spite to make his feats sound trifling, but brief thought should be enough to expose the truth.

My husband always slept at home, save when he was traveling. He left at eight in the morning, came home at one, left again at four, and returned at about eight in the evening. Every time he left the Palazzo Venezia, a telephone call to the Villa Torlonia, where we were living, informed me that the Duce was on his way home. If he went elsewhere, I was given the precise location.

So when and where did he have his affairs? I suppose I know where: at his office, where he'd furnished a little room, not with a bed, but with a couch to rest on. And when? In his spare moments.

That was Mussolini's great love life. Many men must have done as much. Indeed, some men have greater scope. They can go to a hotel, tell their wives they intend to have a drink with friends, or invent that late meeting at the office. One other thing is certain. At no time did Mussolini pursue a woman. Women were drawn to him on physical grounds, because they hoped to profit by the relationship, or just to shock their friends by saying, "I'm the Duce's mistress."

Two anecdotes bear this out. One day a young widow came to the Duce's office in the Palazzo Venezia. Her husband, an airman, had met a hero's death in combat. Benito was extolling her husband's virtues and intending to console her when suddenly he realized that the widow was regarding him with sensuous eyes unmarked by tears. He put an end to the interview as soon as he could. When he told me about it that evening, he was so obviously disturbed that I never had a moment's suspicion.

On the other occasion, he showed me a letter written by a princess, which contained some particularly offensive remarks because he'd spurned her. Seeing that I couldn't conceal a trace of suspicion, Benito pulled up his sleeve and said, "Look, Rachele. I have gooseflesh just thinking about it. If I was lost in a forest with that woman and a monkey, I'd take the monkey. Not that I don't like women, but I don't want her. So she's taking what revenge she can."

After Benito's death, I met this woman's husband and revealed to him my opinion of his wife and why; I mentioned, moreover, that I considered her attitude scandalous—an assertion he didn't dispute.

And yet my husband was no saint. I knew practically all there was to know. I didn't make a fuss when I heard that Magda Fontanges braggingly claimed to be Benito's mistress. It happened that her tantrums so annoyed Benito that he wouldn't let her return to Italy. That was why she shot and wounded the French ambassador who had the responsibility of telling her. I also kept calm when Cécile Sorel was seen leaving my husband's office, flushed, disheveled and radiant.

I knew my husband better than anyone. I'd known him

since his adolescence, when he took money from his sister's purse to buy ice cream for his girl friends and take them dancing. After that, ironically, she had to comfort them when they cried on her shoulder because he'd left them. Before I met him, he'd left a trail of broken hearts in Predappio and Forlì, then in Tolmezzo, Onaglia, Gualtieri, in Switzerland—in fact, wherever he went. He never denied that he liked women, but he mentioned one reservation. He said to me one day: "After you, I'll never look at another pretty woman. Beauty is not to be trusted, it makes you lose your reason."

I don't think he ever lost his reason. If a woman found him attractive—or vice versa—the relationship would be passionate, reckless, but short. Mussolini couldn't be bothered with the women he'd seduced. I think women were drawn primarily by the way Benito looked at them, with those eyes that had subdued me as a child. Moreover, he carried himself well and had a deep, melodious, almost spellbinding voice. Once he had won them, it was his roughness that kept them. Like all Italian men, he thought that a woman's place in society was in the home. Accordingly, he tended to treat his mistresses like objects and never became deeply attached.

Even so, there were three women who hurt me: Ida Dalser, Margherita Sarfatti, and Clara Petacci. I summoned all my strength to fight each one of them.

It was an anonymous letter I received that first made me anxious about Benito's extramarital flings. My husband, the letter revealed, was involved in an affair that was potentially troublesome. I decided to meddle in his life a little, but before I could do so, I was overtaken by events.

Benito had gone to Genoa to borrow money from a friend, Captain Giuletti, who was in charge of the seamen's union, when a strange woman came to the house. She was no beauty and despite her garish makeup looked older than I. Curiously, she declined to give her name but brazenly asked for details about our private life. She even asked Edda if Daddy loved

Mummy. This visit greatly disturbed me, and on Benito's return I told him about it.

"That's the Austrian woman Ida Dalser," he said. He confessed to their relationship, of which I had been completely ignorant till then. He had first met her in Trent and then again in Milan, and since then she'd been pursuing him—even to the office, where everyone knew that if she called Mussolini was "out."

"She's dangerous," he said. "She's a fanatic."

When she told him she had borne him a son in November, 1915, he immediately recognized the child, whom she named Benito Albino. We thought that matters would rest there. But one day in December, 1915, when I was out shopping, the police came to our house telling my mother they'd a warrant to take the furniture. My mother was too bewildered to protest. I was equally puzzled, for only recently I'd received a letter from Benito, then at the front—for this was during the war against Austria-Hungary—saying that all was going well.

I soon discovered what the warrant was about, for later that day the police came back to arrest me and take me to the station.

"Are you or are you not Signora Mussolini?" they demanded.

"Yes, I am," I answered.

"Then that's it, you're the guilty woman."

I was very taken aback. I asked what I had done, what I was guilty of. With heavy sarcasm, the officer "reminded" me that I had set fire to a hotel room in Milan.

"But I've never been to that hotel," I protested. "I've only left the house to go shopping. How could I have set fire to a hotel? Why should I want to?"

Surprised by my indignation, the superintendent asked for further identification—my name and forenames, date and place of birth, parents' names, and so on. He then realized that they were seeking another Signora Mussolini. He checked what I had told him against his information about the mysterious woman, and we discovered that she was none other than Ida Dalser.

Shortly afterward I was notified from the front that my husband had contracted paratyphoid and was in a hospital in Cividale. I went there in a cattle truck and told him about my adventures.

"There's only one way to keep Ida Dalser from spreading the story that she's Signora Mussolini," he said. "We shall have to get married."

"I'll think about it," I replied, deliberately casual to punish him for my troubles. "But I warn you, I am quite capable of saying no at the last minute."

"The awful thing is that you would," he sighed, taking my hand.

In 1910, revolutionary doctrine recommended common-law marriage. I remember Benito's getting very angry after he had registered Edda's birth at the town hall in Forlì in 1910. He'd asked that the certificate should read, "Edda, daughter of Benito Mussolini and another," but the registrar had spread the story that we were legally married, to hurt his reputation. Benito had gone to see him and squared the record with two sharp blows.

Naturally, under pressure of the Ida Dalser situation, I agreed to a civil wedding, and the ceremony took place on December 16, 1915, in the hospital at Treviglio. Benito was in bed with jaundice and looked very apprehensive under his woolen cap. When the time came, he pronounced the formal "Yes" in a clear and joyful voice. But I said nothing. I pretended not to have heard, though I was watching Benito out of the corner of my eye. When the official asked me a second time, I was as silent as before. Benito looked at me, wild-eyed, wringing his hands with fear. Finally, at the third request, I said yes. Benito sighed deeply, falling back onto his pillows as if the strain had overpowered him.

"Were you afraid?" I asked. He just glared at me.

I thought the Dalser episode was dead and buried, but I was wrong. Two years later, on February 23, 1917, Benito was seriously injured when a shell exploded during exercises, giving him forty-three shrapnel wounds. There was even talk of amputation, though that did not prove necessary; and after several weeks of intense pain he was moved to the military hospital in Milan.

One morning, on my way to visit him, I noticed a dark-haired, disagreeable-looking woman. I didn't recognize the Austrian fire-raiser Ida Dalser, but she remembered me. When we reached my husband's ward, she jumped on me, hurling insults and crying, "I am Mussolini's wife. I am the only one who has the right to be with him."

The other patients found this performance highly amusing. I was furious. I lashed out with fists and feet and even began to squeeze my hands about her neck. Benito was so trussed up in bandages that he could hardly move, and in trying to stop us he fell to the floor. Luckily, the hospital staff intervened, or I would have strangled her. She fled, and I burst into tears.

Then Ida brought an action against Benito, and the court ordered him to pay a monthly allowance of two hundred lire for the bastard child, followed by 100,000 lire when he was twenty-one. Ida Dalser came to a sad end. She died in San Clemente, a mental hospital in Venice, in December, 1937. Her son was studying radiotelegraphy in La Spezia, but he too died, on July 25, 1942, in Milan.

When Margherita Sarfatti began to pose a threat, in 1918, I determined to keep the affair from getting out of hand. But I had to be tougher and more cunning with her, because she was a more dangerous and more intelligent woman than Ida Dalser. She worked as a journalist, having covered the literary and artistic columns of *Avanti!* and then of the *Popolo d'Italia* since 1914. Whenever I mentioned my suspicions about Margherita Sarfatti to Benito, he told me that she was too intellectual, too cultured, for him to get involved with. But after my experiences with Ida Dalser, I kept my ears open, for

I realized that in Benito's case the danger came not from him but from the women; they didn't want to leave him.

One day in 1921, while Benito was recovering from his airplane accident with his flying instructor, Redaelli, Margherita Sarfatti came to see him at home for professional reasons. I pretended to be quite ignorant of the affair, while she behaved impeccably. Yet the mere fact that she'd dared to come angered me. So as I settled Benito back into bed after she'd gone, I let slip quite casually, "Some people have the most incredible gall. All you can do with them is throw them out of the window." Benito must have felt a pang of guilt, because he merely remarked—in an unconvincing voice—that I must be imagining things.

In fact, from 1922 to 1926, my husband continued his affair with Margherita Sarfatti in Rome while the children and I lived in Milan. The more persistent the rumors became, the more I determined to fight back. So when I heard, in 1925, that Benito was ill with a stomach ulcer, I decided to visit him in Rome. Rather surprisingly, I was turned back at the station by none other than the quaestor of police himself. I listened to the rigmarole about how my presence at my husband's bedside might be misinterpreted as a sign that his illness was worse, which would lead to all sorts of political speculation. In the national interest, therefore, I ought to stay in Milan. I finally agreed, though I was not at all convinced. In my mind I'd merely postponed a confrontation with Margherita Sarfatti.

In 1926, the children and I spent Christmas in Rome. Benito could not have been more charming or attentive. The children have glorious memories of that visit. I myself was particularly happy, because he had sworn that his affair with the journalist had ended. And he did break off all links with her, even dismissing her from the paper with a pension. Indeed, I thought that peace had returned at last, especially after my husband burned all the woman's letters before my eyes at the Villa Torlonia.

Mussolini's office at the Palazzo Venezia.
Syndication International

Rachele and Benito rowing. *Keystone*

Signora Mussolini in the 1930's.
Syndication International

One day in 1931, however, I opened the *Popolo d'Italia* and was astounded to see Margherita Sarfatti's name at the bottom of an article on an inside page. My blood ran cold and I thought, So *she's* back. Well, we shall see what we shall see. I could not ask Benito for an explanation in person, as I was in Merano. I had gone there for eczema treatment and to conduct some discreet inquiries into Austrian sympathies among the authorities. But I could send a telegram.

Seeing me grab my coat and handbag and dash out of the room, Carolina Ciano, my son-in-law's mother, realized I proposed to create a fuss. She followed me, already fearing the worst, because she knew my fits of temper. At the post office I took a telegram form and wrote in detail—regardless of the expense. The counterclerk openly shuddered when she saw my message and, more than that, the name and address of the man I was sending it to. Carolina Ciano, who'd been reading over my shoulder, was deathly pale. She exclaimed, "Rachele, you're not going to send it."

"And why not?"

The postmistress was both horrified and highly indignant. "I can't send a telegram like this. I refuse to take it."

After all these years I cannot remember the message. But every woman will know what one says to one's husband at such times. "You will kindly take it and send it immediately," I replied emphatically. "If you want any more details, then you may as well know that my name is Rachele Mussolini and the gentleman I am writing to is my husband."

When she refused again, I took another form and filled it in like the first, addressing it to Benito's brother, Arnaldo, the editor of the *Popolo d'Italia*.

That very evening Benito phoned me. "What is all this?" he asked, half angry and half worried. "I don't know which article of Margherita Sarfatti's you're talking about. All I do know is that I have nothing more to do with her, and I don't want to hear her mentioned again."

I recognized the ring of truth in his voice, but this did not make me any less angry. I determined to strike while the iron was hot.

"All right," I said, "but I am telling you once and for all, and you can pass the message on to Arnaldo. If I see the name Sarfatti in the paper just once more, I shall go to Milan, get hold of a bomb, and blow up the *Popolo d'Italia*. And you ought to know, Benito, that I'm quite capable of it. What's more, it'd be a public service. Nobody likes the *Popolo d'Italia* any longer. It's getting tedious."

My threats must have left their mark, because Margherita's name never appeared in the paper again. Not that she suffered unduly. She later sold Benito's letters for seventy million lire. If I had done the same with all the letters he received from women, asking improbable favors, I'd be rolling in money now, especially as some of them were signed by well-known figures —"society women," as they say.

The third and last of Benito's affairs—which possibly caused me most suffering—was with Clara Petacci. I should also say that, since my husband's death, whenever I have prayed for the rest of his soul I have also thought of Clara Petacci, for I believe one should have the magnanimity to forgive, more so from the other side of the grave. Of all the women who were infatuated with my husband, only she paid for the affair with her life. She was executed along with Benito, on April 28, 1945, when she could have fled abroad and benefited from Mussolini's generosity—as Margherita Sarfatti did. For that reason, I do not feel resentful as I tell her story, merely sad and immensely compassionate.

For a long time I knew nothing of the relationship between my husband and Clara Petacci. Everyone else knew— my children, the staff, and so on. There was a conspiracy of silence about it, more to spare me pain than to protect the relationship, and the few times I was near to discovering something through my private police network, I came up against this barrier. It worked so well that I remained in complete ignorance until I read the newspaper reports on July 26, 1943, after my husband's arrest. Whenever an idol has been toppled from power, everything about him becomes public property, and the Mussolini-Petacci affair provided an ideal target for the enemy press. It was through this medium that I found out that my husband had installed a direct line between our home, the Villa Torlonia, and the apartment where Clara Petacci lived with her family. He never realized that all their conversations actually went through the switchboard and were recorded.

I believe my husband met Clara in about 1936. She came from a very good family, her father being the doctor to Pope Pius XI. From what I subsequently discovered about her, I have no reason to conclude that Mussolini regarded her any more highly than various other women he had known. He never formally presented Clara to other people or appeared in public with her. They met only for brief moments, usually in a little apartment he had furnished—as I later found out—in the Palazzo Venezia. Throughout this affair, Benito continued to sleep at home.

I made no move to interfere until 1944, and even then it was one of the most difficult situations I have ever had to deal with. At that time Benito, the children, and I were staying at the Villa Petrinelli, in Gargnano, on Lake Garda. Clara had also come to live in the area, in a villa a few miles away.

Both Benito and his government were insecure at this stage, toward the end of the war, and it had come to my knowledge that certain antagonistic Fascists intended to use Clara's presence at Gargnano to reflect damaging discredit on my husband. So I decided to see her myself and warn her of her possible fate.

Before leaving for the villa where she was staying, I phoned Benito, telling him of my intention and arranging for two friends to accompany me and the chauffeur. I wanted Guido Buffarini, the minister of the interior for Benito's precarious Salò Republic, to come with me as well, and therefore I stopped at the Ministry on the way. I had no love for Buffarini, since

I knew that he was a schemer and was in contact with Clara. But I wanted him to be present at our meeting for those very reasons.

When his secretary announced my arrival, he came rushing out in his shirtsleeves, anxious to know why I was there.

"Finish dressing and come with me," I said.

"Where are we going?"

"I'll tell you when I consider it necessary. Come along —quickly!"

We drove off and in due course drew up at the main gate of Clara Petacci's villa, where I rang the bell. Buffarini wanted my friends to leave, but they refused. It was pouring rain at the time, and our excited little group at the gate must have looked rather sinister.

I had to ring several times before a German officer appeared, informing us, through the gate, that we could not enter. Furthermore, he added, it was pointless to insist. I spent over an hour trying to find some way through the railings, but it was no use. Finally, my friends had to threaten Buffarini with violence before he signaled, sweating with fear, to someone at the window to let us in.

Seeing my fierce expression, he asked, "Are you armed?"

"I never take a weapon when I go visiting," I answered.

I was shown into a small room. Buffarini, the German officer, and another soldier stood nearby while I sat vainly trying to regain some composure. After some minutes I glimpsed a wraithlike figure descending the stairs. It was Clara Petacci. For some reason her frailty, her hesitant, almost awkward walk, and the way she was clutching at a handkerchief completely disarmed me. I managed to hide my anger by avoiding her eyes, for I knew she would be able to read my feelings in them, and asked quite calmly, "Signora or signorina?"

"Signora," she replied, in a low and slightly harsh voice that belied her apparent physical weakness.

"Signora," I said, "I shall endeavor to remain calm. I

have not come here as the jealous wife to insult you, much less to threaten you. Our personal feelings have nothing to do with the crisis affecting our country. I am therefore asking you to make a sacrifice. My husband must have a quiet mind so that he can work. But more than that, I am determined to put an end to the scandal arising from your presence here so close to our house. Love should be capable of sacrifice. As Benito's wife I would be quite prepared to go away, to live alone far away from him, in a castle or on the top of a mountain, if my leaving would help to save him. You say you love him. Well, then, stop seeing him. Let him live in peace. I'm not asking you for my sake, so that I can have him to myself, but for his."

Clara sat curled in an armchair, listening in silence. I went on, "You must know, too, that my husband adores his children and that, since our son Bruno was killed in the war, there are only the four of them. So for their sake as well, I am asking you to go, to stop upsetting the family. Leave Lake Garda."

I wished she would fight back, refuse to go, defend herself. But instead she broke into convulsive sobs, shaking her head as if she could not bear to hear more. Exasperated by her weakness, I told her exactly what I was feeling: that I couldn't tolerate women who thought tears solved everything; that I considered it quite appalling of her to have deposited photocopies of my husband's more compromising letters in Switzerland and Germany; that she should never have agreed to a direct line between her villa and ours when recordings of all conversations were sent to Berlin; and, finally, that she was obviously incapable of caution, seeing that she had even formed contacts with unreliable people.

Still she said nothing. I caught hold of her arm and shook her till she spoke. "The Duce loves you, signora. I have never said an unkind word about you. He would not have tolerated it, because he loves and respects you."

I could not help pitying her. Out of her depth in such a

situation, she had only her unrequited love for Benito to urge
her on. All anger left me, and I remembered her courage when
Benito was arrested on July 25, 1943. Marshal Pietro Badoglio,
now our common enemy as the titular head of government in
Rome, had even imprisoned her in Novara. So I begged her,
"If that's how it is, signora, why don't we both try, together,
to do something to help my husband at such a difficult time?"

She got up, went upstairs, and returned some moments
later with a bundle of letters. Handing them to me, she explained, "Here are thirty-two letters your husband sent me."
I could see at a glance that they were only typed copies. Then
I completely lost my temper. I shouted at her. I told her just
how seriously she was compromising Mussolini by talking to
him while the Germans listened in on their conversations, how
the partisans and Allied spies were using her for their own gain.

Clara's reaction was to fall from one fainting fit into
another, while Buffarini bustled about with a bottle of cognac.
She had only the strength to whisper that my husband could
not live without her.

"That's not true," I protested. "My husband knows I'm
here. Call him and ask."

She took up the challenge and heard him say, "Yes, I
know my wife's there, and she's right. We must end it."

I got up, my eyes blazing, and fired my parting shot:
"You will come to a bad end, signora. They'll put you on the
Piazza Loreto." It was there, in Milan, that the Germans had
executed Italian hostages as an act of reprisal, and there that
the partisans had threatened to put us. Unfortunately, my
warning was truer than I knew at the time, for on April 29,
1945—the day after they executed Benito and Clara Petacci
—the partisans did expose both bodies on the Piazza Loreto.
They hung my husband by his heels, and his mistress upside-
down beside him.

Outside in the darkness, my friends were waiting in the
rain. I went back to the Villa Petrinelli. My husband was still
in his office at the Villa Orsolina. I sent word that I had re-

turned home, having done no injury to Clara. Then I locked myself in my room, and, for the first time in my life, I wanted to die.

Later I found out that Benito had phoned several times. Finally he wrote me a little note asking if I would agree to see him. He spent hours trying to appease me, holding my hand, kissing me tenderly, begging me to forgive him. I'd won my husband back yet again, but I was sure he knew how close we'd been to disaster.

8/ Mussolini and Money

Some time ago, I read in a newspaper that Mussolini's wife had collected jewelry and furs. I found this highly amusing, since I've owned only a bracelet in my life. Even that we had to sell in 1931 to pay back a loan from the bank. In any case, the very fact that I owned it was unusual, for we never made a habit of giving presents in the family. For special celebrations, Benito might receive a tie from the children and bring me a signed photograph of himself. Once, however, my brother-in-law, Arnaldo, bought his wife, Augusta, a bracelet, and Benito felt obliged to give me something too.

As for fur coats, I never possessed one. Whenever I attended social functions, I borrowed a coat from Edda. Hers were a little long for me, but I managed.

After the war there were endless anecdotes about the Mussolini fortune. If we'd cached money anywhere the children and I would never have experienced such financial straits after Benito's death. When I returned to Rocca delle Caminate, I realized how deeply the myth had taken root, for the walls were in ruins, the gardens dug up, and the paneling torn down.

Anyone who once thought or still thinks that Mussolini hid a fortune somewhere need search no longer. There is no Mussolini treasure to be tracked down at the bottom of Lake Garda or anywhere else.

During its two years under the Duce, from 1943 to 1945, even the insecure little Salò Republic in northern Italy had its own economic structure and banking houses and functioned like any other state. The ministers didn't walk about with their pockets bulging with notes any more than my husband lugged the crown jewels about with him.

Once and for all, I can declare that Mussolini never received one scrap of his salary as prime minister during the twenty-odd years he held office. He even refused his parliamentary pay—to the advantage of the Chamber of Deputies and their expense fund. None of this was meant as an ostentatious sacrifice, nor did we have to live on thin air. My husband owned a successful newspaper, the *Popolo d'Italia*. He wrote articles for the foreign press—especially the American press— and was highly paid. He also received handsome royalties for his books, some of which were even translated into Chinese.

This meant that we had enough to live on comfortably, more so when we resided in Rome. Despite Benito's protests, Prince Torlonia insisted that we occupy his villa for a paltry annual rent of one lira. The government provided our cars— apart from those the children, my husband, and I had bought for our personal use.

We even accumulated some savings, with which we bought plots of ground in Romagna and Ostia and a villa at Riccione: Altogether my husband was offered several houses, including one in Naples, the Villa Roseberry (the gift of an English family and now the summer residence of the President of the Republic); another in Rome, the Villa Chiara (today a public park); and Rocca delle Caminate. Benito gave all these to the state—except Rocca delle Caminate, because it had been donated by the people of Ravenna and Forlì, and each townsperson had contributed one lira toward the cost.

Any gifts or legacies that came his way were automatically assigned to charitable organizations or religious orders. In 1924, Benito decided that all the large sums that people paid to acquire an aristocratic title should also be made over to charity. Until then such underhand dealings had lined private pockets; now the sales had become official. Mussolini presented each case for the King's assent, since only the Crown could confer a title.

All this seemed so extraordinary that after World War II several commissions looked into Benito Mussolini's administration of public money. Giulio Andreotti, the present prime minister, announced their findings in an interview published by the Leftist weekly *L'Espresso*, which stated that Mussolini was innocent of any fraud in this area during his term of office.

My husband's disinterestedness arose simply from his belief that money was no more than a means of coping with one's needs. Over and above that, it was a useless burden.

I must admit that this attitude created friction between us, for I rigidly hold the view that anyone who works deserves a wage, and therefore could not accept my husband's refusing his. But I could not change his basic nature. He'd always shown the same lack of self-interest, even as a young man.

In 1909, when Cesare Battisti appointed him editor of his paper in Trent, Benito was offered a salary of 75 lire a month. He actually replied that 50 lire would be enough to live on and the other 25 could go to the paper. He repeated this trick on me twice more after we'd set up house together. On the first occasion, when he edited the *Lotta di Classe* at Forlì, his salary was 120 lire a month, but he gave 20 to the party. The second time was at *Avanti!*, when he took only half the allotted salary.

When he was appointed head of government, Benito assumed that the office of prime minister was purely honorary. Guessing that he'd refused to accept his rightful salary, I took the precaution of saying, "That's all very well. You can do what you like, but I have a house to run and children to feed. Besides, some people on your paper are doing very nicely, while I have to go without. I never worried while you lived in Milan, but now that we are to live apart, I want a regular allowance from the paper for our expenses."

That was how I came to receive 6,000 lire a month. The

newspaper also paid the rent, as well as the cost of the car and the chauffeur's salary.

I was glad that I had this security after my first slightly disturbing trip to Rome, in 1926. Benito had been living alone in the capital for four years, and I in Milan with the children. When he came to see us, he was very much the solid citizen and family man. But in Rome he behaved like a playboy, with his stylish clothes, his sports car, and a puma on a leash to impress the ladies. When I opened the drawer of his bedside table and found 12,000 lire, I lost my temper. After a terrible scene, he explained that when he received money, he just put it there for want of anywhere else. Previously he had given it to me. This incident served a purpose, as it was probably the origin of Arnaldo's attempts to persuade Benito to lead a more orderly life.

Once the family settled in Rome, Benito resumed his former practice of giving me a monthly sum for the housekeeping—about 15,000 lire, and anything else I might ask for. Like a true Latin, however, he never told me exactly what he earned.

Concerning the kind of life we led in Rome, I remember that on the day after the Duce was arrested, on July 26, 1943, an officer approached the Villa Torlonia, where I was still living. When I came in from the garden with my apron full of eggs and vegetables, he mistook me for the maid.

"I would like to visit the Mussolini house," he explained. "Will that be all right?"

"Of course," I replied. "I'll come with you."

I put down the eggs and vegetables and, as I showed him the way, asked him for news about the situation. He told me that Mussolini's wife had been arrested on the Duomo square in Milan with a suitcase full of banknotes and jewelry. I pretended not to be interested and we continued on our way. In one of the rooms the officer noticed a photograph of my son Bruno and smiled.

"What a marvelous boy he was," he said. "Very simple and kind. We went to school together."

"Yes," I sighed. "He was a marvelous boy."

Perhaps the tone of my voice gave me away, for the officer stopped, looked me closely in the face and said, "But who are you? Are you one of the family?"

"Yes, I'm Bruno's mother, Signora Mussolini."

He grasped my hands, kissed them, and asked me to forgive him for what he'd said about my arrest in Milan. "I never thought I'd meet the Duce's wife with an apron around her waist. If anyone had told me, I wouldn't have believed them," he kept saying. "And I was sure Mussolini's house was a palace full of magnificent furniture. There's nothing luxurious here. It's like anyone else's house."

He seemed almost disappointed, but perhaps he was also glad to discover the truth; for when he left he was obviously affected by his visit and asked if he might kiss me.

There were hundreds of other examples of this kind. But we couldn't arrange conducted tours of our house, open cupboards and drawers, and say to the world, "You can see how simply we live. We're not *nouveaux riches*, you know." As far as we were concerned, our life was quite ordinary—the way we had lived since we were young.

Incredibly enough, one of Benito Mussolini's greatest delights on becoming head of government was to be able to change his sheets every two or three days. One morning he said to Irma, the maid, "And yet it would be wonderful to be able to change them every day."

The exterior of the Villa Torlonia was attractive, if a bit solid. The house was located in the residential part of the Via Nomentana in Rome, and the grounds were vast, with a great variety of plants that grew so thick and fast the place was like a forest. There were also large greenhouses and a charming little antique theater.

I was disappointed by the house's interior. Admittedly, it was large, but there was so much wasted space, so many nooks and crannies, so many useless little rooms. Every time I entered a room I collided with a pillar. The furniture was dark and heavy, and, quite frankly, in Benito's room it was black and ugly. But my husband would not interfere, because it was not our property; by no means was Prince Torlonia to be annoyed. Gradually I managed to change things, starting with the chairs. I disliked to see them broken by Germano, one of my nephews, who damaged them every time he came to see us. Commandeering the help of relatives and friends from Romagna, over a period of months I modified the whole building—from the plumbing to the decorations—until the villa was cozy and pleasant to live in.

On the ground floor there was a large reception room, where we watched films in the evening. It was a lovely, high-ceilinged room, with two wide staircases leading up each side to a pillared gallery on the next floor. The children found the design particularly useful when I chased them to scold them for some naughtiness, for they had two escape routes to choose from. Also on the first floor were smaller reception rooms, each dotted with candelabra, and the rooms the children made their work area. Vittorio produced his first newspaper there. A delightful feature was that the rooms opened onto the grounds through large bays and French windows.

The second floor contained the oval dining room and our bedrooms—my husband's in the right wing, with a bathroom and study; mine in the left wing, communicating with his through a dressing room. On the top floor, the children's rooms occupied the left wing, while the linen room and the staff quarters were in the right.

Our way of life had changed since the days in Milan. Vittorio and Bruno were growing fast, and Edda was by now a young lady, whose boyfriends already gave us trouble. After a romance with a young Jew, whose life and whose father's life she saved during the war, she was almost engaged to a young man from Forlì named Orsi Magelli. But the betrothal collapsed after the man's private talk with my husband.

"Duce," he said, "I'd like to speak to you about the dowry."

"What dowry?"

"Your daughter's dowry, Duce."

"But she hasn't got one, any more than her mother had."

Edda never saw him again. On April 24, 1930, she married Galeazzo Ciano, whose father, Constanzo, an admiral with a distinguished record, was one of my husband's closest friends and his only official successor.

I had a larger house to run, and while I could escape public life in Milan, in Rome I had to remember that I was the wife of the head of government. I had less freedom of movement, though I managed to create my own little Romagna in the grounds with hen houses, rabbit hutches, and even some pigs.

My husband's pattern of life had also changed. After 1929, he became a family man again and dropped the minor eccentricities of his years alone in Rome. On Sundays the family would drive out to Ostia or into the mountains. During the week we sometimes went to the theater or the opera. But unlike the children, we were not free to go to the cinema. We had to contend first with the security police, who followed us everywhere, and then with the frenzy that greeted Benito's public appearances. Early on he'd enjoyed it, but eventually it began to pall.

I remember several stories that confirm this. Once, on the way to his office in the Palazzo Venezia, Benito stopped his car at the top of the Via Nazionale. His escort of three policemen in the car behind had no time to intervene before he was on the pavement, calmly walking down the street and enjoying his sense of freedom. His "guardian angels" were helpless, not daring to press too close to get him back into his car. He continued on his way as if it were the most normal thing in the world.

After a while the passersby began to wonder if they were seeing things or, more daringly, began to call his name and move to shake him by the hand. Benito was forced to stop. Suddenly there was a crush of people reaching to touch him, cheer him, kiss him. When he told me about it, I could see that he'd been really frightened, not of an attempt on his life but of the surging torrent of people. There is no knowing what would have happened to him if the police had not interfered. He never repeated the experiment.

Twice during the holidays, we tried to evade our security guard. One day in 1933 we went, just the two of us, to La Fratta, a small town between Forlimpopoli and Bertimoro, to see the thermal baths. At about one-thirty in the afternoon, we parked the car to continue our way on foot, still without our guard. While waiting for the spa's director, we chatted quietly with the manager of the Godoli Restaurant. I remember Benito was expressing his dislike of the theater's facade (which he thought badly built), when the police descended on us, creating pandemonium.

"So, they've found us," my husband sighed. "Come on, Rachele, our walk is over."

Some days later, at Riccione, I suggested going for a romantic stroll on the pier. We'd gone only a couple of yards when we heard the plodding footsteps of the police behind. "You see," Benito said, "there's no point in trying. They'll always be on our tail. I can't relax knowing that some fellow's keeping me under his eye. I wonder if they're here to protect me or spy on me."

"To spy on you, you can be sure," I declared.

We found ourselves increasingly turning inward during our leisure time. Benito really relaxed and became himself only at home. And he built an impenetrable barrier between his private and public lives.

In the fourteen years we spent at the Villa Torlonia, we invited no one for a meal whom the family didn't know intimately, whether they were ministers, friends of my husband, or important foreign visitors. Usually, the only people we entertained were friends of my sons. Even journalists and photographers were barred from the house. On the rare occasions when the villa's interior was filmed, Benito agreed to the pres-

ence of the cameramen—only because they were American—
and even then he resented the intrusion. He once said, "When
I go home and hang up my hat I become Signor Mussolini and
nothing else. The Duce, the head of government, stays at the
Palazzo Venezia."

I remember that someone—Galeazzo Ciano, I think—
asked him why he did not entertain at the Villa Torlonia. My
husband replied, "Everyone already thinks I am Duce twenty-
four hours a day. If I start believing it too, I'll go mad. I must
have a minimum of rest and quiet to clear my head and keep
my identity. I'm not a robot, and I'm not wedded to Italy.
Hitler may have said he was married to Germany, when I asked
him why he didn't make one of his gorgeous lady admirers his
wife. But I'm a normal man who wants respect for his privacy
as well. Basically the English are right not to want strangers in
the bedroom. It's a symbol of their private life. They're right,
and I'm like them."

9/ The Minor Mysteries of a Dictator

My husband's day began about six-thirty, when our maid, Irma, woke him by drawing the curtains. He didn't loiter in bed, and while she was laying out his clothes, he shaved and drank a glass of orange or grape juice. All this took no more than ten minutes or quarter of an hour. Then he went down into one of the reception rooms for a quick bout of gymnastics before going into the grounds to join Camillo Ridolfi, his fencing master since the dueling days, and now his riding master as well as close intimate—a sort of confidential friend. Every morning Ridolfi came to the Villa Torlonia with three or four horses and, depending on his mood, Benito would jump a series of fences or take a ride in the grounds. This recreation never lasted more than half an hour at the most.

At about seven-thirty Benito went up to his bathroom, took a shower, rubbed himself down with eau de cologne, put on the clothes Irma had laid out for him, and went to the dining room to gulp down his breakfast—a meager diet of whole-wheat bread, milk, with a dash of coffee, and fruit. Often he would send Irma to ask if I wished to eat with him. I usually answered that I couldn't, because, already busy with the housework, I lacked the time.

I remember that one day, after I had answered him in this way, Irma came back to me, quite overwhelmed. Benito had confided to her, "You know, Irma, my wife is like that. But under her rough exterior she's a wonderful woman, a book telling a marvelous story. The trouble is that it won't open, so you can't read what's written there."

When Irma passed on this comment I just grunted, but deep down I was very moved, because Benito may have been right. And to be quite honest I think that, although he gave me a difficult time, I wasn't very easy to live with either.

I feel I ought to pass on a few anecdotes and some personal details about my husband's clothes and habits, if I am going to observe the rules of the game and really tell the truth about Mussolini.

I shall begin with his clothes. My husband never paid attention to what he wore. It was Irma who had charge of this side of his life. Every evening Benito's personal secretary gave her a list of his appointments and public appearances for the next day, together with the uniform, decorations, and civilian suits he ought to wear for the occasion. If Irma had ever made a mistake he might quite easily have gone to a military ceremony in a dark suit or received an important foreign visitor in uniform, which would certainly have caused a sensation. But both Benito and I had complete confidence in her, and we never had cause to regret it. I still recall how panic-stricken she grew when she had to make a choice from among the fifty uniforms and formal suits in my husband's wardrobe.

The only items of dress in which Benito took a keen interest were shoes and gloves, and, in the early days, hats. Benito was noted for the original headgear he sported, which often bore no relation to anything else he happened to be wearing. It was his personal touch, his reaction against convention. He might choose to dress in a bowler hat and a riding habit, or a Basque beret and a dark suit with a stiff collar. But as the years passed, he began to pay more regard to established rules, keeping the hats—which amused the children so much—for holidays at Rocca delle Caminate.

The white spats that he was so fond of also disappeared. These, incidentally, had a story of their own. In January, 1922, when my husband went to Cannes to cover an international conference as editor of the *Popolo d'Italia*, he also called on Aristide Briand, whom he greatly admired. Just before his interview with the French statesman, he noticed that his shoes were somewhat dirty. Resourcefully he solved the problem by resorting to fashion, hurriedly buying a pair of spats to conceal most of his shoes. Appreciating their practical use, he started to wear the spats quite a lot—so much so that it was hard convincing him that in certain circumstances he should leave them off.

Benito used to wear his shoes without laces "to save time when I put them on," and to ensure comfort, he always bought them one size larger than he needed. Later he began to wear boots that zipped up the side, because an old wound in his right leg, dating from World War I, caused him pain. One of these boots is above his tomb. The partisans opened the sole to see if anything was hidden there. Being very practical, he would refuse to throw away a pair of shoes he liked. In 1930, I think, I had to have one pair resoled four times simply because he felt good in them.

He also had a weakness for gloves. He had quite a collection of them, given by Italian tradesmen, particularly in Milan and Rome. But his favorites were the doeskin and soft leather ones. The others, made of peccary, wool, and so on, stayed in his drawers for years.

There have been many unlikely tales about Mussolini, one of which would have you believe that he used to pour pints of eau de cologne into his bath. To start with, he seldom took baths, but almost always showers. And then, he would never have indulged in this kind of eccentricity, because he was far more down to earth than he was made out to be.

On the other hand, he did take particular care of his body, as much for hygienic reasons as for vanity. He went regularly to the dentist, and every Thursday he received a manicure and pedicure. He always said that he couldn't tolerate a man whose hands were uncared for, and an ingrowing toenail made regular chiropody essential. When I teased him about his morning rub-down with eau de cologne, he replied that if he didn't keep his body in perfect condition women would not like him any longer, and a man who was no longer attractive to women was worth-less. This explanation hardly served to put me in a good humor for the rest of the day.

Because they have become legendary, I would like to set the record straight on two small points relating to the Duce's physical appearance and enormous vigor. Comment has been rife about my husband's Roman-style head and about the mis-chievous pleasure he derived from rushing upstairs four steps at a time, leaving a whole procession of generals and other dignitaries puffing in his wake.

The fact is that my husband shaved his head because he was losing his hair. According to him, after he'd worn a helmet during World War I, his hair had begun to drop out. For a while he convinced himself that, by using various lotions, he could prevent this deterioration or even perhaps grow more hair. Each morning he cast a critical eye to see what effects these lotions were yielding. When there were no apparent re-sults, after some weeks, he decided on a drastic course: he shaved his head completely. And thus was born the Duce's image in the manner of a Roman emperor. I must admit that it suited him well enough, but the ones who got the greatest pleasure from it were our children and later our grandchildren, for it was thus that they discovered their favorite pastime— playing with my husband's wart.

Benito's staircase sprints date from the day he found him-self stuck in an elevator. After this mishap, he had reservations about such contrivances and preferred to walk up stairs. And so did all who were with him, for they dared not do otherwise. I must confess that he enjoyed watching them puff and blow, for it was his desire that the whole nation should engage in sporting activities.

Each morning Benito left the Villa Torlonia at about eight o'clock, with two or three security officers in a second car. His chauffeur (for a long time Ercole Borratto, about whom I shall have more to say) reached the Palazzo Venezia within minutes, for the traffic police changed all the lights to green as soon as they saw my husband's car.

When he arrived at the Palazzo Venezia, Benito found reports from the Carabiniere, the police, the prefects, and the party awaiting him on his desk. Reading them quickly, he habitually made annotations with a large red or blue pencil, which he used right down to the stub. If he needed to make other notes, he would frequently use the envelopes of letters he'd received, unsticking them to write on the back.

Next came his daily talks with the ministers of the interior and foreign affairs, the director-general of the police, and, during the war, the army's chief of staff. In theory, mornings were set apart for important interviews, such as the reception of foreign-governmental visitors or ambassadors, while the afternoons were given to less important visitors, parties, students, distinguished tourists, or people from the provinces.

Monday and Thursday were the only days when my husband was not the first in the office; on those mornings, at ten o'clock, he went to the Quirinal to confer with the King. About two he returned to the Villa Torlonia. As he left the Palazzo Venezia there would be a telephone call to our caretaker, who would signal the house by ringing a bell when he saw the car approach. What followed was like a chain reaction. The cook would put the pasta in boiling water, and a duty policeman (standing in an antechamber by the entrance) would descend the steps to open the front door and take the briefcase that my husband always carried. It was still with him when he was executed on April 28, 1945.

Except on Thursday and Saturday, when Benito and I had lunch together, the children and I had always finished our meal by the time my husband arrived. We didn't leave him on his own, however, but kept him company during his meal.

Before sitting down at the table, Benito glanced through the newspapers for some minutes in his study. He had a good command of French, English, German, and Spanish, which he had tried to teach. This review of the press was always accomplished at the same speed as when he was in Forlì. With the customary red and blue pencils (which nobody was allowed to touch at home "because they are state property"), he circled or underlined the passages that interested him. He kept the papers he had marked and threw the others down to the right of his chair—an indication that he didn't want them any longer; we could then destroy them.

Finding it beneficial to his health, my husband fasted on one day a week, maintaining this practice for several years. And when he did eat, it didn't take him long—a few minutes at the very most.

An ulcer caused him pain from time to time. Because of that and the treatment his doctors prescribed, Benito drank only mineral water and milk. He didn't eat dishes with sauce or much meat, and his diet was composed of pasta, sometimes eggs, a lot of vegetables, and fruit. Preferring his vegetables raw, he would eat them in a rather unusual way, mixing large quantities of all kinds in an enormous salad bowl. Near him stood a salt dish, in which he would dunk the salad before eating it.

When Benito had to attend an official dinner, he would come and "pick" from our plates before we left, so that he would be less hungry when later he sat down to eat. He would say, "I can't eat with some fellow standing behind me, watching my every move and taking my plate away before I've finished. It makes me lose my appetite."

Once, after tucking his napkin into his collar, he brought

Mussolini on his motorcycle in 1932. *Keystone*

a horror-struck silence to the King's table. "When I eat," he said, "I like to be comfortable. With all their fuss and bother, they make a real sweat of those few minutes. And then, how tedious it all is!"

I can still recall the smoldering expression on his face when he first caught sight of the butler we had hired at home. The man had stood there, spotless in white jacket, waiting to serve us. "I'll end up eating a sandwich in my room," he grumbled, glancing ominously at this imposing figure. Happily, he soon got used to the extra presence at meals, and for over ten years we possessed our own butler.

Benito relaxed at home with the family until four o'clock. When the weather was bad, the children dragged their father off to play billiards, or maybe he and I went into his study for a chat. From experience, I found afternoons the ideal time to get his acceptance to a costly bill, to plead a cause, or to wring some agreement out of him. There were the children's problems to talk about too. The youngest boy, Romano, had his work cut out trying to explain why he didn't always do well at school. His brothers also had their difficulties, particularly when they came home with low marks for mathematics, because Benito was emphatic about the importance of that subject. But we always settled everything in the end, even when Romano, rather than show his report card, hit on the idea of forging his father's signature. At his first attempt he made a mess of the "M" in Mussolini and crossed it out to start again alongside.

"Do you suppose the Duce makes mistakes when he signs his own name?" his teacher scoffed, for he wasn't deceived.

If the weather was fine, my husband liked to walk in the garden. He would put a mint leaf behind his ear and stroll down the paths. In the vegetable garden he picked peas, beans, and radishes and wiped them before eating them just as they were. Or he would visit our menagerie, for we were often given wild animals, which we housed there. Fortunately, we didn't have to find accommodation for all of them at once, and usually they

Il Duce bathing in the sea at Riccione, 1935. *Keystone*

stayed with us only a matter of weeks—two or three months at the most—before going to zoos in Rome or Milan. The only animals that we kept permanently were dogs and cats.

Apart from Pitini, a dog that Vittorio brought back from Ethiopia, we owned Charlie, a marvelous mongrel that stayed with us for seventeen years, I think, and that had the intelligence not to bark, because it disturbed my husband. Charlie had been a family celebrity since the day when Vittorio and Bruno had invented a pedigree for him, after a neighbor asked what species of dog he was.

"He's a spangled dog," Bruno replied.

"Ah, I know," exclaimed the man, "that's a great breed, the spangled."

We never knew which one was getting the best of the other.

There was also Brock, a Canadian dog, and some cats, one of them given to my husband by a female admirer, the wife of a distinguished and elderly aristocrat.

When it came to wild beasts, we had, in succession, a couple of lions, Ras and Italia, which were particularly affectionate toward the Duce and delighted us by producing three cubs; then a jaguar, a lovely royal eagle, the monkey Coco (who remained for some time), a stag, two gazelles, a falcon, some parrots, a few canaries, and two adorable ponies that had come straight from England.

Sometimes I did not appreciate the leisure afternoon hours at all. This was especially true during the "football period," when Vittorio, Bruno, and their father used to play with a ball after lunch. From the moment I saw my husband take off his jacket I trembled for the windows. And with good reason, for Benito came in looking rather sheepish quite regularly having heralded his arrival with the noise of breaking glass. "You know, Rachele," he would say, "I didn't do it on purpose. I was aiming at Bruno and the shot went crooked. But don't worry, the glazier will come. We've already told him."

Then, trying to wring a smile out of me, he would add,

"The glazier likes us. He's working with us. Besides, we have to stimulate the national economy. Glaziers must work like anyone else."

"One day I'll come and break the panes of your Palazzo Venezia, you'll see."

"All right. But be careful of the windows on the right, they're mine."

I was happier when they gave up lunchtime football for tennis. Even so, soccer remained one of the family's favorite sports; so much so that Vittorio organized interclass matches in an arena, with his school friends. These matches taxed the overworked security forces even more, but my husband would not budge an inch; his sons' friends, he ordered, could come to his house even if it was the Duce's residence.

One must not imagine that the Mussolini family spent all their leisure hours in sport, sport, and still more sport. My husband and I also had our moments of privacy during the day—after lunch, to be precise. Then, like two schoolchildren, we would slip away quietly to the terrace steps. Because Benito always felt the cold keenly, we stayed in the sunshine, under an old fig tree, which listened to our secrets. If that tree had the power of speech, I'm sure it would have plenty to say. There we settled our small marital problems. Benito also told me his news, both good and bad, and I in turn revealed any disturbing rumors about the activities of various Fascists, ministers or not. It was common knowledge in the family that I was the secret agent, the archsleuth.

One day, hearing us laughing, the children asked to know the reason for our amusement; we refused to let on, for fear they might tell their friends that Benito Mussolini had just entertained his wife for some minutes with his impressions of a Japanese minister who was then in Rome with a delegation. The minister had called on my husband that very morning, and Benito regaled me with details of the interview. "Think of it," he said. "For nearly half an hour I had to strain myself to avoid laughing. Several times I was startled during his speech, when the minister shouted in a shrill voice: 'Kokode! Kokode!' or something of the sort. And somehow I got it into my head when I heard this cry that he was going to lay an egg. It's stupid, but the more I reasoned with myself, the more I felt like giggling."

On another day he told me that the American child prodigy Jackie Coogan, the famous "Kid" of the Charlie Chaplin film, had paid a visit to the Palazzo Venezia. "At the end of his visit," Benito explained, "he asked me for a signed photograph, and so I took one and wrote on it: 'Benito Mussolini— to the greatest of the little men.' He promised to send me one of himself for the children."

It was beneath that fig tree that my husband broke the sad news of my inevitable separation from the children during the Ethiopian war, and then from Bruno in the Spanish Civil War. It was also there that we assessed the chances of our daughter Anna-Maria when she was gravely ill in 1935; there, too, that Benito told me of his anxieties before World War II.

Not long after our afternoon conversation, at about four o'clock, Benito would go back to the Palazzo Venezia. Before he left, Irma had some milk taken to him, for it was his habit to drink it in the afternoons. As I have already mentioned, his schedule was less tight at this time of the day, and while he ate some fruit he liked to watch the traffic from behind the windows of his office. What fascinated him was the policeman in white gloves who marshaled the hundreds of cars on the Piazza Venezia with his gestures. "If you only knew, Rachele," he once said enthusiastically, "it's really wonderful. Sometimes he makes grand sweeps over his head like a robot, and at particular moments he creates a kind of unspoken sympathy between himself and the drivers. He uses a discreet a little gesture behind his back to signal them to go forward, to pass, to wait. On this level it becomes an art."

Having learned that the Duce took an occasional interest in the traffic on the Piazza Venezia, the police authorities hastened to assign officers who were particularly proficient and brought a military bearing to the duties. Everybody benefited from it: the traffic, the drivers, the tourists who used to gaze in wonder at the sight—and my husband.

At nine in the evening Benito came home to the Villa Torlonia. Eating his dinner as quickly as his lunch, he would have vegetable soup, sometimes a little meat or some eggs, vegetables, and fruit. In the evening our practice was to re main at the table chatting for a few minutes while the film projector was set up in the great drawing room. In fourteen years at the Villa Torlonia, this routine changed only a dozen times or so; then there had to be a worthwhile reason—like Edda's marriage, for instance. (After that celebration I de cided that any similar functions must be held outside the home. The wedding created such turmoil, and the house felt even emptier after all the excitement and the departure of a child.) Sometimes the routine was varied for an eminent visitor, like Gandhi, Chamberlain, Hitler, or Laval, or finally, because of the war.

Otherwise, the routine was inflexible. After dinner we would watch a film in the drawing room, where everyone gathered, including the staff. There would be no question of protocol: indeed, my husband used to sit in an armchair at the back of the room chatting quite naturally with all and sundry. I remember we had two relations who disliked each other in tensely. One day Benito mischieviously called both of them over to him and deliberately put one next to the other. He then awaited results. Now and again during the film he gave me a sly nudge, drawing my attention to the way they were taking furtive glances at each other and scowling. Quite sensibly, they patched up their quarrel in the end.

The program started with newsreels. My husband was in trigued by the foreign ones, and for this reason he arranged for the projectionist to show documentaries about the Soviet army and the occupation of Poland—films that he'd secured from Vittorio or other people. I believe it was while he was watching these films, in 1940, that Benito came close to deciding Italy's pro-German entry into the war, in June, 1940.

He also interested himself in Italian documentaries produced for foreign markets, wishing to make certain that his country was given the correct image. On his instructions several were shelved.

Finally came a feature film, the choice of which didn't concern him. If it was a comedy or based on history I was sure he'd stay till the end, or, indeed, if Greta Garbo was the star. He would then be attentive and quick to show his appreciation. If the film lacked appeal, he never threw his shoes at the screen or blamed the projectionist from the Luce Institute; instead he would get up and tiptoe out.

While Irma was tidying his clothes, he would invariably drink a glass of milk or camomile tea, then go to bed and fall asleep in a matter of minutes. Nothing would wake him until morning—not even the air raids, as I later saw for myself at Gargnano. To complete the picture, I can even state that Mussolini never snored.

10/ Never Thirteen at Table

Like anyone else, Benito Mussolini had his petty obsessions. He could not bear illness, for example, either in himself or in others.

One day a maid began to cough. I saw him frown, and it was not long before he said, "Let her go and rest. I don't want to hear her coughing in the house." It required a great deal of effort on my part to convince him that the maid's condition was not serious; the poor woman avoided him for several days because every time he saw her he glared at her.

It was the same with the children if he himself had a cold. He would barricade himself in his room and expressly forbid them to visit. "I don't want to see you," he would cry. "If you have something to tell me you can say it through the door."

On the other hand, if his illness was not contagious, he ordered them to keep him company and read the newspapers to him. And woe betide the one who stumbled over a name.

The only person who was exempt from this treatment was myself. So that I should not be left alone when I was ill, he had a table put in my room and ate all his meals with me, whether or not there was any risk of contagion.

Dictator though he was, my husband was obedience itself in the hands of his doctors. However much he might curse them and their medicines, whenever they were in his presence he accepted everything without grumbling; he even agreed to replace his usual nightshirt with a fine pair of pajamas.

Besides the authority of the medical profession, Benito also respected the influence of the *iettatore*, or people with the evil eye—for like every Mediterranean, Benito Mussolini was superstitious. He would never sit down at a meal if the total number of guests, including himself, was thirteen. On Sundays, at home, he checked the numbers himself. And quite often one of the children—usually Romano or Anna-Maria—would be banished to eat in the kitchen when there were guests. In the same way Benito would never start anything important on a Friday, and it was quite usual for him to put his right hand over a specific part of his body, even in public, to ward off bad luck.

He was particularly scared of people with the evil eye. One of his colleagues at the *Popolo d'Italia* had this reputation. Benito liked the man well enough, but in the end he politely made it quite clear to him that he would rather not see him too often. I teased my husband about this superstition, but I must admit that on several occasions when this man came to our house there were small mishaps—lamps shattering, a coffee pot exploding, plates breaking without anyone's having touched them. Then my husband would exclaim, "You see, I told you so! He has the evil eye."

There were several distinguished people whom Benito agreed to meet only because there was no alternative. Once, for example, he had to visit the King of Spain, Alfonso XIII, who was in Rome. This monarch was reputed to be an *iettatore*, and everywhere he went, so they said, disaster followed: bridges collapsed, chandeliers fell down, and so on. On the way home, Benito warned his chauffeur to be especially careful; he did not stop worrying until the following day, when he thought the effects of Alfonso's evil eye must have worn off.

The boys laughed at all this until Romano, the most superstitious member of the family, found a piece of gilded porcelain in the shape of a crescent. He got it into his head that it was a lucky charm, and every time he played cards with Vittorio or Bruno he held it in his hand. Despite this precaution, he consistently lost the game. He therefore gave the charm to one of his friends, who, when he had found it equally useless, in turn gave it to another school friend. After going all around the class, the charm came back to Romano. One day he suggested to his brothers that they should try an experiment. During a game of cards they took turns holding the piece of porcelain, and to their astonishment whoever was holding it always lost. They had to agree that there was something odd about the pattern.

My husband also believed in ghosts. And so did I. In fact I still do believe in them, just as I am sure that one sometimes has premonitions. I've had them, and they've always come true. My children used to laugh at me when I told them that as a child I saw ghosts at Salto one evening. I explained how my sisters and I had heard singing and got up. Pressing our noses to the windowpanes, we saw men with long beards, in white shirts, staring at us in the dark. We weren't afraid, because they didn't look harmful, and for a while we heard strange music coming from the yard. I'm still convinced that the figures were ghosts.

Benito nodded his agreement whenever I said that there really were ghosts. Sometimes he and I attended spiritualist séances, both in Romagna and in Rome. One evening a table walked around the room, overturning everything in its path, and another time, at the Villa Torlonia, we witnessed something quite extraordinary. Prince Giovanni Torlonia summoned up the spirit of his mother, which said, "As soon as I disappear, Giovanni, violets will flower on the table." And immediately afterward a scent of violets pervaded the table in front of us.

In Romagna there are a great many houses that are said to be haunted, One of them, which stands on the road from Forlì to Predappio, was inhabited for a long time. Each resident left after hearing a mysterious musician playing the violin in the night.

Rocca delle Caminate also had this reputation, and Benito was very impressed that I wasn't afraid to sleep there alone. "How do you do it?" he said. "Aren't you afraid? I couldn't."

"But the spirits are friendly," the caretaker replied for me. "I often hear music in the night myself. So I sit myself down on the stairs and listen. They've never bothered me."

Spirits were once the cause of a fine rumpus at Rocca delle Caminate. It happened in 1927, during the course of additions to the house. The Admiralty was installing a beacon on the top of the tower which would be lit every night, and the work had been assigned to a group of soldiers led by an officer.

Unfortunately, they, too, had heard stories about the ghosts. Moreover, they'd been told that a house a few hundred yards away was also haunted. So they sent for a peasant woman, who informed them that to get rid of the ghosts they would have to heat a caldron of water and plunge a black cat into it. Then they had to throw the water around the house.

Acting on her advice, the soldiers took a caldron, filled it, and started the water boiling. When everything was ready, they thrust in the black cat they had caught. Needless to say, this was not the cat's idea of a joke. With a tremendous leap into the air, it dashed away shrieking—literally like a scalded cat.

The soldiers also ran, certain that the ghosts would take their revenge. Some days later a fresh contingent arrived, presumably less superstitious, for they stayed until the work was finished.

There was another aspect of Mussolini's character that might seem surprising. He was convinced that anything which got off to a bad start could not be put right. That is why he was very shaken when, on June 18, 1940, a week after Italy had entered the war, the plane carrying Italo Balbo, one of the quadrumvirs of the March on Rome, was mistakenly shot

Mussolini's birthplace
in Predappio.
Syndication International

Bruno Mussolini with Gina
Ruberti at announcement
of their engagement.
Syndication International

Family portrait—Christmas in Rome, 1928. L. to r.: Signora Mussolini, holding the youngest son, Romano, Bruno and Vittorio, Signor Mussolini, and daughter Edda. *Wide World Photos*

Mussolini's yacht, the *Aurora. Syndication International*

down by a burst of antiaircraft fire from the Italian ship *Sangiorgio*. He was convinced that this accident was a bad omen and used to reflect on it from time to time.

Much later, when Vittorio, Romano, and I urged Benito to take some action against his enemies, and at the end, when we begged him to take refuge somewhere, he invariably replied with a disenchanted smile, "There's nothing more to be done. I must follow my destiny to the very end."

11/ The Practical Man

Perhaps my husband's idea of governing the country was a trifle unorthodox, but it was certainly extremely effective. As far as he was concerned, the only things that mattered were action and results. He didn't care if the means were out of the ordinary. His tools of the trade were the telephone, the airplane, direct contact with the public, and his presence at the grass-roots level, even if he had to spend hours in the harvest fields, bare-chested among the peasants.

His practical approach came into conflict with the notions of various eminent archaeologists in Rome, but he paid no attention to them. On one occasion, for example, he drove these scholars to despair over the construction of the first subway line in Rome. My husband had given instructions for the work to push forward fairly quickly, because he wanted to build a new city, the EUR, on the fringe of the capital. His aim was to organize a huge exhibition there in 1942 to commemorate twenty years of fascism. At one point, however, the workers were held back by the discovery of some ruins, and shortly afterward the whole project came to a halt. There followed a succession of meetings between the engineers and the archaeologists to decide what ought to be done.

Finally my husband intervened, instructing that the ruins should be ignored and the work resumed. To the horrified archaeologists, he observed that respect for the past was undeniably commendable—but that a country's progress imposed certain sacrifices.

"They accuse me of disliking museums," he said. "It's not true, but I'd be happier if they contained more standards captured from the enemy than antique statues. We always want to live off our past. Why shouldn't we ourselves build for future generations? Whether we're capable of it or not, we'll only know by trying."

Even on the personal level, Benito was guided by this same practical approach. I remember once, when he was already head of government and I myself still lived in Milan, he tried to convince me that women in Rome were wearing their hair tomboy style, or cut very short. I had little enthusiasm for this cut and stubbornly continued to brush my hair into a chignon or wear plaits at the side. One day as I was passing the barber's salon where Benito was being shaved, he called me. When I went in, he asked me to come closer, ostensibly to whisper in my ear. I leaned forward, quite unsuspectingly, and suddenly, while he was murmuring some trifle, he cut off one of my plaits with one clip of the scissors. I had no alternative but to do the same with the other. I was furious, but he had got what he wanted.

One morning in the Palazzo Venezia, Benito received a report that the milk supplied to schools, hospitals, and nurseries by a particular cooperative was watered down. He ordered an inquiry at once to find out the people responsible. When proceedings dragged on to no effect, he made a decision that astounded everybody—that is, all except myself, because I knew his temperament. Since no one was prepared to confess, he fired the cooperative's entire staff, from the porter to the director.

I have already mentioned that I was compelled to have the same pair of shoes resoled several times because Benito felt comfortable in them. His attitude toward dress generally was very much in keeping. If his clothes were still in good condition but no longer fitted him, he saw no reason why they shouldn't be made into suits for the children. Therefore Irma, a skillful dressmaker, cut clothes for the boys out of their father's suits for many years.

My husband's ideas about his tailor were also in character. Galeazzo Ciano once suggested that, as head of the government, Benito should now go to a well-known tailor. Benito answered scornfully that his present man gave satisfaction, and he didn't see why he ought to change. "When I go out, I don't walk about with a board on my back saying where I buy my clothes," he added.

For him the most practical answer to any problem won the day. He realized that his presence among the people was an incentive to production, for example, so if he had to go into the field to solve an agricultural crisis, he went.

One notable instance was in 1933—the year of the famous "wheat war." Italy had always imported an excess of grain and produced a surplus of rice, which the inhabitants of some areas refused to eat. Benito therefore decided to step up the production of wheat and absorb the excess rice.

Having introduced his plan in 1932, during the following year he sometimes spent several hours daily in the fields reclaimed from the Pontine Marshes, working bare-chested among the peasants. In the evening he collected his wages like the others—three lire, I think. Surprisingly enough, he was really happy when he came home with his few lire. As an incentive to the fairness, he instituted special honors and competitions and danced with the peasant women who were good workers.

This behavior may seem childish now, but it was effective at the time. And by the end of 1933 the struggle for grain had been won. That year 179,805 hundredweight of cereals were imported, as against 1,091,866 the year before. I found these figures in the newspapers.

Benito then had to find a way for Italy to absorb the surplus rice—to persuade Italians to eat it. His strategy hinged on an official press campaign with the cooperation of the medical profession: he knew that people would listen to the advice of a doctor. Referring to the successful technique of a campaign for the consumption of grapes, inaugurated at a Fascist medical congress held in Rome in 1932, he explained that rice was not, as was thought, exclusively a poor people's diet, but was an energy-giving form of nourishment, which had sustained Italian soldiers in World War I. He asked the doctors to carry this message into Italian homes and to impress upon Italian women that pregnancy would not make them ugly—as they might fear—but the very reverse.

Simultaneously, Benito organized a vast national campaign to demonstrate the different ways in which rice could be eaten. He equipped thirty coaches as mobile kitchens, carrying young women to the various centers to cook rice in public and offer it for free tasting. He himself declared that if every family ate a small amount the surplus would soon be absorbed. And that is what happened. In a few weeks, it had all gone. Ironically, the areas that were at first most resistant to rice consume the greatest quantity today.

On the other hand, Benito's schemes of a practical nature didn't always achieve what they set out to do—for instance, his one-way system for pedestrians on the sidewalks had disastrous results. From his window in the Palazzo Venezia he had gazed on the jostling crowds in the streets at rush hours. To him the endless pushings and shovings were pointless, and he decided a one-way system would enable the human stream to flow faster. One day I told him about the public reaction as it had reached my ears. People were saying, "Now he wants us to walk in a queue like geese."

He was no more successful when, keen to increase the importance of family life and to create an atmosphere conducive for its expansion, he officially ensured harsh punishments for men who beat their wives. During my activities as a "secret agent" in Predappio, I heard the objections that were being raised. "That lunatic in the government wants to deprive us of all our rights" was the usual comment. "If we're not allowed to beat our wives any longer, what have we left?" Benito burst out laughing when I reported these comments.

In all fairness, I should point out that it was he who created virtually all the motor-racing competitions that are still run in Italy. He never hesitated to make a tour behind the wheel of a racing car. Indeed, he found it an enjoyable combination of the useful and the pleasurable—like the day in 1930 when he opened the first autorail between Rome and Riccione to boost the railways. The previous day he'd said to me, "I've not forgotten that I promised you a long time ago that we should have a honeymoon one day. Well, this is it, we'll go tomorrow." And seeing my amazement he added, "You'll come with me on the first autorail, and we'll go to Riccione. Not only will it be free, but you'll have your own special driver—your husband."

The next day, just as he had said, he made everybody get off the train, ordered the proper driver to sit on another seat, put on a cap, and remained at the controls all the way to Riccione. I don't think many heads of government can boast of having driven an autorail. My husband did, and to great effect.

I could write a whole book of anecdotes of this kind, but I am sure that to relate them in quantity would become tedious. I would like to say, however, that the winter sports resorts in Italy, the beaches on the Adriatic coast (particularly at Riccione) and at Ostia, and the Italian spas were all either promoted or developed by my husband.

At Terminile, a ski resort that my husband and I literally discovered, we had some fantastic times. No matter the effort, Mussolini was determined to promote skiing, and promote it he did. He devoted the same attention to Catie, which he popularized by appearing in person, for people would rush to see the Duce bathing. It was the same at Riccione, where we went for family holidays. The children and I always knew when Benito entered the water from the shouts we could hear.

Eventually my husband had to arrange for part of the beach to be private so that, in theory, he could get some peace. And once he was in the water, he swam as far as possible from the beach so that at least he left the nonswimmers behind. Even so, this didn't keep him from coming home with lipstick marks on his arms and neck. Anyone who saw those frenzied scenes knows how Mussolini's presence could give a boost to some venture.

I remember another of his unconventional but very logical and essentially practical decisions. It concerned the ancient rivalry between two parishes in Romagna—Castrocaro and Terra del Sole. Visitors had long since ceased to patronize Castrocaro's thermal baths, and both the economy and the administration of Castrocaro were accordingly controlled at Terra del Sole. For over three centuries this curious situation had fanned friction between the inhabitants of the two parishes— until my husband visited the area himself. Sending for surveyors to work out the precise halfway point between the two communities, he marked the spot and announced that a new municipality embracing both towns was to rise there. The cemetery and the church would remain on Terra del Sole land, next door to the town hall and exactly opposite the registry office, which would be on Castrocaro land. "That way," he decreed, "you'll be married here, and when you're dead you'll go there." And that is how it has been ever since.

Whenever my husband told me what he had been doing to promote a campaign or a town, he always said the same thing, "And now I must find something else."

Before ending this chapter, I would like to relate two more interesting episodes. One of them is of a private nature and shows clearly how indifferent Benito was to souvenirs and presents; the other gives an idea of his way of helping people. In the second instance the Duce's practical approach was overshadowed by the common sense of a nun, the mother superior of a convent.

The first episode occurred in 1931. Sometime before, my husband and I had visited the homes of the peasants who worked on the land we had bought after moving into Rocca delle Caminate. The peasants' living conditions made a deep impression on Benito, and he told me that something had to be done to improve them. He asked Camillo Ridolfi to secure a bank loan so that the houses could be repaired and made a little more comfortable. He got the loan without any difficulty, a total of 300,000 lire—quite an appreciable sum in those days.

Benito promptly forgot all about the final settlement date, and when the time came he didn't have enough money to pay it off. He could have earned the sum by writing for the foreign press, especially for the Americans, who paid well. But he either didn't think of this possibility or didn't have the time. His dual position as prime minister and editor of a leading daily paper (which printed six or seven weekly publications as well) would also have enabled him to raise the sum in one way or another. But there it was. My husband considered the debt a private matter to be settled—privately.

One day, after deliberating for hours, we decided to sell some of the many presents we'd received, which were now hoarded in a huge room—christened by Benito the Chamber of Horrors—at Rocca delle Caminate. There was something of everything there: vases, carpets, knickknacks, trays, pottery, pictures, and so on. We were convinced that among that lot we would find more than enough to raise 300,000 lire.

The same evening a jeweler arrived from Forlì, and we retired to the Chamber of Horrors. It must have been an extraordinary scene, for there we were—the Duce, his wife, and a jeweler, haggling like carpet sellers, judging the weight of things and evaluating every article from the smallest coffee spoon to the tiniest piece of Saxe porcelain. But it was no good, we couldn't accumulate 300,000 lire. Even a magnificent tray —the gift of the town of Genoa—which we'd been told was gold, turned out to be plate. "More junk," said Benito, laughing.

"Do you realize, Rachele, from all this we can't even raise 300,000 lire. When I think of all the time that must have been wasted in discussion before giving me these presents! And what do we find? That it's tinplate!"

Each discovery really amused him, but for my part I couldn't see the funny side of it at all. We had to find a solution.

"Tell me, Benito," I said, "suppose you were to sell your decorations . . ."

"No, absolutely not. Never. Can you imagine what the Shah of Persia would say if he ever found out that Mussolini had sold the Order he sent him?"

"Wait, I've an idea. There's the bracelet you gave me."

Benito looked at me, hurt. "That's the only present I've ever given you."

"Well, you'll give me others. In any case, I'm not very fond of it, and Arnaldo's wife, Augusta, has one exactly the same."

"All right, go ahead."

So with the sum raised from the glories of the Chamber of Horrors, we finally had enough to repay the loan.

The second incident took place in 1935, in a Franciscan convent. Perhaps I should start by explaining that when I accompanied my husband on his visits to the working-class areas of Romagna, he used to tell me to hand out discreetly a few notes to the needy. His common sense told him that a gesture of this kind was more useful than fine words. When I wasn't there, his secretary or the police commissioner escorting him fulfilled this mission. On this occasion, Benito and I had gone to a little town near Rimini, accompanied by the prefect of the province, to inspect some irrigation works.

While Benito was talking to the engineers, I went to a Franciscan convent that befriended destitute children. I had never forgotten the poverty of my childhood and was trying in my turn to lighten the burden of others. If every rich person could remember, even if only occasionally, his own times of personal suffering—and everybody has had some unhappy experiences—I am sure there would be less misery in the world.

When I was about to leave the convent, the mother superior took me by the arm and said, "Excellency, couldn't you ask the Duce to come and see us before he leaves the town?"

"But, Reverend Mother, he can't," I replied. "Your order forbids you to receive men in the convent."

"Come now, what's forbidden to others doesn't apply to the Duce. Ask him to come, we'll be happy to see him."

She was so emphatic that I had no choice but to agree, and when I rejoined my husband I passed on the invitation.

"You're joking, Rachele," he said. "You know very well that a man may not enter a Franciscan convent. Do you want me to get into trouble with the Vatican, when everything's going so well? I'd like to come, if only to please them, because they make a real effort for the children, but I'll go no farther than the door."

On reaching the outside of the convent, we saw that the door was wide open and the mother superior was waiting for us. Benito and the prefect were very surprised. What was more, there were refreshments laid out in the courtyard.

At the end of his visit the Duce asked the mother superior if she needed financial help. When she answered in the affirmative, he turned to the prefect, instructing him to arrange for a donation to be sent to the convent. At this juncture there was an even greater surprise. The mother superior murmured to the Duce that it would suit her much better to receive the donation there and then.

"But, Reverend Mother," he replied, "we don't have that sort of money on us."

"Couldn't you give me a check then?"

"I haven't a check on me either."

"And what about his honor the prefect?"

Astounded, my husband turned to the prefect, who put his hand in his pocket and brought out a checkbook. The Duce told him the amount. The prefect signed the check and gave it to the mother superior. "Now, will you please tell me why you've been so insistent on having it right away when you can't do anything with it?" my husband asked, slightly angry.

"To start with, Duce, don't you worry about our cashing the check. We'll get around that somehow. As to why I insisted, that's simple. With you, we can be sure of getting the money, but with the government one never knows."

"And who'd think these holy women have no contact with daily life and know nothing about the workings of government?" my husband commented in amusement, glancing at the prefect, who was still clasping his checkbook.

Through personal publicity and by promoting new ventures himself—in a way, incidentally, that not even people who disapproved could ignore—my husband was achieving the aims he'd pursued since 1922, when, returning from his first and only trip to London, he said, "If people want to see me now, well, they have only to come to Rome."

He must have succeeded in this, for the other day I made some calculations. During his twenty years in power, he received 229,000 people, shook them by the hand, and talked to them individually or in groups. That comes to about forty people a day.

I can't recall all the names, but many foreign tourists came to visit Mussolini as they might the Colosseum or St. Peter's, among them several near-public figures, like Roosevelt's son and the Count of Paris, of whom my husband said later, "He doesn't seem very intelligent, but he has marvelous eyes." There were artists in every medium—painters, filmmakers, writers, novelists; Walt Disney brought a life-sized Mickey Mouse for Anna-Maria. When it came to political visitors, I need say only that chief among them were all the prime ministers and heads of state of the day, not to mention the ministers.

The important guests included Haile Selassie, the Emperor of Ethiopia, to whom the Duce had given an airplane; Benito even planned—as I can now reveal—to keep Haile Selassie on his throne after the Italian conquest. "I'll put a governor alongside him," he said. When the Emperor left his country, Benito added, "The English have urged him to run, for worldwide propaganda purposes. They're afraid we'll interfere with their empire in Africa. It's not Ethiopia they're interested in, but the countries surrounding it."

There was also Mahatma Gandhi, who came to Rome in 1931 to attend a concert. As very seldom happened, my husband organzed a reception in his honor, in the same huge room where we had our film shows. I can remember this visit quite clearly, not only because Gandhi was an unforgettable figure, but also because he was one of the men who made the biggest impression on the Duce—perhaps more than Hitler himself.

I can still see the faces of the society people who had also been invited. When Gandhi came into the room with his little goat on leash, there was utter silence. Everyone was struck dumb, first by the few clothes the mahatma was wearing and then by the goat. During the few days he spent in Italy, Gandhi and his goat were headline news.

At home, too, all conversation revolved around them, especially among the children. There were Gandhi's adventures (at the Colosseum, where the goat nearly dragged him away); the problems of protocol involved in keeping a watchful eye on the goat to protect the carpets (actually it was extremely well-trained); and people's astonishment on being confronted by a small half-naked gentleman with a little goat. The children found it all very amusing and laughed so heartily that their father sharply rebuked them. "I want you to stop your jokes," he ordered them. "Don't you realize that the little man and his goat, whom you find so funny, are undermining the British Empire between them? Gandhi is a saint, a genius who is using a political weapon unheard of till now. And that is goodness."

Gandhi, on his part, was quick to pay tribute to Mussolini. Eventually, after hearing Mussolini's praises sung so often, I wondered how he managed to bewitch all these people, Italians or not. To discover Benito's secret I even went to the length of hiding behind a half-open door at Rocca delle Caminate and listening to his conversation with a visitor.

Here is how my husband's psychological tactics worked. His visitors would be left waiting in a reception room. When they were shown in, Benito would get up and stay behind his desk or walk forward to welcome them, depending on the circumstances. During these few seconds he would not take his eyes off the visitor, who, faced with this searching scrutiny, immediately became embarrassed and unnerved. Then Benito began to speak. He usually started with a few words of greeting, but soon came to the point of the interview and let the visitor have his say.

While the guest was speaking, Benito showed no sign of impatience. He never fiddled with his pencil or paper knife, never pulled at his shirt collar. Very relaxed, with his forearms resting on the desk, he used to listen, leaning his head a little to the left, frowning slightly, and never taking his eyes off his visitor.

When he spoke, my husband could be persuasive, mollifying, or harsh as the occasion demanded, but his voice was always smooth, very warm, rather low, and even a little shy. And when the interview came to an end, he would administer the final blow in the form of a warm clasp of the hands, a smile, and a last spellbinding look.

All the commentaries I have read written by those who met Benito give the impression that people simply surrendered to his charm. Even Churchill recognized that Mussolini could inspire sympathy and respect. In one of his volumes on World War II, he wrote, "On the two occasions in 1927 when I met Mussolini, our personal relations had been intimate and easy."

Hitler was not of the same opinion. He thought that strength should be more in evidence than charm. He once said, "What a shame the Duce loses all the strength he generates during public speeches as soon as he has a private conversation. Then he turns into a charming man." In public my husband was quite different. His low, well-modulated voice became harsh and clipped. I must admit that, for anyone who knew him well, he was more pleasant to listen to in private than in public.

Stories have been circulated about Mussolini's practicing in front of a mirror, as Hitler did, before he made a speech. This is absolutely untrue; Benito began speaking in public when he was just sixteen, and by the time he became head of government, he knew all the ropes. He could sense the mood of the crowd, and, when he wished, he could touch off the cheers, the shouts, and the frenzy.

He knew exactly when to stop, throw his head back, thrust out his chin, put his hands on his hips, or cross his arms. I believe he had an inborn talent, and that there was a sort of invisible link between him and the crowd.

I became even more aware of this on September 18, 1943, when Benito addressed the Italian people on the Radio Munich wave band, from a studio set up in the ground floor of the Karls Palast Hotel. I was quite close to him, I remember, and was trying to catch his eye as he spoke into the microphone. For I knew that having to speak into a vacuum without any contact with his audience made him inarticulate. It was only while I was staring at him that he could think of me as a listener and regain his confidence.

There has been much criticism of Mussolini's delivery, of the panoply of the demonstrations, the tone he gave his regime. Agreed, but one has only to look at the televised ceremonies in democratic countries—in the United States, France, England, and even in the USSR—and to note the impressive public appearances their leaders make, to realize that Mussolini's showy style was no great matter, all things considered.

12/The Story Behind the Lateran Treaties

Benito Mussolini once said of the kingdom of Italy: "It is a marriage bed for two." He would have done better to say "for three," since after February 11, 1929, when the Lateran Treaties were signed between the Holy See and Italy, the Vatican became as powerful a party as either the King or Mussolini.

For me, on a personal and family level, this important phase in the history of my country began on December 29, 1925, when Benito and I had a religious wedding. Three of our children, Edda, Vittorio, and Bruno, had received holy communion in 1924, from Cardinal Vannutelli in an old Franciscan monastery at Camaldoli, a little place in the Apennines where we were spending our holidays at the time.

Then one day in Milan, while I was in the kitchen cooking tagliatelle, Cina, our maid, came in. "The prime minister has come," she said, "with the editor [Arnaldo], a priest, and Marquis Paolucci. The prime minister would like you to join them in the drawing room right away."

I answered that I was busy and would go in a minute. After a while Benito himself came in. "Off we go, Rachele. That's enough now. Don't make me insist."

And as I pretended not to hear, he undid my apron himself and pushed me toward the sink to wash my hands. Then

123

he swept me off into the drawing room. And there, in that very room, which had become a chapel for the occasion, Monsignor Magnaghi, rector of the church of San Pietro de Sala, celebrated our religious marriage, with my brother-in-law, Arnaldo, and Paolucci di Calboli as witnesses.

When the ceremony was over and Benito had kissed my hand, I remember saying to him with some sarcasm, "And now I hope we've finished getting married."

I wasn't particularly excited by the idea of a religious wedding; indeed, every time Benito had spoken about it I had evaded the issue. But for him this ceremony was of consequence, both in view of his plans to reach an agreement with the Holy See and because he wanted to put our marriage on a regular footing.

In fact, since 1921, when he was still only a deputy, my husband had made his attitude toward the Vatican plain. In one of his first speeches to the Chamber, he'd attracted notice by the friendly terms in which he spoke of the Holy See and the necessity of reaching an agreement.

On February 5, 1922, the day before the election of Pius XI, he went to St. Peter's Square with Constanzo Ciano and Chamber Deputy Giacomo Acerbo in the hope of seeing the white smoke that was to announce the decision of the Conclave. It was then, eight months before becoming prime minister, that he said, "It is incredible that the liberal governments should have been so blind to the fact that the universal nature of the Pope is the heritage of the universal nature of the Roman Empire and represents the greatest glory in the history and tradition of Italy." Consequently, as soon as he came to power, he strove to make a comprehensive plan of conciliation between Church and state succeed.

I do not think he was motivated by clericalism. My husband remained basically irreligious until the later years of his life. But the idea of cooperation with the church appealed to that aspect of him that wanted to put everything to rights, and to his common sense. I should perhaps explain. For some years Mussolini had been a revolutionary. Then, faced with pressure from the Reds, the civil disorders in Italy, and the weakness of the government, he became a defender of law and order, believing a social revolution could be brought about only through legal means.

Once he had become head of government, he undertook to put Italy back on its feet. He started social reforms, put the functions of the authorities on a solid base, and brought stability to his own family life. It remained to settle the position of the Church by bridging the gap that had separated the Holy See from the state since 1870.

There were practical considerations. The Vatican was the center of attraction for Roman Catholics throughout the world. So why not use this interest to advantage, and ensure that Rome could profit by the Church's universal appeal? The Duce would engineer a return to the ancient Rome that had inspired him in his building of the Fascist regime.

These were the underlying ideas. The time had come to put them into effect, to erect a bridge between a Church and a state that had been separate for half a century. In the achievement of his rapprochement important human and personal factors came into play.

First there were the major personalities. Pius XI and Mussolini were both of humble, peasant origin, and therefore had more mutual understanding than some of the others involved. I remember Benito's saying of the Pope, "Basically, what helps things along is that both of us have the mentality of the peasant."

Then there were the middlemen: Benito's brother, Arnaldo, who played an enormous part, the lawyer Francesco Pacelli, the brother of the future Pius XII, and Cardinal Pietro Gasparri, secretary of state to Pius XI, who signed the Lateran Treaties with my husband. I almost forgot Professor Barone, a councillor of state, who set the machinery of the negotiations in motion.

According to Benito, the negotiations were not always easy, for there were people on both sides who were opposed to the venture. My husband had to reckon with the old republican tradition that he had once personified. There was also the King, who was not very keen, various Fascists who were no more enthusiastic, and members of the other creeds, not to mention the Freemasons and the Popular Party of the time —now the Christian Democrat Party—which was led by the famous Don Sturzo, whom my husband described in 1919 as "a little long-nosed Sicilian priest who might talk well of paradise but would achieve nothing on earth." Others at the hub of the Vatican were not in favor of the plan. Finally, there were certain foreign governments that would have preferred to see the Treaties remain unfeasible.

After 1922, the slow haul to a normalization of relations began. My husband took the first steps by restoring the crucifix to schools and law courts and by strengthening the laws against blasphemy. Later, religious instruction was given in the primary schools and he had accorded equal status to both state and parochial schools. In 1924 and 1925, the government voted a subsidy of 6,500,000 lire for the Catholic churches in the new Italian provinces, like Trentino and the African regions. Then the Catholic University of Milan was officially recognized, and the authorities took part in religious ceremonies. Better still, chaplains were appointed to the forces, and the clergy was exempted from military service. In 1925, a law was passed giving an allowance to priests—to the benefit of thirty thousand members of the clergy.

In 1925, another momentous law declared Freemasonry illegal because of its anticlerical bias. Mussolini had to suffer the consequences of this much later, for through this law he lost the support of a secret society that had numerous branches and numbered the King and Marshal Badoglio among its members.

Then we had our religious wedding, and there was the plenary indulgence. Everyone did well out of that. Millions of tourists from many parts of the world brought foreign currency into Italy and were able to learn about the new Italian regime, because the government lent every support.

The Church benefited because these measures encouraged Catholics to come into Italy in greater numbers, and Pius XI made his satisfaction plain in a speech to the Consistory.

The atmosphere was right. All that remained was to surmount the last hurdle. Today this belongs to history, but I can add a footnote by pointing out that most of the negotiations never took place—as might be thought—in formal surroundings, under gilded ceilings and sparkling chandeliers, but quite simply in my husband's apartment in the Via Rasella in Rome. To guarantee privacy, Francesco Pacelli came around nine in the evening and left at about one in the morning. Some hours later, he would inform the Pope of the latest stage in the negotiations, and this went on for months. Cardinal Gasparri also met Benito, in a monastery on the outskirts of Rome. The *Popolo d'Italia,* on Mussolini's behalf, and the *Osservatore Romane,* for the Pope, sustained public interest and enlivened the atmosphere whenever necessary.

Finally, the great day arrived, on February 11, 1929. My husband and Cardinal Gasparri, one for Italy and the other for the Holy See, signed the two treaties at the Lateran Palace. The Duce delivered a speech lasting forty-five minutes, during which, as he later told me, Cardinal Gasparri nodded his approval several times.

That evening, when Father Facchinetti arrived, I was busy with the children at home. An old friend of the family, this Franciscan monk had been delighted when my husband made Francis of Assisi patron saint of Italy, in 1925. But on this February day, Father Facchinetti was radiant with happiness.

"What's happened to you, Father?" I asked. "Have you found a fortune for your poor people?"

"It's even better than that, Donna Rachele."

As he spoke he produced two bottles of champagne from

his soutane and set them, religiously, in the middle of the table.

"Where did you get that, Father?" I asked.

He didn't answer right away, and I carried on feeding soup to Romano, who, at fifteen months old, kicked up a fuss every time I stopped. Then, looking up, I saw Father Facchinetti kissing everybody—the children as well as Cina and Pia, the two maids.

"But what's happened, then?"

"That is it," he exclaimed with a tremor in his voice. "The government and the Vatican have signed the agreement. The Duce has succeeded where men like Cavour and saints like Bosco failed. He can be proud, Donna Rachele. Can't we phone him? I'd like so much to congratulate him."

I wanted to make him happy, but I was afraid of disturbing my husband. I never called him, except in emergencies; instead he usually called me. It had always been like that, even during his official travels. And the same rule applied to everybody, including his ministers.

At that moment the telephone rang. It was Benito outlining the news. "Rachele, the golden age of fascism began today," he proclaimed. Then he told me what had happened and was full of praise for Pius XI—"so sympathetic, so simple and sincere in his ways, and so intelligent!" Now that I am reflecting on all this, I must say that the men who invented the sordid story that Mussolini assassinated Pius XI, when the Pope died, in 1939, didn't know my husband at all. They should have conjured up something else, for he would never have endangered the life of someone who had given him so much joy.

I congratulated my husband, and because Father Facchinetti was gesticulating in front of me, making signs that he wanted to speak to Benito, I handed him the receiver. I couldn't see Benito's expression, though I knew he didn't like long telephone conversations. But I sympathized with the father's elation and dared not ask him to hang up. Marvelous

Father Facchinetti! He was the very picture of a lovable priest
—lively, cultured, good, capable of giving those on earth a
glimpse of the paradise beyond.

I prefer not to dwell on this story, for it reminds me of
those twelve years my husband lay without a Christian burial,
after he had done so much for the Church.

There has been much comment about the Lateran Treaties,
with discrediting remarks that Mussolini was the only one to
profit from them. That is untrue, for several people benefited.
My husband certainly did, though he had to overcome some
hostility among his friends. Indeed, eventually he had to be
emphatic and say, "I am only happy when I do something
useful for Italy." Other beneficiaries were the King, who was
finally recognized by the Pope as sovereign, and, most of all,
the Vatican.

If I wished to be malicious, I might say that the Pope
would never have signed the agreements if he had seen no
personal gain. Certainly he was officially renouncing Rome,
which the Church now, for the first time since 1870, accepted
as the capital of the Italian state. But he was not losing his
authority.

Added to the advantage of increased exposure abroad,
there was the financial support that the Vatican received as a
result of the treaties; it was not merely a matter of exchanging
smiles. Finally, from 1929 on, the Holy See figured increasingly
in the exercise of power in Italy. I don't mean that a cardinal
or a bishop sat at the table each time a treaty was made. But
after the Lateran Treaties had afforded official means of reaching the country's farthest corners, the Vatican became a weapon
—a spiritual and a temporal force—that could sway Italian
politics one way or another, influencing the course of events
as it chose. For these reasons, I suggest that after 1929 the
government of Italy changed from a marriage bed for two
—shared by the King and Mussolini—into a bed for three.

I will restrict myself to giving just one more example of
the Vatican's strength. After 1937–1938, when Mussolini

drew closer to Hitler, the Pope dissociated himself from the Fascists, not hesitating to put them in the same category as the Nazis whenever he condemned them. To that point the treaties had been strictly adhered to. The Church remained the defender of ideals, of international morality, and of respect for the liberty of the peoples. But then for some reason the Vatican released information about Italy to the Americans, with whom we were officially at war.

The Holy See performed a humanitarian role, I agree. But to interfere in favor of a foreign country—which perhaps it considered more deserving—and against the man who had hoisted the papal flag higher than ever, was going too far.

Of course, there is always the rejoinder that I have no proof, that my contention is a slander or, at least, an accusation of intent rather than action. But these are logical arguments. Meanwhile, I would be glad to know what President Roosevelt's special envoy, Myron Taylor, came to do during his week in the Vatican—for if I am not mistaken, he landed in Rome on September 20, 1942, and left again on September 28. Although few people are conscious of it, certain enemy countries kept an ambassador in the Vatican during World War II. As the Holy See had no airport, these people traveled to and left from Rome, which meant that they could with impunity move through the capital of a country in conflict with their own.

And the Vatican stayed where it had always been—in its 480,000 square meters in the very heart of Rome. The Pope, with more than thirty thousand priests scattered throughout the country, was the best-informed person in Italy. I'm not saying that these priests were spies in enemy pay. Absolutely not. But within the precincts of the Holy See, it must have been difficult not to let some information filter through.

However harmless these bits of information appear to be, they were valuable to those people who made it their business to draw conclusions that were not apparent to ordinary mortals. That is what dear Myron Taylor did. On his return to the United States, he assured President Roosevelt that the Italians were growing weary of the war; by intensifying the pressure the Allies could bring them to their knees. That is what actually happened. Anyone who doubts it has only to recall the period when Allied air attacks on Italy escalated—after September, 1942.

From our own information services, my husband quickly learned of Myron Taylor's activities in Italy. He was extremely angry, and to Galeazzo Ciano, the foreign-affairs minister, he declared, "This joker, Taylor, has told the Americans that the Italians have had enough of the war and that stepping up the treatment will break their resistance. You can tell them in the Vatican that, Concordat or no Concordat, if Myron Taylor sets foot in Italy again I'll lock him up."

Needless to say, Taylor never returned to Italy—at least not while my husband was in power.

I have often been asked why the Duce allowed the ambassadors of enemy powers to travel freely round Rome. They did not have access to the entire capital but only to the Vatican, yet all the same, the opportunities open to them were endless and, even if they couldn't quit the Holy See, people could visit them. My husband tolerated this state of affairs because he had no good alternative. Otherwise there would have been dramas. Besides, he knew that the Vatican gave sanctuary to Jews and others escaping from the Germans. He preferred that the refugees should be there rather than in Italian territory, for that would have strained relations with Germany, which were already tense enough because of my husband's reluctance to embark on racial persecutions.

There was a third reason why he couldn't prevent enemy ambassadors from crossing Rome: after February 11, 1929, the Lateran Treaties guaranteed the Vatican the status of an independent state in relation to Italy. Even if the Holy See was geographically inside Italy, the Vatican was free to keep up diplomatic relations with any country it chose. The Italian government itself had its ambassador in the Holy See. In fact, the first such ambassador was a member of the quadrumvirate

—Cesare de Vecchi—whom the Duce appointed to signify the importance of the relations between the two states. Consequently there was no question of forbidding these diplomats from entering a state where they represented their countries.

These explanations may seem puerile and useless to the experts, but many people lack knowledge of the special situation existing between the Italian government and the Vatican. The government was obliged not to interfere in the spiritual role of the Church, while the Church's self-imposed duty was to grow offshoots, as indeed it did, all over the country— precisely because of that spiritual role which the Duce's government could not oppose, since he himself had ensured that the Catholic religion was the state religion of Italy.

I must stress that Mussolini never communicated with enemy nations through their ambassadors in the Holy See. He was opposed to asking the Vatican to fulfill anything other than a humanitarian function. It was only for the sake of others that, three days before he was executed, in April, 1945, he agreed to negotiate with the National Liberation Committee through the arbitration of Cardinal Schuster, archbishop of Milan. The National Liberation Committee was a Socialist political and military organization formed in Rome in September, 1943, and dedicated to freeing Italy from all armies of occupation. Benito's purpose in negotiating with the committee now was to surrender to the Italian Socialist Party the power invested in the Salò Republic, the minority government in northern Italy which Benito had maintained for two years in opposition to Marshal Badoglio's government in Rome. A first scheme for such a step had been rejected by Sandro Pertini, the present president of the Chamber of Deputies, who was then a member of the National Liberation Committee.

For my husband it was a question of saving human lives, now that the war was virtually over, and of finding a legal solution to the problematic division of Italy. He was not negotiating to save his own life, for he would never have agreed to fall into Allied hands alive. "I'll never go to the Tower of

London or Madison Square Garden, where the English and Americans would put me on show like a freak after they've caught me," he said. "I couldn't, ever!"

The facts of the meeting with Cardinal Schuster are well known. In one of the reception rooms of the archbishop's residence in Milan, Cardinal Schuster and my husband sat down on a couch facing, on one side, the representatives of the National Liberation Committee—including Luigi Cadorna, the son of the World War I generalissimo who had given his total support when Mussolini formed his first government—and Schille Marazza. On the other side were the Fascist delegates accompanying the Duce, including Marshal Rodolfo Graziani, the minister of defense of the Salò Republic.

The talks had begun and Marshal Graziani was explaining why the military surrender demanded by the National Liberation Committee could not be signed, when Ugo Bassi, the prefect of Milan, who had just entered, whispered in his ear. Bassi, it transpired, had heard from the cardinal's secretary that the Germans, having already negotiated the surrender of their army in Italy, were waiting in another room for General Wolff to sign it.

My husband immediately put an end to the meeting, declaring that he had been betrayed both by the Germans and by Cardinal Schuster. "It's July twenty-fifth all over again, only much more serious," he shouted, alluding to the occasion of his own arrest and Badoglio's betrayal of the Axis. "The Germans are paying us back for September eighth, 1943, in our own coin."

He was sincerely accepting the responsibility for the signing of the armistice between the Allies and Badoglio. Even if Badoglio had had Mussolini arrested, Badoglio was now the legal head of the Italian government in his eyes.

Three weeks earlier, the same Cardinal Schuster had said to Vittorio, my son, "Your father has almost always had poor backing, but his name will be written deep in the history of Italy. With the Conciliation, not only did he bridge the gap

between Italy and the papacy, but he also found a definitive solution for the problem of the temporal sovereignty of the Church
in Rome, which has been with us since 754. With the Lateran
Treaties," Schuster went on, "the papacy has regained the
freedom to rise higher in the people's minds. Nobody can take
this exceptional achievement away from Benito Mussolini."

If he felt like that, why didn't he tell my husband about
the German surrender, seeing that everything was over? He
could have done so, if only out of gratitude for what the Duce
had done for the Church, and it wouldn't have changed the
situation at all.

I suspect that, leaving his humanitarian duties apart,
Cardinal Schuster had chosen which side he proposed to support.
Since the Allies and the partisans were winning, he intended
to join them and deliver Mussolini to them. The Duce had
declined to admit this. He was therefore all the more offended
that Cardinal Schuster could have listened so coolly to Graziani's
speech without consulting the Germans.

A few years ago I said to a French lawyer whom I greatly
respected that the devil must have gobbled Cardinal Schuster
when he died. I added that if ever I heard that he'd been
canonized, I'd go and throw a bomb at the Vatican myself.
I'm too old to do it now, and I've finally found peace of mind.
But I can't help feeling a little bitter when I think that my
husband, who had given so much to the Church—and I'm
quite prepared to repeat myself—lay for twelve years in a box,
and I mean a box, without a Christian burial. Since he was
buried, near his family in the San Cassiano cemetery in Predappio, several priests, to my knowledge, have refused to say
a mass for his soul. Admittedly, they were once chaplains to
the partisans.

Neither can I help feeling profoundly sad when I think
about two other episodes in my life, separated from each other
by about thirty years.

The setting of the first, which arose because of a river in
flood, was a monastery in Predappio at the time the Duce was

at the very peak of his glory. Sitting on the back of a motor-cycle driven by one of my security officers, I arrived at this monastery to ask the abbot if he would take in peasants of the Rabbi valley; their homes had been devastated by the floods. I had myself donated money for the restoration and expansion of this monastery, but it was soon obvious that the abbot didn't remember me. He ran out in front of the motorcycle, shouting, "Go away, go away this minute! Women are not allowed to come in here."

Even when we tried to explain who I was and the purpose of my visit, he stubbornly refused to listen. To get rid of me, he said at last, "Write to the Pope then. He'll give you his per-mission to use this monastery."

I was fuming and left him with the retort: "That's a good idea. I'll do that and then we'll see!"

Driving to the main post office in Forlì, I phoned the Duce in Rome, describing to him the details of the situation. He answered that he would do what was necessary right away. Two hours later, the astonished abbot was opening his monastery to the homeless peasants.

The second incident happened in 1959 or the following year. I wanted to go to the Vatican to meet Pope John XXIII. It so happened that I knew his brothers. They had explained what a good person he was, but by all accounts he was very unhappy as Pope. No longer could he drink the good wine he loved, or have the freedom to go about; in fact he felt like a prisoner. An image formed in my mind of a priest unlike the rest, to whom I could bare my soul, and perhaps make my confession also. I wanted to go not as Mussolini's widow but as a woman who had important secrets to disclose. Furthermore, I could do so only to a Pope, since besides being head of the Church he was also a statesman who could understand the significance of various messages and certain secret information.

My confidence that I would be given an audience was backed by the fact that I had sent regular telegrams to the Holy See since my husband's death on the anniversary of the

Lateran Treaties. For the audience I proposed to wear a lovely black dress and a black mantilla—a gift during a trip to Spain and an outfit in which I wish to be buried. One day, however, a bishop arrived at my home. Very embarrassed, he explained that the Holy Father could in no sense see me, because "politically it was not feasible."

I was overwhelmed. I had never used my husband's name or his authority to my own advantage except to do good. Under the circumstances I was unable to appreciate how the Pope could possibly imagine that, fifteen years after Benito's death, his widow would use an audience at the Vatican, with political and other reasons in mind, as an excuse for self-glorification. I had always been assured that the Holy See was not involved in politics, and now I knew to the contrary. There had been a time when the Vatican's doors opened at the mere ring of a telephone; now they were hermetically sealed.

13/Mussolini and Hitler

As soon as the tide of World War II had turned, there was criticism of Mussolini—both in Italy and elsewhere—for his alliance with Hitler. He made a convenient scapegoat. If we turn back to April 28, 1945, the day Mussolini was executed by the partisans, we might ask why all the false patriots (who sang hymns to victory as soon as they were out of danger) and the foreign military and political leaders did not give Mussolini the public trial that was planned for Hitler.

Because the partisans had arrested him, Mussolini was essentially in Allied hands. There was no longer any doubt as to how the war would end, and the partisans could have put a spectacular end to fascism by trying my husband. Instead, they contrived a hasty execution for him. By carrying it out in total secrecy, they scratched away his chance to put up a defense and publish the documents in his possession, which might have compromised a number of his Italian opponents and foreign enemies.

The victors might have been embarrassed to realize that, for as long as Mussolini's friendship with Hitler was to their advantage, several nations—including France, England, and America—made use of my husband. Churchill, along with many others, might have been annoyed to see the leader of fascism expose the letters they'd written to each other—even after the beginning of the war, when they were supposed to be enemies.

It was more convenient to silence Mussolini than to blame him for his alliance with Hitler; indeed, to keep him from explaining why he'd agreed to this alliance. Benito's revelations might have spoiled the happy atmosphere of the Yalta agreement, when Roosevelt, Churchill, and Stalin divided the world among them like fellow thieves dividing their spoils.

In fact, Mussolini was never obsessed with Hitler, as Allied propaganda would have had one believe. From the beginning, my husband greatly admired Germany—not the land of the Third Reich, perhaps, but the country that had given the world Beethoven and Wagner, Kant and Nietzsche, Frederick II and Bismarck, Goethe and Schiller, Luther and Marx. It was they who had been his spiritual masters and shaped his pattern of thought. In my husband's mind Germany was the nation of nations. Europe could only gain from an alliance with her, as far as the construction of a western dam against the tide of bolshevism was concerned. But Germany was also the country Mussolini had encouraged the Italians to fight, the country he had himself fought in World War I.

Such was my husband's attitude when he first met Adolf Hitler, in Venice, in June, 1934. For Benito, there was no question of love at first sight. When he returned to Rome, he said of Hitler: "He is a violent man with no self-control, and nothing positive came out of our talks."

A fortnight later, Benito came home with a bundle of newspapers under his arm. Throwing them onto his desk and underlining the headlines in thick red pencil strokes, he indignantly exclaimed, "Look at this. That person makes me think of Attila the Hun. Those men he killed were his closest supporters, who raised him to power. It's as if I were to kill Federzoni, Grandi, Bottai, and the others with my own hands." Taking one of the papers, I read that Ernst Röhm and other recalcitrant German politicians had been executed by

Hitler. Compared to the Führer, Mussolini was never a real dictator. He never had that kind of blood on his hands.

If the English and French had shown greater vision in the two months after Hitler and Mussolini first met, World War II might never have broken out. For after his initial impressions of the Führer, Benito would have missed no chance to make war on Germany, especially after the Nazis' assassination of Engelbert Dollfuss, the chancellor of Austria, on July 25, 1934. For the Duce, this was not only an appalling crime but a personal affront, in view of Hitler's assurance at their meeting in Venice that he would drop the Anschluss—his plan to annex Austria. Moreover, Dollfuss had been an intimate friend of ours.

We learned of his death on July 26. Frau Dollfuss and their two children had already been residing for several days in Riccione, where we'd rented a villa for them. Her husband was to have joined them on the twenty-fifth—the very day he was assassinated in his office while preparing to leave.

When the news reached Benito the following afternoon, while he was visiting some public building works near Forlì, he hurried back to Riccione, pale and shaken. "They've murdered Dollfuss," he shouted from the doorway. "Come with me. We must tell his wife and see if we can help her."

We went straight to the villa and found Frau Dollfuss resting while the children played on the beach. Benito didn't inform her of her husband's death right away, but the poor woman became distraught when he told her gently in German that Dollfuss, now lying seriously wounded, needed her. I held her hand and tried to comfort her, but, as always at such times, I felt awkward, especially as I knew the truth.

That same evening, on the Duce's orders, a special plane took Frau Dollfuss back to Vienna. It was then, during the flight, that she learned in an odious manner the bitter truth of her husband's terrible death. The children's governess, who in reality was a Nazi spy, callously told the children of their father's tragedy, and they in turn had the sad privilege of informing their mother.

On our way home from the airport, Benito gave me further details. Dollfuss, he revealed, might have lived had he not been left bleeding in his office. That evening, Benito telephoned orders from Riccione launching a hostile press campaign and concentrating troops and aircraft on the Austrian border. Temporarily at least, these precautions sufficed to stop Hitler from advancing into Austria.

But the Duce had discovered that he could not rely on the other great powers, notably France and England. He said, "I have been disappointed by the friendly Western nations. I had expected a more energetic response. Less apathy on their part, and things might have been different. As soon as Hitler realized I meant business, he disowned the murderers of Dollfuss, but I'm still wary of him. He wants Austria, and he'll have it, especially if I'm the only one to march on the Brenner. The other powers ought to show some interest in Austria and the Danube basin."

Shortly afterward, Frau Dollfuss brought to Rome the keys of Venice, which Austrian forces had taken to Vienna after the conquest of Venetia. With her came some toys that her husband had intended for our children, and his letter asking Benito to protect his family if tragedy befell him. The Duce honored this last request. When the Nazis raped Austria, in 1938, he arranged sanctuary for Frau Dollfuss and the children in the United States.

The Allies had missed their chance to nip Nazism in the bud. Even later, when the situation changed, the French and English governments were too obtuse or biased to grasp whatever opportunities presented themselves. Perhaps, too, the English thought—as did the French—that Mussolini's Italy would wage war on Germany alone and that both countries would exhaust themselves in the process.

After these events, three years elapsed before Mussolini and Hitler met again. Their second encounter occurred in

Germany. By now Hitler fully understood the true meaning of Mussolini and fascism. When the League of Nations imposed sanctions on Italy after the Ethiopian campaign, Hitler alone offered economic and political aid, and he was the first to recognize the Italian Empire. The Führer had made a profitable investment; he would gain in political capital when Italy came to decide about the German alliance. For the Duce remembered this support when Hitler made overtures for the latter. It was a determining factor, along with the vision of what such an alliance could achieve against bolshevism—something the world had already seen graphically demonstrated in the Italian-German intervention in the Spanish Civil War in 1936.

The wind seemed set fair for Benito's next visit to Germany. He left Rome on September 23, 1937, expecting a cordial welcome; he returned overwhelmed. In those five days, Hitler was his constant companion, attending to his slightest needs. He ensured that Benito had the hard pillows he liked to sleep on and personally supervised the sleeping arrangements every night. He made sure my husband had warmth, because Benito was susceptible to cold. Indeed, Hitler showered the head of protocol with endless questions. Were Benito's curtains too dark, and had the picture that his guest might not like been removed? Nothing was overlooked—right down to the flowers in the Duce's room and the train stops to allow adequate rest. From the first evening, when Benito phoned me as usual, he expressed his amazement at the tumultuous welcome he'd received. He was particularly impressed by the parade on the Königsplatz in Munich.

The visit reached a climax in Berlin with one vast demonstration after another. My husband made a speech in German and called me immediately afterward to ask if I'd heard it and what I thought; he ended by saying, "You wouldn't believe what I've seen here. It's all so well organized, and the people are extraordinarily tough. With that kind of support Hitler can embark on anything."

Hitler, realizing that his show of strength had impressed the Duce and anxious to strike while the iron was hot, immediately laid the foundations of an agreement that was to become the "Pact of Steel"—the military alliance that Germany and Italy signed on May 22, 1939.

When he returned to Rome, Benito told me every detail of his trip. What surprised me most were his words about German war power. "If you only knew, Rachele," he explained, "it's unbelievable. I've never seen such a military machine with all the wheels turning so smoothly."

Obviously, the man who'd welcomed the Duce had changed a great deal since the day he'd hesitantly left his plane in Venice—in his badly fitting, putty-colored raincoat, awkwardly clutching his gray hat. A French journalist had described him as "a little plumber holding a chamber pot [his hat] in front of his stomach." Benito had laughed on that occasion, but this time his German visit had confused him. He'd found an awe-inspiring leader backed by a whole nation—and a well-oiled military machine.

Faced with these incontrovertible facts, Benito realized that if Italy was to oppose Hitler, it must not do so in isolation. The Duce had to reconsider his whole attitude. An alliance with Germany might not be attractive, but in the framework of an anti-Comintern agreement it might be a necessity. Benito told me, "We're trying to create an anti-Bolshevik front stretching across Europe from the North Sea to the Mediterranean. The Führer and I agree about Russian pressure in Spain. For the first time we are, so to speak, on the same level of defense against bolshevism. We shall try to enlarge this defense system and strengthen it."

However, my husband added a qualification that he stood by until Italy entered the war, in 1940. "For my part I see this plan from a solely defensive point of view, as a nonaggression pact without any immediate military objective. If we succeed in forming a bloc of really powerful nations, it'll be easy to persuade Moscow to limit its field of activity to within its own borders. Italy and Germany represent the Latin and Teutonic worlds. Their mission is to defend European and Christian civilization against all Bolshevik, atheist infiltration."

Perhaps they were just words, but I stress that after 1937 Mussolini looked upon Germany as a power better to ally with than oppose. From then on, he was totally preoccupied with preventing a war, but equally determined that Italy should not suffer for her neutrality. When it was crystal clear that the unreasonable attitude of France and Britain prevented this, Mussolini was forced to become entangled as well.

One other thing had impressed Benito during his German visit—Hitler's sense of humor. During the Berlin parade, the officer conducting the fanfare dropped his baton, which struck a soldier on the head. The man's sharp reaction startled a horse, which bolted right to the rostrum where the Führer and the Duce were standing. At first the incident embarrassed Hitler, but on seeing that Benito was appreciating its humorous aspect, he relaxed.

"I told him," Benito said, "that such incidents were not unknown in Italy either. Then Hitler whispered: 'Imagine what the fate of that poor soldier will be. Our perfect organization will already be grinding into motion. The general will reprimand the colonel and he the commander, who will take the same disciplinary measures against the captain. The captain will punish the lieutenant, who will punish the adjutant. The adjutant will certainly reprimand the sergeant, who will then take it out on the corporal. The corporal . . . that poor soldier.' "

Seven years later, in June, 1944, Hitler revealed a similar sense of humor in more dramatic circumstances. He was showing Benito and Vittorio the damage caused by the bomb that had almost killed him. "You realize my trousers were torn to pieces," he said. "Luckily there were no women around, or they would have been treated to an unusual sight."

I saw Hitler for the first time in May, 1938—from some distance, admittedly, as I was standing on the first floor of the Palazzo Venezia. But that was close enough for me. For, on one hand, I loathed appearing in public, and, on the other, I felt no great sympathy for the Führer, though he never treated me badly. Indeed, whenever the occasion arose, he was very attentive, and generous with gifts. After his visit in 1938, he sent me a bouquet so vast that it couldn't pass through the gates of the Villa Torlonia and had to be dismantled. Unthinkably, I compared it to the bouquet the King had given me the previous year, when the Empire was proclaimed. With my usual malice, I reflected how little the Empire had cost.

Much later when I joined Benito in Germany after his rescue from the mountains of Gran Sasso d'Italia, where he was imprisoned by the conspirators who threw him out of office in 1943, not a day passed without my receiving the Führer's flowers and presents of all kinds. When my husband returned to Italy, before the creation of the Salò Republic as an independent state in northern Italy, Hitler courteously put his personal car at my disposal. The SS guards at Rocca delle Caminate even thought that Hitler himself was in the car and were terribly scared. But this is digressing from the point.

On Hitler's arrival in Rome, Benito told everyone—including the staff at the Villa Torlonia—to go to the Palazzo Venezia. It would be a sight, he thought, that no one should miss. Without adding to the many existing accounts of the visit, I must say that the six days Hitler spent in Rome tested my husband's patience and tact to the full. The main cause of tension was protocol, which dictated that Hitler's official host must be no less than the King himself. But Hitler and Victor Emmanuel shared a mutual dislike, and the Duce was caught in the crossfire of their remarks.

The trouble began the moment the Führer arrived at St. Paul station. On leaving the train, he was received by the King in full-dress uniform, surrounded by his generals. My husband, observing protocol, stood slightly apart. Hitler was at a loss. In his view, the Italian ruler—whom he had received so magnificently in Germany—was Mussolini. He was mystified why a little king with glittering generals greeted him while his friend, the Duce, waited to one side. His bad temper toward the King began that moment, worsening outside the station. He asked for Mussolini, but the Duce had left separately to satisfy protocol, because the Führer was to stay at the Quirinal with the King. Hitler's exasperation merely increased. He grumbled about everything—discreetly enough not to be rude, but he grumbled all the same. He commented on the horse-drawn carriage, asking if the House of Savoy had ever heard of the automobile. He hailed the Quirinal as a museum of antiquities, and thought the court reactionary and anti-Fascist. He even criticized the King's table, claiming that both service and dishes were rather poor.

When Benito repeated these comments, I half-agreed with Hitler. But before I could utter a word, Benito cried, "Don't you start! I already have Hitler and the King on my back." For Victor Emmanuel was equally biting in his remarks about his guest. He repeated endlessly that Hitler was a psycho-physiological degenerate and had even asked a maid to remake his bed in his presence. The Duce was in constant fear of a diplomatic flare-up.

Hitler did not regain his good humor until May 9, when he left Rome for the relaxing atmosphere of Florence with my husband. The Führer was so enthusiastic about Florentine art that he promised to return if he ever needed a rest. His admiration for whatever he saw nearly led to an accident at the outset. While driving through Rome with Benito, Hitler was so overwhelmed by the spectacular floodlit Colosseum that he leaned too far out the window and would have fallen had Benito not grabbed him.

When he returned to the Reich, Hitler was determined to cement the Italian-German rapprochement, especially after watching the impressive naval display in Naples on May 5. As the procession of submarines, cruisers, and battleships passed by, Hitler remarked to the Duce that Italy could control the seas—more particularly, the Mediterranean. And he must have been right that our naval strength was intimidating, for soon after Italy entered the war, the English hastily sank three of Italy's finest ships in the harbor at Taranto.

Hitler's and Mussolini's personal feelings for each other surprised me. Hitler, oddly enough, considered the Duce his superior. His office in the Brown House in Munich possessed two adornments: a portrait of Frederick II and a bust of Mussolini. The Führer actually adored my husband, and when he spoke of Benito, to either his own supporters or the Duce's, the tears welled in his eyes. Ciano noticed this during a conversation. My husband noticed, too, that Hitler was on the brink of weeping when he left Italy in May, 1938. In 1943, when Edda arrived in Germany, she saw the Führer shake with emotion as she told him of her father's arrest. "But why didn't he tell me?" he kept asking. "How could he have . . . ? Why did he take his life into his hands and go to the King's villa? And after I've always told him not to trust that hypocrite."

Some weeks later, Vittorio, then in Germany, had a similar experience. Hitler's face was wet with tears when he learned that the Duce had been rescued by the Führer's own man, Capt. Otto Skorzeny. When Benito arrived in Germany, after the rescue, the Führer made no attempt to hide his feelings. While Nazi officials saluted stiffly, Hitler shook Benito's hand warmly, then drew back to allow Vittorio to embrace his father.

Benito's explanation for this diffidence in the Führer was that, on coming to power, Hitler had recognized his master in Mussolini and his ideal in the Italian regime. He therefore borrowed many of Benito's ideas, imitated many of his achievements. The theory of *Lebensraum*, or living space, was originally Mussolini's. After his youthful experiences and his discovery when he came to power that numerous Italians had to emigrate to survive, it was a logical step for him to provide them with land on which to live and work. Hitler took this idea to the extreme, destroying the native characteristics of occupied countries, instead of adapting to them as the Italians did.

From the Fascist "Balilas" was born the Hitler Youth Movement. The Fascist salute, which Benito began for hygienic reasons, in order to discourage the skin contact of handshaking, became the Nazi salute. The Nazi Brown Shirts were the German version of the Fascist Black Shirts.

Hitler clearly idolized Mussolini, but my husband was more reserved about Hitler. He was touched by Hitler's courtesies, he respected German military strength and the single-mindedness of the people who had invested Hitler with power, but he was slightly afraid of the change in Germany. He saw his alliance with Hitler as a marriage of convenience.

Mussolini's fear centered on his dwindling influence after 1940, as Hitler began to call the tune. There were many reasons for this. Hitler was a dictator, Mussolini was not. Hitler's supporters were a belligerent people, but Mussolini had not forgotten his hero's welcome for preventing war after the Munich conference in September, 1938. Whereas the German generals owed total allegiance to Hitler, their Italian counterparts owed allegiance to the King, and they would use this obligation as an excuse at a point of crisis. And, to be harsh, the Germans were militant to the core, while some Italian leaders were only as militant as their uniforms made them.

Benito often said that, had the German general staff had their way, they would have removed the Italian army from the front, dispatched the King to some backwater, and sent a Nazi governor to rule Italy—as in the case of Poland, Czechoslovakia, and elsewhere. Only Hitler's respect for the Duce averted this.

The German attitude toward Italy became clear to me when I returned from Germany to Rocca delle Caminate, on November 3, 1943. Benito had preceded me. I was stunned to find that, though back in his own home, he'd retreated into a modest room, while the German officers assigned to serve and guard him ostentatiously occupied most of the house. Their well-shined boots stood sentinel-like outside the rooms they'd taken over. They had eaten virtually all the food, and our poor maid was driven to distraction. I lost no time in acquainting them that my house was not a hotel, even less a barracks, and that they would have to leave.

They left at once. I concluded that the highly disciplined Germans had either to respect or to destroy anyone who stood up to them. On that occasion they had listened to me, and I think Hitler would have done as much for Mussolini if the Duce had not at that point shared the leadership with two partners—Marshal Badoglio, who had assumed control of the Parliament when the Grand Council voted to oust my husband, and the King, to whom Badoglio had restored full command of the armed forces.

Hitler was now in the habit of acting on his decision before he informed Benito, and when my husband reproached Hitler for this, the Führer had a stock reply: Mussolini lacked total power in his country. Now that—since the arrest—Mussolini's authority in Italy had been challenged, Hitler trusted neither the Court nor the Italian general staff, of which Victor Emmanuel was supreme commander, and he preferred that his plans remain secret.

And yet no member of the German general staff suspected Mussolini's loyalty for a moment. There lay the paradox. My husband was governing a country and was negotiating, as a leader, with an ally who admired him greatly. Everything should have been for the best in the best of all possible worlds. But because Mussolini respected existing institutions, he had to stay his hand against the monarchy in Rome that since July 24, 1943, had obstructed cooperation with Germany.

I must admit that Hitler's skepticism was borne out by events, especially when it concerned the King's loyalty to my husband.

14/Mussolini and the King of Italy

In a sense, Victor Emmanuel III and Mussolini were almost old acquaintances when they met on October 30, 1922, the day of Mussolini's greatest triumph, at the Quirinal Palace.

They had met twice before this historic encounter, the first time in the Cividale Hospital during World War I. My husband, who was then in the army, was being treated for paratyphoid, when the King came to inspect the hospital. They didn't say anything to each other on that occasion, but six months later, in Ronchi Hospital, they chatted for some moments.

My husband was confined to bed, hovering between life and death and ravaged by fever. The doctors had recently removed the forty-three shell splinters he had sustained when he was wounded in training on February 23, 1917.

Victor Emmanuel asked to see Sergeant Mussolini, and for a specific reason. He was undoubtedly well aware that in civilian life Mussolini edited a newspaper of weighty influence and had always been fiercely antiroyalist. But now Mussolini was no longer attached to a political party, and there was no knowing which path he would take next. The King may have been mulling over these ideas as he walked toward the bed where Benito Mussolini lay, pale and with his eyes protruding from their sockets.

149

"You must be in pain, Mussolini," said the King.

"It's agony, Your Majesty, but one must keep going."

"Do you remember, I saw you six months ago at Cividale Hospital? General M. told me many good things about you."

"Thank you, Your Majesty, but I've only done my duty like all the other soldiers."

"I know, I know. That's fine, Mussolini."

And there the conversation ended, however significant it may subsequently have become. Five years later, on October 30, 1922, the King and my husband met again, this time at the royal palace of the Quirinal.

Two days before, the March on Rome had effected a dramatic change in the power structure in Italy. Today, one of these men was the conqueror; the other, having lately sustained what amounted to a defeat, had summoned Mussolini only because, under the pressure of events, he was afraid of losing his throne. Victor Emmanuel had no option but to give assurances of friendship and loyalty. Mussolini wanted to rule the country, to make Italy a great power, and to put the machinery of state back on the rails—with or without the King. It didn't make much difference to Benito what happened to the monarchy, but since the sovereign was there, and was willing to cooperate, there was no reason why he might not become a nucleus for Mussolini's unification of the country.

The King would not suffer by his involvement with my husband, since Mussolini constituted an effective barrier against the advance of the Bolsheviks—the Communists of the time—who, if they had gained the upper hand, would doubtless have swept away the House of Savoy just as ruthlessly as they had deposed Czar Nicholas II. Besides, Victor Emmanuel was killing two birds with one stone: by sheltering behind Mussolini he was also disposing of the whole array of politicians he'd had to reckon with as a constitutional monarch, who were of no further use to him now.

My husband also profited from the arrangement: he avoided a violent revolution and took power without violating democratic procedures, while remaining the victor. Later he made this comment on the event: "The House of Savoy has been towed into Rome for the second time. First in the wake of Garibaldi and now of fascism."

The first few minutes of the meeting on October 30 set the tone for future dealings. The King wore uniform, thereby signifying his intention to remain at the head of the armed forces. In contrast, my husband had discarded his Fascist black shirt, favoring instead a white shirt with stiff collar and a rented frock coat, the correct dress for the occasion. This formal attire subtly indicated that he was willing to recognize the existing authority.

In this way, the two men shared the leadership of the country. The King reigned and retained command of the army, while the head of the administration governed.

For the first seven years of his rule Mussolini's seat of government was in the Palazzo Chigi; after 1929, he governed from the Palazzo Venezia. Every Monday and Thursday, right up until the war, my husband donned his frock coat and top hat and went to the Quirinal to obtain the King's signature for decrees and the nominations of ministers or military leaders. The King would study the papers closely, muttering to himself, before he signed. But sign he always did.

In the main, the King and my husband managed to establish a fairly honest partnership. It had its ups and downs, for the King was basically suspicious, but the prime minister, as my husband was called, had almost no mental reservations. To be perfectly honest, I think the Duce regretted only that the King was not tall and well-built, like the Scandinavian monarchs. When he was angry with Victor Emmanuel, Benito even went so far as to say, "He's much too small a fellow for an Italy on the path to greatness."

My husband wished to make Italy into a great, powerful, and respected country. And because he was moving toward this goal on the political, social, and diplomatic levels, the King left him alone to do as he wanted in those areas. Indeed, whatever comments the King made stemmed from friendly concern, as when he criticized the Duce for traveling by air too much. "If he carries on trying to stop me doing what I want, I shall turn republican again," my husband grumbled. But that was more of a whim than anything else. At the time of the Matteotti affair, when Fascist thugs assassinated a prominent Socialist minister, in 1924, Victor Emmanuel played fair, refusing to act on the counsels of various politicians that he should get rid of Mussolini. Five years afterward, on February 7, 1929, Mussolini made the King a gift of the Conciliation between the House of Savoy and the Throne of Saint Peter. I should point out, in this context, that my husband was given special dispensation from kissing the Pope's ring during his audience with Pius XI preceding the Lateran Treaties.

The serious quarrels between the King and the Duce began when my husband tried to alter one of the main elements in the expansion of Italy, namely, the army. Although Benito merely wanted to improve the armed forces, the hackles of Victor Emmanuel rose at once; everything of a military nature was the province of the Crown, and therefore jealously guarded.

On one occasion, for example, Benito designed a new uniform. Until then the Italian soldiers had worn battle jackets with tightly buttoned collars that they opened as soon as they could—and with their necks bare the soldiers usually looked untidy. With his practical intelligence, my husband figured that a change of collar would keep the soldiers from fiddling with their uniforms. The result was a terrible fuss, involving months of explanations, surveys, and committee meetings before the King would finally acknowledge the wisdom of Benito's suggestion.

In another instance, my husband was keen to abolish the wearing of puttees. He had worn them himself during World War I and condemned them for two reasons. Several minutes were wasted, he argued, while the soldiers unrolled the puttees before putting them on, and the puttees also endangered health—

a matter of primary importance to Benito—in that they interfered with circulation and were a source of infection in themselves. There were further tensions, further meetings, and explanations, but the King finally agreed, and the Italian army began to wear boots.

The first really big crisis between Victor Emmanuel and Mussolini flared up in 1928, after a vote in the Chamber of Deputies made the Fascist Grand Council, chaired by my husband, a constitutional organ. Under the new measures, the Grand Council became the chief machinery of the state, since its opinion had to be sought in regard to all constitutional questions. These embraced such matters as the succession to the throne and the prerogatives of the Crown—so the King could dismiss his prime minister only after consulting the Grand Council. Fifteen years later Victor Emmanuel applied this law to dispense with my husband, but when the law first went into effect, he did not value it at all.

Furiously, he declared that the Fascists had no right to interfere in the affairs of the Crown. According to him, the question of the succession was settled under the constitution, and if a party meddled in the succession that was the end of the monarchy. But that was as far as he went. In fact, from what my husband said, Victor Emmanuel feared that after his death the Fascists might give the throne to the Duke of Aosta, his nephew, whose Fascist sympathies were well known. In fact, the Duke of Aosta had taken part in the Black Shirt procession before the Quirinal after the March on Rome in October, 1922. Since his presence on the balcony, behind his uncle, was essential, he'd ascended by a private staircase, holding his jacket collar tightly closed so that the King wouldn't notice his shirt.

From 1928 to 1938, there were virtually no problems between the Duce and the King. Every Monday and Thursday "Mister President," as protocol demanded the King should call Benito, met His Majesty at the Quirinal. Their relations on a personal level even seemed to grow cordial. Once, when Victor Emmanuel was ill, Benito went to his bedside only to be asked

point-blank, "Tell me, my dear Mussolini, how do you manage
to have lovely apples at your table? The ones they bring me
are so small you' wouldn't believe it. I don't understand it at
all."

Making discreet inquiries, the Duce discovered that the
King, believing the palace bills to be excessive, had decided
on a fixed sum to cover all expenses. But he'd neglected to allow
for the fluctuations in prices and in the quantities and kinds
of products purchased. Consequently, the staff were sometimes
obliged to pick cheap examples of some items so that they
could pay for everything else. When Benito told me about this
situation, I found it easy enough to believe, for I'd already
heard rumors about the King's stinginess. Besides, I didn't find
him very likable; on several occasions Benito had to interrupt
me when I began to explain that the King of Italy needed a
ladder to mount his horse.

At the same time, I had great respect for the Queen and
was fond of the Queen Mother, Margherita of Savoy. In 1926,
I met her in Milan, where I was still living, during a concert
at the Palace of Sports, to which Margherita had also gone.
I was quietly pointing her out to Edda, Vittorio, and Bruno
when an aide-de-camp approached me and said, "Her Majesty
the Queen Mother asks if you would kindly join her in her
box. She would like to meet you and the children."

At first I refused. "I'm not used to being in the presence
of queens," I answered. "Would you kindly convey my excuses to Her Majesty, but I cannot and will not disturb her."

The aide-de-camp was so insistent, however, that in the
end I accepted the invitation, and pushing my children before
me, went to the royal box. The Queen Mother was extremely
friendly, and I can still remember how she greeted me. "I
wanted to meet the Duce's wife," she said, "to tell her that
the House of Savoy should always be grateful to her husband
for all he has done and continues to do for our country." When
she died a few months later, I learned that the Queen Mother
had made my husband an executor of her will. She had also

bequeathed to me a small medallion of St. Anthony, which Benito wore continuously until he died. It was then stolen, together with everything else he had with him.

In the spring of 1930, during the period of peaceful relations between the King and the Duce, I got to know Victor Emmanuel III and Queen Helen, his wife. When we first met, at a reception in the Quirinal, I was dutifully whiling away the time among the ladies of the bedchamber—who, incidentally, were not very forthcoming—when the King approached me. Pointing to a chattering group of elderly ladies, he said jokingly, "You'd think we were in a hen house." That was the only noteworthy remark I heard him make, and I found it amiably down-to-earth.

A few weeks later, Queen Helen invited me to a performance given in honor of her daughter, Princess Maria, the Queen emphatically asking Benito to make certain that I accepted. I therefore went, but in a terrible state because I had to feed Anna-Maria, my youngest child, who was only a few months old, and I was afraid I'd forget to keep an eye on the time. In fact, it was the Queen herself who put my mind at rest. Every now and again she looked at her watch, and when the time came she gave me leave to go, after presenting me with a lovely rose. I was very touched by such great kindness and simplicity. Later the Queen offered the Duce the use of an apartment in the hunting lodge at Castel Porziano on the outskirts of Rome, so that he could relax there whenever he so desired.

Everything seemed to be for the best in the best of all possible worlds. Between 1937 and 1938, however, there were two difficult incidents, of which one, the second, amounted to a serious crisis between Mussolini and the King, who never forgot it.

The first quarrel was of the puttee-and-battle-tunic type. This time it concerned the parade step. My husband had always been outraged by the way the Italian soldiers marched. "With their rifles at the end of their arm, they look as if they're carrying a suitcase and are going to catch a train," he grumbled. He added that the Italian army was the only one that didn't have a parade step. After he visited Germany in 1937, he came back full of enthusiasm for the military carriage of the German soldiers. Their way of marching had also impressed him, and he decided to introduce a *passo romano*, which was a less rigid sort of goose step, in our army. He thought this slight innovation would give the troops a more military bearing, but for the King it was another encroachment on the prerogatives of the Crown, which included those of supreme commander of the armed forces and therefore the right to dictate how the Italian forces marched. However much my husband explained that every army in the world had a parade step, Victor Emmanuel III and his general staff didn't wish to know. The step might have been an impressive one, but it remained the "German step."

That was one of the rare occasions when Benito lost his usual reserve with me and made an acid comment about the King. "It's not my fault if the King is pint-size," he exclaimed. "Naturally he won't be able to do the parade step without making himself ridiculous. But the height of the King is no reason for stunting the army of a great nation as he has done."

Finally the storm blew over, and the King agreed to sign the new measures. But what mountains he made out of molehills!

The Duce's concern did not stop at puttees and battle dress, but he had a much more grueling time when he wanted to reorganize the Italian army completely, changing both its weaponry and its outlook. March, 1938, saw the eruption of a major crisis between him and the King, and this conflict remained unsettled until July, 1943, when my husband was arrested. On March 30, 1938, Benito made a speech in the Chamber praising the army. When he had finished, Constanzo Ciano, president of the Chamber, proposed the creation of the new rank of Marshal of the Empire, to be conferred on the King and the Duce simultaneously. The law was passed by acclamation, and the senate approved it on the same day.

The drama broke when my husband went to the Quirinal to ask the King to ratify the law. He found an extraordinarily irritated man. "This law is another mortal blow at my sovereign prerogatives," Victor Emmanuel protested. "I could have given you any other rank as a sign of my admiration, but to place you on the same footing as me puts me in an impossible situation. If it were not for the imminent international crisis, I would rather have abdicated than submit to such an insult."

My husband didn't want to aggravate the situation either. But he said to Ciano, "I've had enough of this. I do the work and he does the signing."

The title meant little to Benito, although it must have pleased him that he was now—in one detail at least—on the same level as the King. But Victor Emmanuel found the new law especially offensive, because he was afraid that this title would indirectly enable the Duce to establish a Fascist control of the army, for which Fascist veterans had yearned for some time. In order not to offend the King, the Duce generally avoided wearing the uniform of Marshal of the Empire in the King's presence.

Sometime later, after Hitler's visit to Italy in 1938, Victor Emmanuel told my husband that he would be glad to visit us at Rocca delle Caminate. Crown Prince Umberto had already been there, in 1936. The whole atmosphere had been very warm, and Umberto had spent a while meditating by the graves of the Duce's parents during a visit to the house where Benito was born.

Despite his old revolutionary ideas, Benito was very flattered by the King's suggestion, especially as the monarch was to come to our private home, in our region. This arrangement made the visit different in Benito's mind from an official visit to places owned by the state.

I was responsible for my husband's first bout of nerves.

A few days before the King's arrival he said: "We must provide something special. Don't forget it's the King who's coming to the house." Then, on June 8, the day of the visit, he asked me, "Well, Rachele, is everything ready? Have you organized everything properly? Have you thought about the drinks?"

Because his fretting was beginning to exasperate me, I became edgy too. "Of course I've thought of the drinks," I said. "I've thought of everything. I've ordered orangeade and sandwiches from the buffet at Forlì Station. Is that good enough for you?"

He was stunned, poor man. "But is that all? Nothing else? We are talking about the King after all, Rachele."

"King or no King, that doesn't cut any ice with me. As far as I'm concerned, whether it's the King or Minghini [a peasant friend of the family] it's all the same."

While this conversation was taking place, the King was paying a traditional visit to Predappio, with speeches from the Baccanelli *podestà*, flags in the streets, and a cheering crowd of local people. I must say that, in the lovely June sunshine, the view from Rocca delle Caminate was rather beautiful with the countryside all green, flags along the winding roads, and the Romagnoles dressed in their Sunday best.

Finally, the King dispelled all my husband's fears, when he and his retinue reached the main door of Rocca delle Caminate. He was carrying a big bouquet of roses, which he held out to me, saying, "I'm bringing these from the Queen, but I'm very afraid they've wilted a little in the sunshine of Romagna."

I took the roses with a few conventional words of thanks, and then something funny happened, which would certainly have worried my husband slightly more if he had been aware of it. I gave the roses to my nephew, Germano, to take care of. He didn't want to miss one second of the visit and handed them on to Armando, the caretaker. But Armando also wanted to watch everything. So he ran off and put the flowers in a basin used for the laundry and forgot all about them.

The King walked around the house, complimenting me on the way Rocca delle Caminate was laid out, on the hall of the Grand Council—which was indeed rather attractive—and more particularly on a portrait of myself that had been painted when I was thirty. Very courteously, Victor Emmanuel III remarked that I hadn't changed at all. These gallant words moved me very deeply, as they would any woman who is forty-five and is told that she looks only thirty.

After taking a rest and drinking a glass of orangeade from the station buffet, the King took his leave, but not before he had told my husband how pleased he was by the heartfelt welcome of the people of Romagna. He informed us that no other monarch had received such a greeting in Romagna, and he was all the more moved because he had once been whistled at by a crowd in our region. This had made him so cautious that, during subsequent travels, he'd preferred to make a detour to avoid us.

Once the visit was over, Benito wanted to take the flowers the King had given me to his parents' grave. Armando went to fetch them, and we heard shouts of "What a calamity! My God, what a calamity!"

I thought there had been an accident or something serious. We rushed in, to find Armando weeping over the basin. When he had put the roses in the tub there had been soap in the water, which had made the blue of the ribbon run, had taken the yellow out of the petals, and had withered the leaves. It was not a pretty sight, and my husband was very upset.

"You can at least get a plaque put on the front of the house with the date and time of his visit," he said.

"You can rely on me," I answered. But I didn't put anything up.

This story may be of incidental interest only, and may show aspects of the past that most people are unaware of, who come across only the official and the formal versions. But for my husband the royal visit to Rocca delle Caminate was very important. It was a test. Because Victor Emmanuel had suggested coming to Rocca delle Caminate of his own accord, not at my husband's invitation, and because the visit was a private one, to our home, not our official residence, Benito thought his personal relations with the King were back in equilibrium and that the monarch had forgotten their two crises—the assignment of constitutional powers to the Fascist Grand Council and the creation of the title of Marshal of the Empire. In fact, the situation was very different. But we didn't find out until five years later that the King of Italy bore an inexorable grudge against Benito. And even when he had all the evidence before him, Benito Mussolini could not bring himself to believe that Victor Emmanuel III was capable of sanctioning a conspiracy against his prime minister, let alone of playing an active part in it. Not until Benito was arrested and abducted by men in the King's pay could he admit that all the warnings were more than the product of a wild imagination.

15/World War II Could Have Been Avoided

I have often been asked why Mussolini wanted war in 1940. I have always replied, and still maintain, that he never wanted it. On the contrary, he did all he could to avoid it.

Intimately involved in his life at the time, I saw how distressed he was by the thought of another European war, how disheartened by his discovery that the Italian-German alliance, which he'd signed as an anti-Bolshevik, might now make him the enemy of Italy's historic allies. After the assassination of Dollfuss and the Anschluss, in 1934, when the world had seen Austria almost swallowed by Germany, he was afraid he'd see Italy invaded and sacked if he sided with those weaklings who had neither caught on nor reacted in time, France and England.

He had seen Germany's military strength for himself. Neither French nor English statesmen had even begun to envisage what Hitler had shown him in the vast Krupp factories— now working around the clock to produce every imaginable instrument of war. He knew that if a conflict erupted, boundaries would be swept aside like straw and all Europe would be one enormous blaze. That was why, when Hitler threatened to invade Czechoslovakia in order to annex the Sudeten territory that housed three million German-Czechs, Benito did everything possible to avert this Sudeten crisis before it sparked a world war; he knew that Hitler would stop at nothing.

161

Everything began on September 28, 1938. That was the day my husband saved the peace by making a telephone call. He'd spent the entire day at the Palazzo Venezia, not even coming home for lunch. I waited for him all evening. When he returned late, he looked gloomy. Anxiously, I asked him what stage the crisis had reached.

"There's some hope," he told me, "but it's as slender as a thread. I've tried everything today, but I don't know if the other powers will agree to peace talks. I'm even wondering if there's still time for a conference. Oh, Rachele, how blind the French and English leaders are. They still haven't grasped that Hitler wants the Sudetenland. And to get it he's prepared to go to war. He was to have opened hostilities tomorrow. By some miracle, I managed to persuade him to wait and agree to a conference. That's the last hope."

My husband then told me about his race against time.

"At about ten o'clock this morning," he said, "Ciano came rushing into the Palazzo Venezia. The British ambassador, on Chamberlain's behalf, had asked me to mediate with Hitler. At eleven, I phoned Attolico [the Italian ambassador in Berlin], telling him to meet Hitler at all costs and urge him to postpone the Czech invasion for twenty-four hours. Attolico dashed to the Chancellery, where, he later reported, everything was in great confusion. Although the Führer was locked in his office with the French ambassador, Attolico made the devil of a fuss—eventually managing to get an officer to inform Hitler of my urgent message. The Führer saw Attolico at once on hearing how the British had asked me to act as middleman. Hitler thought for a few moments, then answered: 'Tell the Duce that I accept his proposal.'

"Within minutes of receiving Hitler's reply, I heard of Chamberlain's willingness to go to Berlin at once to discuss the Sudeten problem with us, the French, the Germans, and the Czechs. Again I phoned Attolico, asking him to tell Hitler that I hoped he would approve of Chamberlain's proposal, which had my support. I didn't mention the Czechs, because Hitler would not have agreed."

As my husband spoke, I could not help wondering how long our home, and the tens of millions of homes throughout Europe, would continue to enjoy peace.

"Attolico," Benito went on, "reached the Chancellery just when Nevile Henderson, the British ambassador, was seeing Hitler. Again the Führer left his office and, before he even listened to Henderson's message, told Attolico that he agreed to the proposal and asked me to take part in the talks. He even added that it was up to me to choose where—at Frankfurt or Munich. Attolico phoned me again. I chose Munich and sent him back to tell Hitler. This afternoon the official invitations went out to London, Paris, and Rome. The next three days will be crucial. But peace is hanging by a thread, Rachele, just a thread. The slightest incident could touch everything off, because the German army is ready to march."

I didn't sleep a wink that night. I feared that Galeazzo Ciano, Edda's husband and the foreign minister, might phone, telling my husband of some serious development—a change of heart on Hitler's part or on the part of one of the other two powers involved. Happily, nothing happened.

Benito managed to sleep. He woke rested and with a less pessimistic view of the future. He left very early for the Palazzo Venezia, dispensing with his usual ride, then phoned me during the morning.

"I've done it, Rachele," he cried. "I've finally managed to arrange a meeting between Hitler, Chamberlain, and the French premier, Édouard Daladier." He was obviously excited. "I'm leaving for Munich right away. Pack a bag for me. I shall be with you in a few minutes."

I was delighted to pack his bag, even more than on the day he left for Rome to become the head of government, in October, 1922.

When Benito arrived at the Villa Torlonia, he was radiant.

All the staff knew what was at stake at Munich and wanted to say good-bye. Only Romano—whose birthday fell on September 26—reproved his father as he kissed him for having forgotten the occasion.

"If all goes well," promised Benito, embracing him, "I shall be bringing back a marvelous present for you. You know what? A peaceful world for children to grow up happily in."

"Bah! I'd rather have an electric train," Romano replied, disappointed. He had no experience then with the bitterness of war.

My husband called me briefly from Munich to tell me, "The danger has been averted. There will be no war."

I need not describe the ecstatic scenes on his return, though I can say that Benito felt they were inappropriate, for knowing Hitler and knowing that he would respect only a show of strength, he was afraid that the celebrations would undermine the Führer's opinion of Italy.

At home I bombarded him with questions, naturally enough. He simply gave me a summary of the atmosphere of the talks. "I hadn't dared to hope for so much," he said. "And yet, when Chamberlain arrived, he was skeptical about what might emerge from the meeting. He was most suspicious of our good intentions, and I had to talk to him for some time to convince him. Once he was convinced, his whole attitude changed; he was cooperative right to the end. As for Hitler, he was proud that England and France were waiting on his decision—not that it made him any more open-minded. Daladier was cooperative. France is obviously not ready for war. When he realized that a peaceful solution was near, he was overjoyed. It showed on his face—though I think he was the only one. As interpreter, I tried to round the edges, because Hitler speaks only German, Chamberlain English and French, and Daladier only a little Italian."

That is how four men saved the peace in 1938. By allowing Hitler the right to accupy and annex the Sudeten territory of Czechoslovakia by October 10, 1938, the leaders of the four nations avoided a military confrontation for which none of them was ready. My husband had promised peace as a birthday present for Romano, but he hadn't told me how fragile this toy was. It didn't last long. We had scarcely a year of happiness, but in that time Benito enjoyed one pleasure that derived, at least indirectly, from the Munich Conference: an official visit to Rome, in January, 1939, by Neville Chamberlain, the British prime minister, and Lord Halifax, his minister for foreign affairs. This visit endorsed the British government's recognition of the Italian Empire. The British representative in Rome now presented fresh credentials addressed to the "King-Emperor" and not merely the King of Italy.

During this visit, Halifax gave Benito even greater proof that the English sought Italy's friendship. He asked Lord Perth, the British ambassador in Rome, to show my husband the text of a speech on Anglo-Italian relations which he was to make before Parliament. From what Benito told me, this gesture was a specially significant sign of friendship, since it was outside normal diplomatic procedure. I doubt if one government has ever communicated to another the text of a speech before it was read to Parliament. Yet Halifax did so unofficially. The archives must contain some record of this.

I have emphasized this point to show how glad the Duce was to receive the two British statesmen in Rome. I believe this was the high mark of his career in international politics and the last public show of peace before World War II. The climax of the visit was an evening at the opera attended by my husband, Chamberlain, and Halifax. On this occasion Benito wore evening dress, which he had not done for some time.

Afterward he told me that he was pleased with the outcome of this visit, because he wished to maintain friendly relations with England even if there was some conflict of interests. "The only thing I regret slightly," he added, "is that the Roman people didn't give them a really warm welcome.

They have long memories, and they haven't forgotten the sanctions during the Ethiopian war. Chamberlain realized this, but it didn't make our relations strained."

Every important occasion, however well organized, always has its share of incident. Chamberlain's visit was no exception. It was no serious matter, but it caused a flutter among the police—for the British prime minister's umbrella disappeared.

I already knew that Chamberlain had an umbrella just as I knew that he had a bowler hat, and that these were the distinctive badges of every self-respecting Briton. Besides, when my husband first mentioned the visit, he jokingly said, "On January eleventh, Chamberlain and his umbrella are coming to Rome." Whenever he spoke to me about the prime minister during his stay, he always managed to include the expression "Chamberlain and his umbrella." Then, on the day of the reception, Benito called me from the Capitol.

"Rachele," he said in a solemn voice, "it has finally happened."

"What? Is it serious?"

"Of course. Chamberlain has lost his umbrella. Someone has stolen it from the Capitol, and the police are at their wits' end."

Then he hung up. Several hours later he called again, this time laughing. "I know you must be worried about Chamberlain's umbrella. Well, you needn't worry any longer. It's been found. It wasn't stolen, but someone had placed it with the ones put aside for bad weather."

To return to more serious topics, I remember that my husband always had the greatest respect for Chamberlain, as he had for almost all the heads of state of his time. The only one he never liked was Roosevelt. He thought Roosevelt was a mistaken idealist who was fanning the flames of war and who, like all Americans, hadn't the slightest notion of European problems. He said to a journalist one day, "You'll see. Once the Americans have set foot in Europe it will not be easy to shift them."

He greatly respected Churchill, whom he considered a worthy adversary. "He's a real John Bull . . . a good friend and a good enemy. One of the great living Europeans, who understands Europe's needs for the future, even though, as an Englishman, he cannot meet them." Benito more than once assured his sister, Edvige, that if she ever needed help or refuge she had only to contact Churchill, who had been forewarned.

I know—because he said so on several occasions—that the Duce kept up a secret correspondence with Churchill during the war. Indeed, I remember one day, in 1943, I believe, when he told me that if the Allies won, he wouldn't try to escape but would wait resolutely for them. "I have enough documentary evidence," he assured me, "to prove to Stalin and Churchill that they drove me to war and that even after the war began I tried to restore peace. I have it in black and white."

He was carrying all these documents in a portfolio when he was arrested at Dongo, in 1945. Needless to say, they disappeared when he was killed. There have been endless speculations about his hastily contrived execution. I myself have always wondered whether his executioners had specific orders from Moscow or London to prevent him from falling into American hands and to remove communism's chief enemy.

Similarly, I have always found it odd that after my husband's death Churchill should have come to northern Italy for a fortnight's holiday. Officially he came "to paint." I know that Churchill was resourceful enough to receive his colleagues in his bath, with a cigar in one hand and a glass of whisky in the other, or to paint pictures in the middle of a war. But why did he choose the shores of Lake Garda? And why then? Surely the intelligence agents who accompanied him weren't there to hold his brushes. I suspect that his object was to recover any documents concerning himself that might be stored in the Salò Republic, since they would have embarrassed him if his Allies had seen them.

The documents are officially missing. If they have not been destroyed, they must be sitting somewhere. The Duce has

been dead now for twenty-nine years and can't return from the
grave. Why not then publish the documents that concern him?
If he really was the hateful betrayer of his Allies that his enemies claim he was, why not add weight to this view by disclos-
ing proof of his faults?

My husband naïvely believed that a country that had made
war and kept a code of honor, whose rulers respected international law and humanitarian principles, could not possibly
be trampled on once it was beaten. The former enemies of the
two world wars could not be closer now. Mussolini thought that
Europe would emerge united from its harsh experiences and
avoid its present turmoil. Unfortunately, he was wrong.

On the other hand, he was right in his reply to Vittorio's
question just before the outbreak of the war. Why, having
saved the peace at Munich by discussion, our son had asked,
had he not tried to arrange another meeting?

"Then what? What will that achieve?" Benito questioned.
"Hitler will give us a two-hour speech full of hazy ideas from
Mein Kampf; Roosevelt will pass for a saintly defender of the
peace while he's really pressing for war; Stalin will tell us that
only the people's will can triumph, as if he hasn't crushed his
people already; and Churchill will listen to it all without doing
anything—because he can't do anything. No, Vittorio, a meeting like that hasn't a chance of succeeding—this time. America doesn't understand Europe at all, and doesn't want to,
anyway. Russia's only aim is to export communism. As for us
Europeans, our only chance of keeping out the Americans and
Communists would have been to build a United States of Europe.
But we didn't, and it'll be an expensive mistake."

Benito paused for a few moments; then, wrinkling his
eyes into a smile, he added, "And to be less serious, I think
Stalin, Churchill, Roosevelt, Hitler, and Mussolini haven't a
chance of getting on. Hitler doesn't drink or smoke, neither
do I; Stalin and Churchill smoke like chimneys and drink like
fish; Roosevelt smokes, but drinks only tea or coffee—"

And since I'm passing on the Duce's opinions of the war's

main figures, I should perhaps mention that the military leaders he most ardently admired were Eisenhower, on the American side; Karl von Rundstedt on the German; toward the end, Albert Kesselring, because he held down the Allies for six hundred days; finally, Baron Mannerheim, the distinguished Finnish marshal, for his heroic struggle against the Russians.

16/Why Mussolini Became Hitler's Ally

On realizing that he could do nothing else to stop the war, my husband tried to keep Italy out of it for as long as possible. But he felt trapped by former agreements, because he was still determined to do the right thing, even if it meant—as it once had—selling gifts in order to repay a debt and respect commitments.

I realized something was in the wind when in June, 1939, at the Villa Torlonia, a chance phrase caught my attention. That day, while walking through an antechamber, Benito stopped in front of a painting given to him by a Hungarian artist. At the bottom of the picture ran the words "Treaties are not eternal." Benito read this legend aloud several times, then remarked, "The time for juggling is over. For the first time in history, Italy will have to respect her commitments."

That was his sole comment, but it was not long before I understood its significance. As the days passed, the news became increasingly alarming. Both Attolico, our ambassador in Berlin, and Ciano, the foreign minister, sent reports leaving little doubt that Hitler was determined on war. His excuse would be Poland's refusal to cede Danzig to the Reich, but my husband was certain that Poland would be only the initial step.

First, Benito tried using his military alliance with Germany, the Pact of Steel, to curb the Führer's aggression, but it soon became obvious he was laboring in vain. Then he tried to keep

170

Italy aloof from the conflict. He told Hitler, through Attolico, that his weakened military strength and the fact that the wars in Ethiopia and Spain had sapped Italy's raw materials prevented his giving the Nazis adequate backing.

"I only hope," he said, "that honesty will be enough to restrain the Führer. Italy isn't ready for another conflict, and this time I don't think it will be localized. To tell you the truth, Rachele, I don't know where it will lead. Wars are like avalanches; no one can tell in advance how long they will last or where they will lead. There have even been wars lasting a hundred years, Rachele, but I shall do everything I can to keep this one from spreading."

Benito believed that the nonaggression pact between Germany and Russia, signed in August, 1939, had finally killed all hopes of peace. The Duce was surprised, not that the pact had been signed (since he had always maintained to the Führer that some kind of working agreement between Western Europe and Russia was essential), but that Hitler should have given his signature at that particular time without telling Italy beforehand.

He had said to Ciano, "I'm sure this agreement is a precautionary measure on Hitler's part to avoid Russian retaliation. That means he's intending to take action in Poland."

From that day, diplomatic activity between Rome and Berlin grew in intensity. Once again, the other powers appealed to my husband to arrange another Munich. And I know that he almost succeeded in doing so, although he no longer believed conferences would help. Yet again, the English and the French were too blind to profit from the situation. Unwittingly, they gave Hitler the go-ahead and drove Italy into Germany's arms.

Between August 25 and the night of August 31, 1939, peace hung in the balance. By the twenty-fifth it was clear that Germany was ravenous for war. Ribbentrop had distinctly said so to Ciano during the latter's journey to Salzburg some days earlier. Just before dinner, Ciano asked, "Well, Ribbentrop, what do you want? The Danzig Corridor?"

"No, we want more than that. We want war."

During the twenty-fifth, Hitler sent a lengthy message to my husband through Hans Georg von Mackensen, the German ambassador in Rome, explaining how he viewed the situation in the light of his agreement with Russia. My husband brought all his papers home to have them readily available, and I saw that Hitler ended his letter by appealing to Italy for aid—in accordance with the Pact of Steel—and to my husband for his understanding.

This appeal was all the Duce had to cling to in his attempt to delay the day of reckoning and to keep Italy out of the war. His immediate reply to the Führer took the form of a delaying tactic, advising Hitler that the Germans would need to send armaments and raw materials if they expected Italy to be on Germany's side. Benito's message went in the afternoon. At about six o'clock Attolico gave it to Hitler, who was waiting anxiously to learn Italy's position. On reading the message, Hitler acted swiftly, as he had done over Munich. According to Attolico, General Keitel entered the Führer's office as soon as the Italian ambassador had left, only to emerge quickly, shouting to his aide-de-camp, "The order to mobilize must be delayed."

It was ten in the evening when my husband received Attolico's final message at the Villa Torlonia. Once again he had postponed the day of reckoning, but for how long? During the war Benito often talked to me about that last chance of the Allies, for Hitler was afraid of losing Italy at the last moment. But for the German general staff, the Duce might have achieved even more by playing on the Führer's friendship for him. Proof of this came the following morning, when another message from Hitler arrived at the Palazzo Venezia, asking Mussolini what quantities of armaments and raw materials he needed to prepare Italy for war.

"This may go on for days, for weeks, or for months," my husband said. "We shall have to see."

Benito aimed to remain neutral until 1942, by which time

he thought Italy would be ready to enter the war. Otherwise, he would not have continued work on EUR, the new town under construction just outside Rome, where he intended staging a vast demonstration to celebrate twenty years of fascism. So he sent another message to Hitler, deliberately exaggerating the quantities so that the Führer could not possibly provide them. On August 28, Hitler replied, as the Duce had hoped, that he could not send Italy all she asked for, but that he would agree to her remaining neutral on three conditions that were to remain secret. (I stress the word *secret* because it had a weighty effect on subsequent events.) These conditions were that Italy was not to reveal her neutrality until hostilities opened, so that the French and British would deploy forces to blockade her; she was to indicate that she was building military might, for the same reason; and the Italian government was to mobilize a labor force for Germany to replace men leaving for the front.

On the same day, my husband communicated with Hitler, agreeing with these conditions, and by the evening the fate of Italy appeared to be sealed; she was to remain neutral in the inevitable war. As on every other occasion when he had made a momentous decision, the Duce was unusually calm when he came home.

As I watched him at dinner, I realized that I was close to regretting the good old days of the Forlì demonstrations. This time world peace hung grimly in the balance. The nagging thought that this solitary man who sat eating before me held the lives of millions of Italians in his hands was painful to the mind. Only a woman in a like predicament could assess my feelings.

On August 29, Ciano came in person to acquaint Benito with Hitler's attempt to reach a deal with the British government in London. In return for British neutrality, the Führer guaranteed safety for the British Empire. On hearing of this offer, Ciano had confirmed it in a telephone conversation with Lord Halifax, the British minister for foreign affairs. The Duce was vexed, because he had not been kept abreast of affairs.

But rather than risk ruining whatever chance there might be, he kept his ill humor to himself. He was still skeptical about Hitler's true desire for peace, and thought that the Führer would be deterred only by a power bloc consisting of France, England, and Italy. Yet Benito feared that the idea of open discussions with Britain was quite absurd while Italy officially continued her military buildup—and his fear proved justified as events followed in swift succession after August 30.

On that day Hitler received Britain's answer to his terms. Briefly, it amounted to a refusal. Moreover, there had been a decree of general mobilization in Warsaw. The fuse to the powder keg had been lit.

When Attolico wired at nine in the morning of August 31 that the crisis was desperate, my husband tried one last effort. He was prepared to mediate with the Führer, he told Lord Halifax, if Britain would agree to cede Danzig to Germany. But Halifax replied that annexation was out of the question. My husband tried yet another tack: in the afternoon, he invited Britain and France to reconsider the Treaty of Versailles at a conference on September 5. If they agreed, the Duce might be able to restrain the Führer yet again.

But that very evening, at eight-thirty, while the Italian government still awaited replies from London and Paris, Ciano learned that telephonic communications between Italy and Britain had been severed. The strategy Hitler and Mussolini had worked out to give the impression that Italy was preparing for war had succeeded beyond the Führer's wildest dreams. The British were so convinced that my husband was deceiving them that they lost all confidence in him. So as evidence of our good faith, Ciano revealed to Percy Lorraine, the British ambassador in Rome, that Italy was to remain neutral. My husband went further: he ordered that the lights of Rome should be lit.

As a result, on August 31, 1939, in a desire to help Britain and France—who had not recognized the situation for what it was—Italy actually dishonored a secret agreement concluded with Germany. After taking up a dubious position in relation to the Allies to please Hitler, Mussolini now found himself in the same position with regard to the Reich. He had risked an attack from Britain and France and now ran the danger of German aggression—as Hitler did not fail to point out quite bluntly some months later.

Ciano's gesture of friendship to the Allies on August 31 was one of the reasons for the Führer's persecution of him. After my husband's arrest in 1943, when, through an error of judgment, my son-in-law fled to German territory, Hitler permitted him to leave on one condition: that he fly back to Italy, where he was arrested on landing. Edda, my daughter, tried to plead her husband's cause with Hitler himself, but in vain. The Duce forgave him, the Führer did not.

Even in his predicament between Germany and the Allies in 1939, my husband obstinately strove for peace. Before making new proposals, however, he was anxious to consolidate his position. Early in the morning of September 1, he asked Attolico to arrange for Hitler to send him a telegram freeing him from the obligations of their alliance. This arrived quickly, to be followed by a second telegram, again from Hitler, informing the Duce that the Führer would make no more concessions and was going ahead—into war.

Even at this late hour, my husband raised a last flutter of hope: on September 2 he hinted at fresh negotiations. Contrary to all expectations, Hitler agreed. In the afternoon, in the presence of André François Poncet and Percy Lorraine, the French and British ambassadors in Rome, Ciano phoned Georges Bonnet and Lord Halifax, the French and British foreign ministers, telling them of the Duce's proposal.

At seven in the evening Halifax called back, declaring that the British would not agree unless the Nazis removed their troops from the Polish territory they had begun to occupy the day before. Ribbentrop did not even reply to Ciano's message about the British requirement. And, as if some comic relief were called for in such high drama, on the night of September

2–3, Georges Bonnet asked the Italian ambassador in Paris for a "symbolic" withdrawal of the German forces in Poland.

On the morning of September 3, Britain and France declared war on Germany. That evening Benito said to me, "From now on it will be impossible not to enter the war, and even more impossible and dangerous not to go in on the side of Germany."

After his hostility to Hitler, it was time for Mussolini to be cautious. In the end, there could be only a marriage of convenience—for better or for worse. The Duce had taken nine months to decide.

All the relevant documents that might cause offense are now shrouded in secrecy. But if they are ever published, historians will be able to say who fanned the sparks of war and who tried to snuff them out.

And as for Mussolini's scrupulous respect for Italian-German ties—for which, incidentally, he has been criticized more than once—one queries why France and Britain should have risked declaring war on Germany for the sake of their agreements with Poland, while Mussolini was not entitled to honor those he had signed with Germany.

17/Italy in the War

To imply that Mussolini never entertained the idea of war would be false. In 1940, he felt that Italy should enter the conflict for two reasons: to honor her agreements with Germany, and because conquest fitted in with the Duce's hopes for Italy's political place in the sun. It should be remembered that Germany and Italy considered themselves poor countries beside the great Western powers with their "plutocratic" regimes. So my husband looked coldly on the war as a necessary evil, which would enable him to finish the work of building the Italian Empire—which had been begun in 1935, with the subjection of Ethiopia—by seizing the French protectorates or even a part of France itself.

In 1939, the Duce told a meeting of the Fascist Grand Council that Italy was claiming everything south of the Alps as Italian territory, while the other side would remain French. In fact, this claim didn't mean very much for Italy. I think the frontier would have run somewhere near Menton-Nice. Savoy didn't figure in the Italian government's claims, and this omission was a great disappointment to Victor Emmanuel III, who as head of the House of Savoy wanted that province, if nothing else, attached to Italy.

During the same meeting, the Duce claimed Tunisia as an Italian protectorate, as well as Djibouti and Corsica. In the case of Corsica, he argued that although the island had had historical connections with France since the time of Napoleon, he couldn't allow French territory to remain so close to Italian shores, since it represented a strategic threat. The moment had come to deprive France of these lands so that Italians could have a field of action and more living space.

These claims were never made public, and the Duce's proposals remained a secret. Therefore he was rather annoyed when a speech by Ciano provoked a demonstration in the Chamber and frantic cries of "Tunisia, Corsica, Nice, Savoy!"

"What an intelligent way of bringing the matter to public notice and stirring the people to action" was his irritable comment as he left the Chamber.

Apart from his territorial objectives, my husband felt he had grounds for complaint against the French people as a whole, especially against the Leftist political elements and the various governments that had led France to declare war on Germany in September, 1939. At that time he cared for only four Frenchmen: Aristide Briand, the statesman; Marshal Pétain, the great military commander; General Weygand, whom Benito thought capable of straightening out the military situation in 1940; and Pierre Laval, the foreign minister, whom he had met several times. I received Laval myself at the Villa Torlonia and was deeply impressed by his kindness and his desire for French success within the limits of the situation.

My husband criticized the succession of French governments because they were Leftist and had not been alert to the beginnings of Nazism. The Duce had not forgiven the French leaders for deserting him after the murder of Dollfuss and the Anschluss, any more than he'd forgotten the incidents leading up to the outbreak of World War II over Poland.

The attitude of the French press, which lavished criticism on the Italian expeditionary forces in Spain, even when it was unjustified, had also deeply offended Benito. He was certain that such adverse comments were manifestly inspired by the government of the Popular Front, which then ruled France.

The manner in which the French despised the Italians was another grievance. This hostility went back a long way, to the time when Benito himself had tried to find work abroad. In 1923, he had said to Rossi, who was secretary of the Fascist Party, "We have no friends in France. They're all against us. Every Frenchman thinks of us as just dirty Macaronis." I remember his delight in June, 1938, on hearing that the Italian football team, which was meeting the Hungarians in the World Cup finals at Marseilles, had caused a scandal by giving the Fascist salute as they entered the stadium. "At least we've shown them that the Italians aren't afraid any longer," he said. "The Macaronis will show them what they're capable of."

Above all this, Benito objected persistently to the French Left-wing parties, which not only welcomed Italian political refugees but actively participated in anti-Fascist campaigns. Men like Pietro Nenni, one of Benito's fellow prisoners when they were both members of the Socialist Party, had fled to France when fascism took over in Italy, and was not exactly politically idle there. And at this point, few Socialists basked in my husband's admiration. Of Léon Blum, for example, he said, "He's more a great Jew than a great Socialist."

And yet, though Benito assured himself there was no other course, the obvious need to turn against France worried him, for he'd always rather liked the country. He even gave our younger son the name Vittorio in memory of a French victory during World War I.

In the early part of 1940, the victory bulletins that Hitler sent impressed upon Benito the need to act quickly if he wanted to sit prominently at the negotiating table. But he had a problem: the Italian forces had been weakened by the campaigns in Ethiopia in 1935–1936, and in the Spanish Civil War in 1936–1939, and we were deficient in raw materials for our war industry. One evening my husband told me there was one solution: to delay intervention until 1942. But the snag was that the war might end sooner. He said, "If that happens we will have done nothing and will be on the sidelines, while our chief ally carries off all the prizes. How can I claim part of the conquered territory if Italy is just a bystander? It's a luxury she can't afford in view of her prestige and position in the world. Also, I don't want Hitler to be the only man talking to the British and the French for their sake." Because of all these considerations my husband was in a state of feverish activity, urging the general staff to plunge into the fighting. But like every general staff, ours was obviously not ready. "What good is a general staff that can't make war?" Benito protested.

It took the pressure of events themselves to get our military machine moving, and the Germans, who had begun their steady march from victory to victory, exerted the greatest force. Both the Allies and the Germans were intensifying their demands on the Duce, the one asking him to keep out of the war, the other pressing him to take part. Hitler, who had freed the Duce of his commitments in 1939, while the war was confined to Poland, now threatened that he would not respect our frontier if Italy stayed neutral. In short, Italy was confronted with the starkness of invasion without further ado, as the Duce had always feared might happen.

This new cause for anxiety arose in February, 1940, when Sumner Welles, Roosevelt's special envoy, arrived at the Palazzo Venezia to exhort Mussolini to stay out of the war. As soon as he set foot on Italian soil Welles went straight to my husband's office, where they talked at great length and "very frankly," in the Duce's opinion. "He's a latter-day Colonel House," Benito told me. "Like House, and for the same reasons, Welles's mission is doomed to failure."

It wasn't long before he felt the sharp repercussions of Welles's visit. As soon as Hitler learned of the meeting, he sent his special messenger, Ribbentrop, the foreign secretary, whose habit of speaking without bothering about formalities had already delighted Ciano. Without wasting words Ribbentrop bluntly informed us that German troops would march in and occupy Italy if she failed to abide by her Pact of Steel with Germany.

From that moment, the Duce was convinced that Italy could not remain aloof from the war much longer. If he had had the military means, he would have been glad to abandon the position he once described as "an unstable balancing act on the very edge of the flames." But he tried to be evasive for as long as he could.

In March and April, Hitler stepped up his psychological warfare, first at a meeting with my husband on the Brenner, where he outlined his plans; then through his announcement, on April 9, that he was attacking Norway and Denmark; again with a friendly message on April 11, followed by another on the twentieth; and finally in letters describing the victories of April 28 and May 4.

On May 10, 1940, the major blow fell. Ciano, who had dined at the German embassy, informed the Duce that von Mackensen, the German ambassador, might disturb him during the night, bringing an urgent communication from Berlin. At four in the morning Ciano and the ambassador both arrived at the Villa Torlonia, and Irma showed them into a reception room, where the Duce soon joined them. Handing Benito a sealed letter from the Führer announcing his decision to attack Holland and Belgium, von Mackensen also asked my husband to take any measures he considered necessary for the future of Italy. He clearly meant, Well, I'm waiting to see what you're going to do now. It's your turn to play.

"Do you realize, Rachele," Benito said, "they'll be at our gates before long."

The constant flow of messages from America, France, and Britain was of little use now. On April 24, the French premier, Paul Reynaud, had written to my husband expressing the conviction that France and Italy ought not to fight before the leaders had met for talks. "We should have had discussions before, not now" was Benito's bitter comment. "It's not fine words we need now, but fine guns." He replied, confirming his adamant decision to remain Germany's political and military ally. Therefore it would be fair to say that the French knew in April what to expect from the Italians.

Only a few days after Hitler's ultimatum, Benito received a letter from Churchill. I clearly remember one sentence: "I declare that I have never been an enemy of Italian greatness, nor ever, at heart, the foe of the Italian lawgiver."

"This is a good time to write that," Benito said. "If the British hadn't voted for the League of Nations' sanctions against Italy's invasion of Ethiopia in 1935, we could have formed a European power bloc." And when Churchill warned the Duce about the aid Britain was bound to get from America if she herself entered the war, my husband thought the warning was pointless. "Britain can't withstand the German military machine. As for the Americans, they are too far away, and even if they did intervene, the Germans would have won a total victory before they had time to do anything."

Daily bulletins about the crushing advance of the forces of the Reich were reaching Rome. Nothing less than a triumphal march, the military advance was having an impact on the Fascist Party, the Italian army, and the people. Tens of thousands of letters poured in each morning, all on the same theme: "As usual Italy is coming in last. The Germans will take everything."

One evening Benito told us, "This time the Italians aren't satisfied with snatching suitcases like the Neapolitan *scugnizzi* [street urchins] do. They want to snatch colonies, like the British."

On May 28, Belgium capitulated, and as the evacuation from Dunkirk gathered impetus, Hitler again sent my husband reports of his victory. Two days later, the tension reached its peak. It was then that President Roosevelt sent Benito a personal message strongly urging him to stay out of the war. My husband was rather shaken by this, and in the evening he came home to the Villa Torlonia with a parcel of photos and films, which, procured by Vittorio from film associates, showed Nazi operations in Poland. After dinner we had them shown in the same projection room where we had spent such pleasant hours during the years of peace. That evening all hell broke loose. We sat horrified by the tidal wave of violence, by the steel monsters bearing down and crushing everything in their path, while Stukas roared above, their strident noise piercing the ears.

To be honest, I couldn't sit through this apocalyptic vision. I was torn between admiration for the courage of the Polish soldiers and a horror of war with its aftermath of ruin, death, and tears. I fled to my room and looked from the window at the dark mass of the garden, almost expecting it to burst into flames.

The sound of the door opening made me jump. It was Benito, who had come to find me. He was pale, and his voice betrayed his emotion as he declared, "All those troops, all that formidable machinery, are getting closer. Soon they will be at our frontier, and if they wish, the Germans won't even need to cross France. We have a common border. Within hours they can storm Italy. But, Rachele, there's something else we can be sure of—whether we go into the war or not, the Germans will occupy Europe. If we're not there with them, they'll be able to dictate their conditions to tomorrow's Europe, and that'll mean the end of Latin civilization."

He put his hand on my shoulder, looked me intently in the eyes, and said, "Rachele, we have children as well. We're going to be frightened for them. Millions of Italian mothers will be frightened too. But I can't go back. Not only in the acquisitive interest of Italy, but also to prevent her suffering the same fate as Poland, Holland, and so many other countries, I must fight. God is my witness that I'd have done everything to keep the peace, but I can't spend my time putting chestnuts in the fire for others to pull out." I said nothing. Seeing tears in my eyes, Benito took my hand and said in a deliberately playful way, "Don't worry, we'll try to be as quick over it as we were in Ethiopia."

That was May 30, 1940. On June 10, from the balcony of
the Palazzo Venezia, Mussolini announced to the Italian people
and to the world that Italy was entering the war on Germany's
side. The Duce had asked Marshal Badoglio, chief of the
general staff, to begin operations at once, but Badoglio objected, contending that it would take several days to muster
our divisions. The rest is well known: after four days the
French were seeking an armistice. What my husband had
feared became reality, for the Italian forces were brought to
a halt. "It's a nuisance, that," he cursed. "Couldn't the French
have gone on fighting a little longer? The Italian army has
hardly had time to show its paces!"

Another point had also struck the Duce—the speed with
which the French line had collapsed. "How can an army that
was triumphant at Verdun admit defeat so quickly?" he asked
on hearing about the French request for peace. "And that
famous Maginot Line, what use was that?"

In actual fact, while he wanted victory for Germany,
Italy's ally, he thought that Hitler's troops would be exhausted
after the conquest of France. But not at all. There were further
surprises in store. Hitler didn't see the need for a military
occupation of the whole of France and the French colonies.

"All the Germans have to do is enter Paris and look at the
Eiffel Tower and they think they've won the war," Benito
said when he came back from the Munich negotiations. "With
this free zone they want to maintain, they're in for some fun
and games." Then, commenting on the Führer's refusal to
occupy the French colonies in Africa, he added, "They're a
threat as long as we lack total victory. Hitler has made a
strategic error, because the African colonies can serve as
a storehouse of men and machinery for Frenchmen who still
want to fight. Well, let's hope my fears aren't justified."

I can say quite simply that Italy's great error—and I
haven't the faintest idea if it originated with my husband, the
Italian general staff, or both—was to conduct the same kind

of war as the Germans. In Africa, among other instances, our
general staff were mounting operations without any attempt
at liaison with the Germans. Consequently, a whole series of
temperamental difficulties arose between the two armies. On
the African front, for example, no sooner had Hitler promoted
Rommel to the rank of marshal than the same honor was conferred on General Cavallero and General Bastico, chief of the
general staff and commander-in-chief of the Italian forces, re-
spectively. The sole object of these promotions was to avoid
letting the Italian generals appear in any way inferior. I should
add that the German generals made no attempt to foster good
relations, for they snatched every chance to flaunt their su-
periority over their Italian counterparts. When Italian-German
arms took Tobruk and reached the gates of Alexandria, the
Duce spent a month on the African front—from June 29 to
July 21, 1942—trying to iron out differences and boost morale.
Under the strain of nervous tension he returned to Rome with
terrible stomach pains. That summer of 1942 saw the turning point of the war, for, after success in Africa, the Germans
began troop withdrawals, and in Russia the Red Army began
to take the initiative.

Before I discuss the hostilities in Russia, I should point
out the one error of judgment that my husband believed to
be the origin of the Axis defeat; it concerned the war between
Russia and Finland. I won't go into details, for the same
reason that I haven't written a book on military strategy, but
I am looking back to the end of 1939. At that time the valiant
fight Finnish troops put up against the Soviet army had won
the admiration of the entire world. While that is well known,
few people realize that the Red Army's apparent inability to
engage in modern warfare was what inspired Hitler to embark
on a rapid conquest of Russia. My husband disapproved, confident that "the Russian operations against Finland were merely
a trap laid for idiots. Russia," said the Duce, "could have
swallowed Finland within days if Stalin had wanted it." He
therefore sent Hitler a letter through the Italian ambassador in

Berlin, for he already suspected that the Führer, agreeably surprised by the Red Army's ostensible weakness, envisaged ending the Soviet-German nonaggression pact. He wrote that the Russians were not to be trusted, that they were more powerful than they looked. But under the circumstances, Benito wasn't completely taken aback when, despite his warnings, Hitler informed him of the invasion of Russia.

This was on June 22, 1941. We were staying at Riccione when the telephone rang at about three in the morning, and because it was near my bed, I answered it. The caller, the German military attaché at the embassy in Rome, asked desperately to talk to the Duce. To avoid waking Benito, I suggested that the caller phone back later, but he refused, stressing the urgency with his remark: "I have to tell the Duce that Germany has just declared war on Russia."

I ran to Benito's room and woke him, but when he came to the phone it was not just to listen; he spoke long and irritably in German. When he had hung up, he said furiously, "It's madness. It's our ruin. They should never have attacked Russia. Germany may know how to make war but not politics." He did not return to his bed, but set off for Rome at once.

Hurriedly he set up an Italian expeditionary force under the command of General Messe, to whom he specifically ordered: "It must be a lightning victory. We ought to beat the Russians in a matter of months."

For this particular campaign the Fascists displayed wild enthusiasm, for it meant getting to grips with Marxism itself. That is why the troops of the CSIR, or Italian expeditionary force in Russia, fought better than our soldiers on any other front.

"You see," my husband said to me, "even there they need us. In this way we can show the whole world that it isn't only Germans who are able to win."

Soon afterward, in October, 1941, the Duce informed me that the Führer had called him in person to tell him of the capture of the Russian town of Orël. "That's great," he cried.

"Orël is at the gates of Moscow." Then he added, "They must be careful and tighten the net quickly, for winter isn't far away." And in fact the cold from the Arctic that year was terribly severe; there'd been nothing like it in Russia for twenty or thirty years.

The Duce made some observations about the conduct of the war on the Russian front when he visited the divisions of the Italian expeditionary force in the Ukraine. Accompanied by Vittorio, he flew in the same plane as Hitler, who failed to conceal his fright, though he did not dare say anything when he saw Benito take control of the aircraft. "Do you realize," my husband later observed, "what a hit the Russians would have scored if they'd shot down our plane? In one blow they'd have killed Hitler and Mussolini!"

As the flight took them over German-held Soviet territory in the height of summer, the Duce could see the vast stretches of grain. It clearly impressed him, but he was shocked by the attitude of various units of the army of the Reich.

"They're too harsh with the local population," he later told me. "When they forage they raze everything to the ground. That's wrong, because the victors should always behave humanely toward the inhabitants of conquered countries."

The few months that the Duce allotted for conquest in Russia ran out without achieving his objective. From then on he grew more certain that the disaster in Russia would cause the fall of the Axis. I can now enlighten everyone that my husband spent months trying to induce Hitler, both in writing and by word of mouth, to negotiate with the Russians. He even established contacts with the Russians through Japan, but nothing tangible came out of these efforts. Hitler was never interested in discussing peace with the Soviet Union. If he had been, the outcome of the war might have been different.

Like every mother, I feared for the lives of my three children who had left for the front. Vittorio and Bruno were pilot officers in the air force, and Edda served as a Red Cross nurse. It was she who caused me my first serious anxieties over the outbreak of the war.

It happened in March, 1941, during our Greek campaign, which my husband considered a defeat and which cost Marshal Badoglio his post as chief of general staff. One morning I woke after a strange and disturbing dream in which I had a premonition about some impending disaster. I was telling Ernestine, my maid, about it when the telephone rang. It was my husband. With his customary tact when conveying bad news, he blurted out, "Edda has fallen into the sea. She was in the water for five hours, but she's safe. I'm flying off to see her."

"How did it happen?" I asked, alarmed.

"I'll tell you when I get back."

Then the line went dead. Eventually he phoned again, relating the incident in detail. Hit by seven bombs, the hospital ship on which Edda was serving off the Greek coast had started to sink immediately. Standing paralyzed with fright as the ship capsized, Edda had luckily been pushed into the water by a sailor running by. The fall enabled her to escape from the backwash when the vessel went down. She was rescued five hours later.

On August 7, 1941, I experienced the pangs of grief so many mothers have felt on learning that one of their children has died. On July 30, Bruno had come to kiss me good-bye at the Villa Torlonia before he returned to base. More demonstrative than usual, he had even asked me to keep his wife and their little girl, Marina, with me. The following morning he came to the house again, just as he was about to leave, and I can still visualize him on my doorstep, tall and strong with that innocent look of a child who has grown up too fast. I never saw him again.

So I've had firsthand experience of the despair of parents who have just lost a child, and I know you can't rebel against the cause of your grief, because this sacrifice is the dearest gift a mother can make to her country. Even if this not the appropriate place to say so, I would like all mothers who read these words, whatever their nationality, to know that Mussolini's wife and Mussolini himself were always deeply affected by the grief of those who lost a son in the war.

Apart from my children, many ministers, officials, and others donned the gray-green uniform, usually for only a few months—merely a break in their career. At least that was the pattern at the beginning; later it changed, when a soldier's life became tougher during the North Africa campaign, in Ethiopia, in Russia, and finally even on Italian soil.

As in every country at war, civilian life in Italy had its crop of difficulties. But compared to what I saw in Germany, we Italians suffered less. For example, we had football matches every Sunday until the end of the war, our cinemas were open, our concerts carried on, and our people could get out and about. Obviously we had restrictions, ration cards, and very little gasoline.

The Mussolinis themselves were exposed to the same stringencies as every other citizen, and I can assert most emphatically that neither my husband nor I infringed the current laws or allowed others to do so. Once, after receiving several hundredweight of coffee at the Villa Torlonia—a gift from Italians residing in Brazil—the Duce decided to distribute it to the hospitals. Yet every time we passed near the room where the coffee was temporarily stored, the exquisite odor made us faint with longing. To have coffee—one's national drink—within reach, and not be able to touch it, is real martyrdom.

It would be hard to imagine the severe restrictions the Duce imposed on the family right from the early days of the war. We had to give up our pleasure trips in the car; Benito himself used his only to go from the Villa Torlonia to the Palazzo Venezia or for other official journeys. Because I had parted with my car, the children went to school by bus. Even Anna-Maria, who wore a special bodice—the result of poliomyelitis—did as everyone else. It was my practice to take food to the children in the care of a Monte Mario institution, and in spite of the transport difficulties I refused to end these visits. Instead I went by bus—that is, until Cardinal Pizzardo, learning about my custom from a nun, immediately lent me his personal car, which was representative of the advantages peculiar to the Vatican.

On March 11, 1942, a requiem mass was said in Rome for the Duke of Aosta, viceroy of Ethiopia, who had died in a Nairobi clinic while a prisoner of the British. The King and Queen of Italy attended, as did the highest authorities of the state, including the holders of the Collar of the Annunziata. I had gone there in a bus with my daughter-in-law, Gina, and after the service, when everyone took leave of the royal couple, I noticed that all the other guests remained standing while an usher looked agitatedly for my car. Something had to be done quickly, for according to protocol the next person to leave the church should have been myself, and people were waiting for me. Galeazzo Ciano ran forward to suggest taking me home; he was perplexed that I hadn't come in a car. Calmly, I showed him my bus ticket and went home the way I had come.

These two illustrations will convey our way of life during World War II. To be perfectly honest I ought to mention that, fortunately for us, I still had my chickens, rabbits, and little pigs at the Villa Torlonia, which allowed me to vary our diet and add something extra to what we got from our ration books. And for the record, I should add that—as one might expect—my husband's book was Number One.

Before ending this chapter, I would like to make one thing clear: my husband was never in doubt about the courage of the Italians. His sole complaint related to some of our army's leaders, who had obviously forgotten that one can't wage war in comfort or by creating impenetrable barriers between the ranks. He'd seen signs of elitism particularly on the African front, and had made a point of reprimanding those responsible quite openly. When he went to Russia he was impressed by the close relationship between officers and men. Hitler and he even lunched with the enlisted men and received the same menu.

The foreign press has commented freely about Italian soldiers' surrendering without a fight or deserting during World War II. These reports are completely untrue. For one thing, there were never so few deserters as during that war. For another, the soldiers who laid down their arms did so at the command of their leaders, as happened at Pantelleria and Augusta, two important naval bases. If they'd behaved differently the net result would probably have been much the same, for the Allied forces were much stronger, though the Italian army would have ended the fight with more honor to its name. The Italians who remained in the German ranks after September 8, 1943, and the men fighting with the partisans were magnificent in combat.

18/I Was the Duce's Secret Agent

"Can you explain how you manage to know some things at least several weeks before I do?" The day my husband posed this question I felt extremely proud, for it was his first admission that the information I brought to him had intrinsic value. I had just won my laurels, so to speak, as super-secret agent to Mussolini, a pursuit of mine that few people know about even to this day.

The curious thing is that to acquire my items of intelligence I never directed any kind of police force; it was essentially a product of my feminine instinct and my peasant good sense. I had noticed since 1926, on my first visit to Rome, that certain people in the Duce's entourage failed to inspire the least trust in me. And so I decided to keep them under surveillance.

Later, in 1929, when the whole family moved to the Villa Torlonia, I came up against the snags of protocol: as the wife of the head of government, I was not expected to lead the kind of life I had previously adhered to—even in Milan after my husband came to power. I couldn't for instance, take the children to school, go into the big stores to buy shoes for them, or, more simply, stand over the stove and do the housework. This restriction didn't suit me one bit, because I'd never been accustomed to a lazy life and I found these limitations a real burden.

192

On the other hand, I was soon to discover that few people knew who I was. My photo appeared in the newspapers a few times, but hardly anyone could describe Rachele Mussolini's features—especially as I had rarely been seen at official public functions. I remember, at the wedding of my daughter Edda, some journalists expressed astonishment on seeing what I was really like. Some days later Benito brought me some foreign papers, mostly English and American, observing, "You've been a hit with the reporters, Rachele. They all thought you were marvelous. They were even more amazed because they had thought you were old and ugly."

The compliment flattered me at the time, but it didn't make me any more eager to emerge from the shadows in which I'd decided to live. At the Villa Torlonia, or at certain ceremonies that I couldn't avoid, I was Her Excellency Rachele Mussolini, wife of the head of government; for the rest of the time my name was Rachele Guidi, my maiden name, and I had complete freedom of movement.

And yet there was a minor obstacle. Whether I was Rachele Guidi or Rachele Mussolini, I still remained the Duce's wife and as such came face to face with security problems. In all, three or four policemen were assigned to me personally as bodyguards, and because I couldn't get rid of them I resolved to employ them as secret agents. At least in that way I could keep them occupied so that they didn't bother me much.

Besides, like every wife of an eminent personality who wants to make some useful contribution and isn't just looking for honors, I helped certain people in various ways; and before long I'd formed an information network with offshoots all over Italy. That and the thousands of letters I received each week demonstrate how I soon acquired more information than probably anyone else in Italy.

My husband was quick to appreciate that he could exploit this situation to his advantage. Every now and again he would send me to "take the temperature" of the man in the street or perform some special mission—as, for instance, in the Alto Adige section of northern Italy in 1931. The local Fascist Party secretary had been sending reports criticizing the official authorities, the governmental representatives in that region, for alleged incompetence. The prefect denied these accusations, blaming the branch secretary for meddling in other people's affairs—in short, for exhibiting too much zeal.

The problem was a little ticklish, because since my husband had come to power, he had endeavored to keep the Fascist Party from identifying itself with the state. In this way, he hoped to avoid corruption and maintain respect for the establishment; so much so that every time any kind of dispute arose between representatives of party and government, he almost always decided in favor of the prefect. This practice not unnaturally caused some resentment.

In the Alto Adige, however, it appeared that both sides were less than blameless, and the Fascist secretary's arguments worried the Duce. Seeing that I had to go to Merano for a course of medical treatment, he asked me to ferret about up there. I stayed for a month, and when I came back to Rome, he had my completely objective reports to guide him: neither the prefect nor the local secretary was fulfilling his duties as he should. Both were moved to other posts.

This was one of the few extramural jobs that I carried out for the Duce. Because of his beliefs about what a woman's role ought to be, he thought my activities should be confined to picking up rumors and passing them on to him. And my reports were not to be old wives' tales either, for then they would annoy rather than interest him.

I had no desire whatsoever to stop with eavesdropping on rumors. From what Benito told me, backed by my own intelligence sources, I was becoming daily more convinced that the whole truth never reached him. Some people in whom he placed trust were definitely misleading him, assuring him that there were no problems when the reverse was the case. Under normal peacetime conditions, this situation had no serious consequences, but I wondered what these people would do if Italy was beset by crisis or involved in war.

My fears were all the greater because not a single facet of my husband's nature was hidden from me. I knew, for example, that the last speaker he heard usually left the most indelible impression on him. He was trusting to the point of naïveté, thinking that anyone who agreed to work with him could never betray him. Basically kindhearted, he was opposed to hurting people, always finding an excuse to forgive, whether it was his children or his ministers. His philosophy was such that he felt a more intimate bond with someone like Gandhi or Francis of Assisi (whom he worshipped and had made the patron saint of Italy) than with someone like Stalin or Hitler (whom he admired to some degree but whose brutality and violence he'd always condemned).

I imagine that this pacific trait in Mussolini is virtually unknown, for the world has stopped short at the false image of the dictator. There are many people who will give the lie to my words, but I can prove my arguments with two official, historical facts.

The first is connected with the list of war criminals that the Allies drew up at the end of World War II. Mussolini's name did not appear on it, nor did the name of any other Italian, soldier or politician. Mussolini was Adolf Hitler's major ally, but no one could accuse him of any crime against international ethics.

The second piece of evidence is Hitler's own personal view, as stated in September, 1943. When Otto Skorzeny rescued my husband from the Gran Sasso, where his successor, Marshal Badoglio, had sent him, the Führer received Benito at his general headquarters in Rastenberg. During conversation he summed up Mussolini's paramount weakness. "Duce, you are too kindhearted," he told him. "You'll never make a dictator."

Nowadays such words are a source of comfort to me, especially as not a day passes without someone's saying to me,

"You remember how good the Duce was, Donna Rachele."
Yet for a logical reason, at the time I thought that all his fine
qualities were the worst faults a dictator could have.

Take a strong and forceful man who is firmly in control,
give him all the equipment of command, and you'll make him
a dictator. But for such a man to do everything himself is
physically impossible. He must choose trustworthy associates,
who have sworn their loyalty and who may even have proved
their love for the cause that brought them together before they
reached the heights of glory. Suppose this dictator makes a
mistake in his estimation of these men, or that—driven by
ambition and corrupted by the desire for advancement, riches,
and titles—his colleagues decide to betray the man who has
put his trust in them. Cunningly, they refrain from telling him
that they are no longer what he thinks they are. They spin a
web of lies that will hide the truth from him—the truth about
themselves, because it's not attractive, and the truth about the
outside world, because it might disturb their tranquillity. With
the passage of events, they begin to move from omissions to
deceit and from deceit to treachery. If the dictator is easy-
going, rather than a stern Victorian father figure, he is bound
to lose control of the situation one day; by the time he realizes
that he's been deceived, it'll be too late.

That is what I wished to avoid by keeping watch on some
of the "faithfuls" who were faithful only in name. I might as
well say at the outset that, although investigation exposed a
deterioration that went from bad to worse, the end result was
always the same: my husband would punish the man who had
erred simply by appointing him to another post or by sending
him away. This policy was feeble compared to purges like
Stalin's.

But it is still true that my activities as a female James
Bond were often useful and that they had an edge to them.
For instance, on one occasion I learned that my husband drove
to a farm on the outskirts of Rome every morning. At first I
was somewhat skeptical, but when the friends who were my

informers described the car, driver, and passenger I had to
admit it sounded as though they were talking about the Duce.

In the end I decided to get an explanation. One afternoon while we were taking a stroll in the garden of the Villa
Torlonia—as we often did after lunch—I asked him point-
blank why he went to the farm. I had caught him nibbling at
some peas he had just picked. He stood openmouthed, the
pod in his hand, and looked at me wild-eyed, as if I had suddenly gone mad. I didn't make an issue of it. Obviously the
key to the mystery lay elsewhere.

I quickly put my "secret police" to work and soon wrested
the secret. True, the car was my husband's and the driver was
Ercole Borratto, our chauffeur, but the Duce wasn't the Duce.
Let me explain. As it was wartime and there was rationing in
the country, our chauffeur had devised an ingenious plan for
trading on the black market without being caught. He found
an accomplice who was bald and of the same stature as my
husband, and this perfect double would sit in the back of the
car—the ideal decoy—while in the trunk were the goods, which
Ercole could distribute quite freely.

I considered the matter serious enough to tell Benito about
it, but all he did was grumble and give his driver a dressing
down. He didn't take the matter any further, because he was
fond of Ercole Borratto, having been through some trying
times with him. He forgave the chauffeur, and when I told
Benito that Ercole might be capable of more harm some day,
he began to laugh. He was wrong, but I had no proof of
Borratto's treachery until much later, when my husband was
already dead.

During the time when Benito was still head of government, I often noticed Borratto jotting various things down in a
little notebook when we were in the car. I told my husband
what I had noticed, expressing my fear that any conversations
he might be having with other passengers were being passed
on.

"While there are only the two of us talking," I said, "it

doesn't matter, but any indiscretion about a political conversation could be more troublesome."

"You think so, do you?" he exclaimed. "You see danger everywhere, Rachele. The honest fellow is only making a note of the mileage. That's all!"

Some years later, at the end of the war, Ercole Borratto published a book. In it the "honest" chauffeur described the discussions he said he'd heard between my husband and other people. I am sure that Borratto wasn't acting alone, because his revelations weren't confined to conversations in the Duce's car. Under remote control from various quarters, he had taken part in a small campaign to blacken Mussolini's name, for at the end of the war many people were continually trying to drag my husband into the gutter.

If someone else had been involved I wouldn't have been surprised, but that it should be Borratto, whom my husband had trusted for twenty years, made me sad; it was further proof that a sense of gratitude is something not all men possess. I knew that Borratto had recorded a tissue of lies. And he did so again, a few years ago, when he published another book, containing a series of lies as foul as the first.

If such disloyalty had been confined to chauffeurs, the tale of my exploits would not be very interesting. But there was much more serious treachery afoot than Borratto's.

In 1935, during the Ethiopian War, the Villa Torlonia had a permanent telephone line to the general headquarters of the Italian armies. That was how my husband was able to follow operations hour by hour, to receive reports and to give orders. One evening he got the distinct impression while he was actually speaking that a third party was on the line. One should remember that in those days telephone lines were not as clear as they are now, but this interference, which lasted throughout the conversation, reappeared with such regularity that eventually the Duce tore out the telephone wires in a fit of temper. "This really is too much! Who on earth has the nerve to listen in on my line?" he burst out.

He ordered an inquiry, but the mystery went unsolved, and so I decided to meddle in the affair. Without saying anything to my husband, I instructed a couple of my agents who were familiar with the workings of the telephone to make some tests. In no time I learned that our line was quite simply being tapped by Marshal Badoglio, the commander-in-chief of the Italian forces in Ethiopia, the very man whom my husband most trusted from a military point of view—and one of the men who headed the conspiracy that finally overthrew Mussolini, in 1943.

This investigation cost me five thousand lire, which was quite an appreciable sum at the time, but my men cut the line that enabled Badoglio to tap ours and paid some of Badoglio's agents to keep quiet about it.

We didn't have peace for long, however, because after Badoglio there were others. And astonishingly enough, the marshal managed to listen in to the Duce's conversations even after he had ceased to be chief of the general staff. Stroveglia, one of my private policemen, had to go into action again before we could put a stop to Badoglio's chicanery.

Now that I am on the subject I could discuss Emilio Badoglio for hours. To sum him up, I think he was a typical example of the man who is prepared to do anything to slake his thirst for honor and titles. When my husband made him chief of the general staff in 1925, many people advised him against the choice, criticizing Badoglio for not being entirely trustworthy. During World War I he had not been noticeable for his brilliance. Moreover, he was a Freemason and well known for his lack of concern for anything other than his own interests.

The Duce, however, thought that someone who had pledged his honor in taking on an important command could not betray him. So strong was this belief that he paid no attention to other people's opinions of Badoglio. He would have done better if he had heeded them, for Badoglio had time to do quite a lot of damage before the Duce recognized his blunder. Take, for example, Badoglio's endless delays to the start of military operations in 1940, under the pretext that the army wasn't ready. And there were two more serious instances, which, in any other country, would have meant at least a court-martial for the offender. First, Badoglio never kept the Duce informed of the exact state of the Italian army before the Italians entered the war. Neither did he do so when it came to the French and Greek campaigns. I know it is hard to make such accusations stick thirty years later, when the archives—at least some of them—have vanished, and when the two men most closely involved, Mussolini and Badoglio, are no longer alive. But if Badoglio really did warn the Duce that the army was unprepared and the Duce didn't consider his opinion, then why did Badoglio agree to uphold the Duce's mistaken decision when so much was at stake? In his position as chief of the general staff, Badoglio could have resigned or asked the King, as supreme head of the armed forces, to arbitrate. But he did not.

The second instance is even more compromising. Three months after Italy went into the war, the Fiat factories designed a thirty-ton tank. While it had become clear to the whole world over the past few weeks that German strength lay essentially in this kind of armored vehicle, Badoglio ordered the weight of the machine to be reduced to twenty-seven tons. The Fiat engineers worked frantically, and the twenty-seven-ton tank was soon ready. But then the chief of the general staff asked for further modifications, and they had to reduce the weight again from twenty-seven tons to twenty-four. Such stupidity—assuming that it was never more than that—would have meant a court-martial anywhere else. Not only did Badoglio go unpunished, but he went on seeking honors and sinecures until the Duce's eyes were finally opened, and he relieved Badoglio of his duties during the Greek campaign.

Just for the record, I should mention that one day a telegrapher passed on to my husband a cable from General

Ubaldo Soddu, commander-in-chief in Albania, who had wired that the situation there was causing grave concern. The cable specifically ordered that the Duce was not to be told. Ubaldo was relieved of his post.

Since I am on the subject, I would point out that these treacherous acts began as soon as Italy entered the war. I wish to make this point quite clear, because one might assume that our military leaders began changing sides only in the face of defeat and with the prospect of total disaster. The truth is much more depressing and nauseating. In actual fact allegiance was violated right from the start, when Italy was still powerful and her ally Germany was marching from one victory to the next. The King, some of the military leaders, and various Fascists had irons in every fire, using Mussolini as long as he could serve some purpose but consolidating their position, even if they had to betray him, for what the future might bring.

They were forgetting that before destroying Mussolini, they'd be destroying Italian soldiers—young men who could laugh at life, who trusted them, and who believed that they were dying under enemy fire when in fact their fellow Italians had been their undoing. And nobody can convince me that these devious persons were prompted by idealism. If there had been one leader ordering them to fight fascism, they could have assassinated Mussolini. At least that would have been honorable, if more dangerous than the course they actually followed.

During the war the only attempt on my husband's life— if it really was one—took place in Albania in 1941, when he went to the front line to watch our forces undertake an offensive that never materialized. While his car was crawling to an observation post at the top of a hill, he heard a voice say to him in Romagnole: "Don't go any farther, Duce! Don't go! I'm speaking to you in dialect so that no one can understand."

Benito told me that he disregarded the warning, seeing that he couldn't cancel the offensive. He merely looked around to see where the voice had come from, if for no other reason than to show how glad he was to hear Romagnole, but no one came forward.

Staying at the observation post for a while, he left a quarter of an hour earlier than arranged. He had just gone when a shell came straight down to explode on the very spot where he had been, a splinter even penetrating the binoculars he'd just used. He brought them home, and I kept them as a souvenir. Whether it was chance or whether the soldier who shouted the warning to him was right, we never knew.

After a certain time Benito was well aware of the treachery, but all the inquiries he set in motion resulted in nothing. It was as if some irresistible and invisible force were driving him off course. In fact, those responsible were various influential army leaders who were acting partly out of blind fanaticism, partly because the Duce—having meddled in sacrosanct customs—had disturbed the comfortable tranquillity of the officers' existence, and partly out of opposition to what they called "Mussolini's war."

Sometimes Benito could be ironic about the acts of sabotage. On one occasion he said of the Ethiopian war: "We were so quick that even the traitors haven't had time to betray us." But most of the time he was sadly upset by what he learned, always after the event. He used to groan, "Who can I trust?"

It grew so bad that when the Italian secret service first reported, in May, 1943, that an Allied landing might take place in Sicily during the next few months, the Duce said to me one evening, "I'm sure they won't be able to land, unless everyone is lying to me. I trust the soldiers, but as for the others . . . !" Unfortunately I had graver suspicions, for I, too, had my informers, and my private police force were reporting nothing but alarming news.

During the winter of 1942, for instance, a Carabiniere brought me a rocket made by our Terni munitions factories. There was no powder inside, but sawdust. Again my husband ordered an inquiry. The mass of evidence was all there in black and white, and the report was on his desk, then suddenly nobody could find it; it was as if it had been spirited away.

There was worse to come. On our way home from Terminile, the winter sports resort where we sometimes stayed, the Duce paid an unexpected visit to an air base. According to the lists provided by the general staff, there should have been squadrons of fighter planes at the base, but Benito was astounded to discover that there were no planes at all. After giving him the figures, a general had conceived the idea of keeping up the deception by moving various squadrons from base to base to be ready for inspection. Fortunately my husband discovered the ruse in time. I was so angry about it that I was ill for several days.

Similarly, on another occasion Benito summoned the undersecretary for aviation to Rocca delle Caminate, instructing him to visit the Caproni factory, which was manufacturing new planes. This time, because the factory was close to Predappio, we would have no great difficulty exposing any fiddle that might ensue. The secretary made his inspection, noted the quantity of raw materials required, and promised delivery of several hundred aircraft. Some time later my husband was advised that hundreds of this new type of plane had been produced and were actually ready to fly—yet I soon discovered that in fact the raw materials that had reached the factory were sufficient for only two planes—yes, two planes, not one more.

I passed this staggering piece of news on to Benito, and I must admit I seldom saw him get into such a state. Harsh measures were taken, but he would have had to fire many people to put the situation right. Once again he had to give me credit, which at any other time would have made me happy. "Ninety times out of a hundred," he admitted, "Mamma is right."

Even more depressing than the deliberate acts of treachery were the passive attitudes of some people and, after the early defeats, the common fear of telling the Duce the truth. Those who had the courage to speak up were immediately removed from their posts so that they couldn't make the mistake of reporting to Benito again. Once my own son Vittorio, an officer in the air force, came to inform his father that the radio receivers on some aircraft just weren't working at all. Indeed, the pilots were reduced to using sign language to communicate between themselves, which wasn't very easy during combat. Benito summoned the undersecretary at the air ministry and I don't know how many generals and demanded an explanation. He got one: the receivers were working perfectly. He soon realized he was just banging his head against a wall.

I even wonder about the death of our son Bruno. On August 7, 1941, his plane crashed to the ground on the verge of the runway at the Pisa airport, for some reason which has never been explained. Bruno was a distinguished pilot who had totaled an impressive number of flying hours. He managed to avoid inhabited areas even when his plane was in distress. I shall never be quite free of the idea that Bruno, who was also in a position to notice misbehavior and report it to his father, paid for his powers of observation with his life. Whatever anyone says to the contrary, I saw evidence of too much wickedness to believe that my son's death was only an accident.

In the same way, I don't think it was chance that the *Duilio*, the *Cavour*, and the *Littorio*, three of the finest cruisers in the Italian fleet, were sunk by English bombs in the middle of Taranto harbor in November, 1940, only four months after Italy went into the war. "Without some treason, it's impossible to score such a hit," the Duce was forced to admit. Even then, in 1940, treason was already at work.

So contrary to my husband's hopes, I was worried about our chances of beating back an invasion force in Sicily. But even I, well known for my pessimism, could never have imagined that the Italian resistance in the area would be so weak.

When Admiral Pavesi, the commander-in-chief of the fortress of Pantelleria, insisted that the supreme commander of the Italian forces—at this time, the Duce—should allow him to surrender because, he said, he hadn't a drop of water left and was in an impossible position, my husband was dubious. He gave Pavesi permission out of concern to save human life. A few days later he came home blind with rage. He had a bundle of papers under his arm and threw them on his desk, saying to me, "Read that, Rachele! They're English radio messages that our listening services have intercepted. He may say he's come out of it with honor, that Pavesi! He hasn't lost a single man. He just threw in the sponge. The English say so."

Unhappily it was all too true. In these messages the English had reported to their general staff that the base at Pantelleria surrendered without having suffered any casualties. The same applied to the fortress at Augusta, a highly fortified naval base, where the commander-in-chief hadn't fired a shot. As soon as he saw the enemy, he burned his papers, then opened his gates and his arms wide in welcome.

What could I say to the American officer who, when it was all over and I was in a concentration camp in 1945, asked me, "Can you explain, Excellency, why millions of Italians who worshipped Mussolini for twenty years should have made a complete turnaround in this way?" Could I tell him that the Italian people hadn't changed sides or committed treason? When my country entered the war, the soldiers did their duty with enthusiasm. When the time of defeat and sacrifice arrived, the civilian population showed themselves capable of self-denial and courage. The people had behaved irreproachably even when they longed for peace, in 1943. Thus the Italian people made no contribution to the fall of Mussolini, any more, by the way, than did the anti-Fascists who boasted of it after the event.

Even so, I couldn't admit to this officer, who had been our enemy, that the Fascist regime had destroyed itself; that some officials had weakened through fear of the future or through ambition. After 1943, as part of a well-organized propaganda campaign, we were led to believe that all of these officials had turned against Mussolini. This is untrue, for even among those men who voted against my husband during the meeting of the Grand Council just before his removal from power, there were many Fascists who, while they wanted peace, also wanted the Duce to stay.

But I couldn't tell the officer any of that. So my answer to his question was a silent shrug of the shoulders.

19/The True Portrait of the Dictator

One day during World War II, while we were at Rocca delle Caminate, I did something scandalous. After that I acquired some notoriety as Mussolini's adviser. Benito was receiving some Fascist dignitaries in the hall of the Grand Council. I had sneaked in behind them, and when—as was the custom—they rose, arms outstretched, to salute him with the cry, "At your command, Duce," I echoed loudly, "Yes, to betray you."

Far from being furious with me, Benito asked me to be present at further talks with other notables. He wanted to know if his visitors spoke the truth or not. I would sit on one of the wooden benches padded with cushions, which stood under each window, and follow the conversation without speaking.

Such was the case, again at Rocca delle Caminate, the day Mussolini received the minister of agriculture. The minister had brought sheafs of paper covered with figures and graphs to justify the flour quota he intended to allow the peasants. After listening to the minister's long explanations as to why these allotments should be 100 kilos for adults and 150 for children, Benito turned to me and said, "You know about these things, Rachele. What do you think?"

By chance, some minutes before the minister had arrived in a special coach, an agent had informed me that people in the vicinity were annoyed with the bigwig. His personal cook had been requisitioning stocks of biscuits from local tradesmen. Since he had come to discuss rationing, this stockpiling seemed rather curious, to say the least.

So before I said anything else, I eagerly told the Duce about what I had learned. Then I looked the minister straight in the eye, and said, "One hundred kilos of flour would be too much for you, because you don't need bread. You've got your supply of biscuits. But do you realize that to peasants bread is everything? In Romagna they even kiss it before putting it on the table. Country children eat twice as much as adults, because they're always hungry." Turning to Benito, I asked him if he would guarantee that adults received 150 kilos and children 200. From behind his desk he nodded his approval, while the minister, now on tenterhooks, would have agreed to anything. All he wanted to do was leave—in a hurry. That is how biscuits and my private police gave a little more flour to the Italian peasants during the war.

I could achieve such things only at Rocca delle Caminate, however, for in Rome I never made a habit of going to the Palazzo Venezia. Affairs of state were conducted much more formally in the capital than in Romagna; the whole atmosphere was different. But I didn't abandon my self-appointed mission to keep a watchful eye on the administrative hierarchy, to prevent the ministers from deceiving the Duce. Besides, I began to establish a reputation for fairness and was besieged with appeals to right other people's wrongs.

Nothing is more misleading than hearsay, and for every ten items of information that came my way, probably no more than one or two were reliable—sometimes none at all. It was wise to be cautious, because if some accusation reached the Duce's ears and was later proved to be unjustified, the swindlers went straight into action. I had to check every detail meticulously, and if I thought the affair serious, I did not hesitate to investigate it myself.

That is why, when I heard rumors that an official had changed the facade of his stable to resemble the frontage of the Duce's villa at Riccione, it took me a while to believe that so foolish a rumor could be true. But I went to check. It was false.

Then I was told that a minister had paved the road leading to his house and erected a statue of himself in the village square; I saw red. I could not tolerate anyone who held a position of high social responsibility and behaved in this way. That sort of vanity infuriated me, especially as my husband had always refused even to pave the stretch of road leading to the Villa Carpena, although it was only about three-quarters of a mile long. So I went to see for myself and found that these rumors were absolutely true. I took action at once, I can assure you.

I was just as painstaking when I learned that one of Mussolini's own secretaries was building himself a magnificent villa at Rocca di Papa, on the outskirts of Rome. There were even reports, untrue as it turned out, that Mussolini had given the villa to Clara Petacci, though luckily these reports didn't reach my ears until many years later. As far as I was concerned, the owner of this sumptuous property was the secretary, but I had to have proof that it belonged to him.

I visited the site with Irma and one of my investigators and found that a building was indeed being erected. I urged Mussolini to ask his secretary for an explanation. The man swore that the allegation was untrue and, to prove it, produced a photograph of a small farm that belonged to him. Not satisfied with this, I returned to the site some days later, disguised as a peasant woman desperately seeking work to support her six fatherless children. As I stood chatting with the man on the gate, both full of admiration for this structure and indignant about the cost, Romano (who had accompanied me) tactfully filmed the whole scene. Indeed, I still have the reel.

A week later I suggested that Benito should come and see a little film his grandchildren had made. My scheme worked to perfection, and he followed me into the hall prepared to admire the children's handiwork. Benito sat amazed, though whether his secretary's guilt or my system of detection surprised him the more, it is hard to say. In the face of such evidence, he asked for a further explanation from his secretary, who excused himself this time on the ground that his wife had inherited some money. My husband dismissed him.

It was after inquiries of this kind that Arturo Bocchini, the director-general of the police force, once said that he would gladly use my services if I were not the Duce's wife, for he could do with someone who stuck to the scent. Romano, on the other hand, seeing how tolerant his father was, suggested with childish spontaneity that there should be a coup d'état and I should be made dictator.

Some readers may find these stories disrespectful or even offensive. Others may think that I'm exaggerating and trying to turn Mussolini into a simple man who was deceived by everybody, preached to by his wife occasionally, and most emphatically under Hitler's thumb. I wish only to give an objective account of the Duce, neither for nor against him as his biographers have been.

From the day I first met him to his poignant farewell telephone call forty-five years later, Mussolini always kept his humanity and his good qualities along with the bad. It's too easy to say that Mussolini was ruined because he was Hitler's ally, that his fate was no more than what tyrants deserve, and that he was guilty of every imaginable crime. This book is not intended to make him appear to be a greater man than he was, but only to restore him to his real stature, his true aspect.

I think it is right to censure my husband for pardoning his "faithful" traitors. I hold it against him as well. But very few people know that the man who assassinated him owed his liberty, if not his life, to Mussolini.

Walter Audisio says that he was the instrument of justice when, under the pseudonym of Colonel Valerio, he executed Benito Mussolini—as a beast is slaughtered—against a wall. But Audisio never tells the story of how he found freedom in 1934, after being arrested and interned as a Communist. He quite simply wrote the Duce a letter asking how long his internment would last, because his family was in need. And what did Mussolini do? He freed Walter Audisio and even authorized his employment in a Fascist agricultural cooperative. Obviously, Fascist money was not tainted then.

The Jews are supposed to have suffered racial persecution in Italy. One would do well to view the situation of the blacks and the Indians in America, as well as the life of the Russian Jews, before criticizing Mussolini's attitude toward the Jews. I do not mean that there was nothing against the Jews on paper during the Fascist regime. But there is a wide gap between what is said to have happened and what actually did take place.

I should begin by pointing out that in 1940 the Italian Jews could not be considered a serious problem, for there were only about 50,000 of them, if I remember rightly. And one other thing is certain. Benito Mussolini was never hostile to the Jews. He was simply an enemy of Zionism, whether in Italy or on an international scale, because he thought it made for conflict of loyalties. An Italian Jew could not be wholly Italian in that, as a Zionist, he might be tempted to make over capital to the Zionist movement—capital he had withdrawn from the Italian economy. And if he ever had to define his position—that is, to make a choice—it could not be sure that he would reject Zionism. If he held an important position in his native country, there was no reason to suppose he might not harm Italy. The Duce's attitude to Zionism was more based on these defensive considerations than fundamentally hostile. I can give several instances of his benign feelings toward the Jews, whether Italian or not. The first concerns my husband's dentist. He was called Piperno and was an orthodox Jew. The Duce could have had his teeth attended to by a dentist of another faith, but he never even considered the possibility and continued going to Dr. Piperno. What is more, my children had several Jewish friends. Our doors were always open to them, and as far as I know, we never made them conscious of their race in our home.

On a very personal level, two of my husband's mistresses

were Jewish. There was Angelica Balabanoff, who some people claimed was the real mother of my daughter Edda—an idea that greatly amused us, for I know better than anyone whether Edda is my daughter or not. Margherita Sarfatti was Jewish too.

There were Jews among the founder members of the Fascist Party and in Parliament under Mussolini's regime; for instance, Aldo Finzi, one of the members of Mussolini's first government, and Guido Jung, for several years Minister of Finance, were Jews.

Mussolini was one of the first and, at times, the only man to attack Hitler for his racial policies. In March, 1933, less than two months after Hitler had come to power, Mussolini did what no other religious or political body thought to do. He instructed the Italian ambassador in Berlin to make representations to Hitler about his policy toward the German Jews. There must be documentary evidence of this, since all such business was conducted on an official level. In June, 1934, when my husband met Hitler in Venice, he persisted in making it quite clear that he was against any kind of racial persecution. And though the Führer never gave them a second thought, my husband made repeated efforts to improve the lot of German Jews. Sometimes he facilitated their departure from the Reich on a large scale, with Italy as the first halt on the road to freedom.

It is true that the Fascist government passed certain measures against the Jews. For example, non-Italian Jews were debarred from attending Italian schools. In September, 1938, it was decreed that non-Italian Jews were forbidden to take up residence in Italy, Libya, or the Dodecanese. These two measures followed Hitler's desire for vengeance on German Jewish refugees. But the Italians never returned these Jews to certain death in Germany. Indeed, my husband actually informed the children when these measures were imminent so that they could warn their Jewish chums. Many Jews quit Italy. One of Vittorio's friends went to Argentina. I admit it was hard for a family to be uprooted yet again, but surely that fate was better than the concentration camp—and death—awaiting the Jews in Germany, Poland, Holland, and France.

There is another historical fact which few people know. When the Germans occupying France asked for information about the Jews living in the Italian-controlled zone, Mussolini gave written instructions banning any communication on the subject. And he also ordered that there should be free access to this zone, and freedom of movement within it, for Italian Jews fleeing from German-occupied France and for Jews of other nationalities, though they were not the responsibility of the Italian administration. I remember seeing a letter from the prefecture at Nice acknowledging receipt of these instructions and saying that they had been obeyed. The Vichy government objected strongly to the Italian attitude, and Laval even protested that the Italians had no right to concern themselves with the fate of Jews who were not Italians.

There must still be documentary evidence of all this. If it were published, it might not whitewash Mussolini, but it would give an accurate picture.

In effect, Mussolini introduced measures against Italian Jews also, after the Pact of Steel had been concluded, but never of the extreme kind taken by other regimes. Violently anti-Semitic articles appeared in papers like the *Tevero* and the *Difesa della Razza*, but there was little concrete persecution. Officially, Italian Jews were prevented from marrying Italians of another faith, and forbidden to own or direct enterprises employing more than one hundred people, to own more than fifty hectares of land (about 125 acres), or to serve in the armed forces. That was all.

These measures were not enforced until 1938. And I can give a personal instance of how leniently they were applied even then. In April, 1938, Vittorio took part in the Mille Miglia motor race with an Italian Jew as his co-driver. This person didn't try to conceal his origin, and even if he had wanted to, he would never have succeeded with his surname. But he was not harassed in any way.

Anyone who wishes to moralize—and many do in retrospect—may think that whatever Jewish persecution prevailed in Italy was still enough to bring condemnation of the Duce from the enemy nations. It makes no difference whether I agree or not—and, I repeat, I am not an apologist—but I am trying to give things their true perspective and explain the whys and wherefores of events. One need only consider the Nazi persecution of the Jews in Germany and the occupied countries to realize that it was no small matter for Mussolini, Hitler's main ally, to diverge from the Führer's policy in this area.

Any Jewish person reading these words will be aware that the Duce afforded protection as long as he was in power, since from 1943 (when he was dismissed by the King and the Badoglio clique) to 1945—that is, until the end of the war —the Germans applied the same harsh measures in Italy that they'd enforced elsewhere. Even though my husband was not influential enough to oppose all the Germans' activities, he continued to try to save the Jews.

Before ending this chapter, I would like to shed some light on three more points.

Nobody has disclosed until now that Mussolini almost founded the state of Israel after the conquest of Ethiopia. He held several secret meetings with Chaim Weizmann, who later became the first president of the Jewish state; and their talks were about to bear fruit, since Weizmann and Mussolini were in agreement, when they encountered a financial stumbling block. The American Jews refused to finance any such project, though God and the American capitalists alone know why.

A training camp for Jews was set up near Rome on my husband's orders, and it was there that the nucleus of the Jewish terrorist organization against the English occupation of Palestine was created. Some of the main leaders of the Irgun were schooled by Mussolini's Fascists. That surely must have been some help to them.

There is an Israeli admiral today who was one of the

leading commanding officers in the Italian fleet under Mussolini's regime. It is significant that he was never victimized for
being a Jew.

One might suppose that Mussolini took all these steps to
harass the English—such a purpose was quite possible—but
one should appreciate that he could also have turned to the
Arabs. I believe Benito's decisions were tactical, but they also
sprang from his respect for individual peoples. This interpreta-
tion is borne out by the specific orders he gave to Italian
forces in the Ukraine and all along the Russian front—that
they should always behave humanely toward the inhabitants of
occupied areas.

The second point I would like to clarify concerns the
role of Victor Emmanuel in all this. If it is true that he disagreed with Mussolini about racial policies, one might wonder
why he never declined to countersign the anti-Jewish laws in
Italy. All decrees had to be signed by the King. If he had
thought them immoral, or at least contrary to his own standards
of morality, he could have refused his assent. As far as I know,
never did Mussolini on his twice-weekly visits to the Quirinal
force the King to sign at revolver point. Victor Emmanuel
might have risked dethronement, but he, too, had his ethical
responsibilities to bear. Moreover, once the King had signed,
the ministers enforced these laws. It is noteworthy that none
resigned because he disagreed with Mussolini. It is curious,
too, that no amendments were drafted when the laws were
passed by the lower house. I would like to think that Mussolini
had faithful friends, but the men who raised the first cries of
"Monster!" were the very men who had always said amen
to Mussolini, while it suited them, and that includes the King.

There is a third point I must make, and that concerns the
Nazi extermination camps.

In all conscience, I can say that Mussolini never knew
anything about these vile centers. He knew that there were internment camps, where the Italian laborers in Germany were imprisoned as enemies of the Reich after the Badoglio government

signed the armistice in 1943. Indeed, on behalf of the Salò Republic he made strenuous efforts to bring 600,000 Italians back from Germany when Badoglio abandoned them to their fate. It was not until some of them came home, in 1944, that he heard rumors of certain special camps, but there was never any precise information. In any case, it was 1944 and too late to try to find out.

I have said that my husband respected peoples. He also respected persons, even his enemies and political opponents, like Saverio Nitti and Pietro Nenni, who benefited from his humanity and generosity when Benito interceded with the Germans on their behalf at the end of the war. And one must not forget the Matteotti children, whose survival after their father's assassination was due solely to Mussolini's financial help.

It would have been easy for Benito to arrest his opponents, even those in German-occupied France. Indeed, after the Germans arrested Pietro Nenni and handed him over to the Italian authorities, Mussolini could have arranged a fate far worse than surveillance on the island of Ponza. Nenni's sentence may not have been freedom, but neither was it a concentration camp, or the death sentence carried out on Mussolini.

It was when I saw how my husband was killed that I was fully convinced that his fine, humane qualities were really defects. Nobody remains a true dictator for long unless he ruthlessly strikes his enemies down. The men who killed Mussolini in 1945 knew only too well what they were doing.

20/Betrayal

Before going into the details of Mussolini's fall from power in 1943, I should probably give an idea of the background against which the conspirators planned and carried out the plot against him.

The first consideration is the Duce's state of mind and health in 1943. Physically, he was not in very good shape. The nervous ulcer that had already given him some trouble, particularly in 1926, when I was living in Milan and he in Rome, was again causing him terrible pain. Sometimes it was so unbearable that he would roll on the floor trying to ease it. Often he would sit on the edge of his chair and fall back, bringing his knees up to his chin and holding them there with his hands. This extraordinary position brought him some relief, he said. When he returned from a month on the North African front, on July 22, 1942, the pains were fiercer than usual. As a man who was accustomed to having only two colds a year—one between winter and spring and the other between summer and autumn—he found this ordeal particularly trying. On my own initiative I attempted to nurse him by deleting all fat from his food, but I soon had to call in one of his physicians, Professor Castellani. There followed an infernal round of prominent medical men, and every conceivable diagnosis was put forward: an ulcer, cancer, a virus, a nervous infection, and heaven alone knows what else.

So in 1943 my husband was in no condition, either physically or mentally, to withstand the critical news arriving from every front. There was no military defeat as yet, though that hovered on the horizon. In Africa, all my husband's cherished hopes of recovery had gone up in the smoke of scuttled boats, British and American offensives, and the wrangling between the Italian and German commands, both of which persisted in conducting the war as if the other didn't exist. North Africa was falling in May, 1943, and the Axis front was shrinking to nothing.

Since April, the Italian secret service had been reporting that the Allies were preparing to land in Sicily at any moment. My husband was therefore in a dilemma, for he could recover the military situation only with support from the Germans, who alone could provide him with the materials Italy needed. But Hitler himself was having to face serious difficulties in Russia, and the German generals, who distrusted the Italian high command and our government, were unwilling to take the risk of trapping troops in Italy unless they had total control of the country. The Führer couldn't agree to this, because of his confidence in Mussolini and his regard for him.

Such a state of affairs could only profit the British, the Americans, and the traitors. A number of Fascist leaders wanted either to fight or to put an end to the war, but not to stay where they were. It was all very well that they wanted to fight, but the morale of the troops was low. A break with Germany and withdrawal from the war was a solution the Duce had entertained, but there was still, as in 1940, the vision of Marshal Kesselring's troops just marching in and occupying the country.

It was this fear, a human fear, that made Mussolini appear weak and indecisive to some people. In the face of impending disaster, strength of will was weakening, emotion was taking over, and the leaders were fast losing their sense of responsibility.

By February 25, 1943, the news was becoming so alarming that the Duce chose to leave Romagna, even though his health demanded that he stay there, and to return to Rome. From then on he spent hours at the telephone, both day and night, organizing relief work for the civilian populations of Milan, Turin, and Naples—the victims of air raids—never stopping until he knew that shelter had been provided for the homeless. I, meanwhile, was making lists of clothes and provisions I could accumulate to send to the local authorities. Benito, naïvely imagining that everyone who had a duty to perform in the overall defense of the country was actually on the job, said to me: "I must ask for complete information about the towns which have borne the brunt so that we can make amends to them. It's encouraging to see how resilient and patient the Neapolitans are. It's at moments like this that I feel I'm not alone."

But I can recall his anger and bitterness when one night, after a boat loaded with munitions had exploded in port, he had to take sole charge of the relief organization; the Duce was compelled to work on his own, for the prefect was simply not there. There was also one evening when he had to call various ministers at their homes some twenty times or more to settle urgent business. One or two had the effrontery to reply that they weren't in. It was with this kind of laxity that my husband was struggling. Obviously he could have worried a little more about his political future, started a witch-hunt, and paid attention to the information I brought him of plotting in Rome, but he said, "It's not the conspiracies that worry me, Rachele, but American tanks."

And yet the conspiracies were ripening. Since January, 1943, when the first real rumors had started, several plots had taken root. Gradually I learned that the schemes intended not only to depose my husband—whom they regarded as the villain responsible for our disastrous commitments in World War II—but also to betray our alliance with Germany. The conspirators were going to hand Italy over to the Allies.

Among the most dynamic of the conspirators was Dino Grandi, president of the Chamber and a former minister of justice. Grandi was a lawyer whom my husband had brought out of obscurity, making him an ambassador to London and minister of foreign affairs after teaching him how to take his place in society. An eternal chaser after titles and honors, he would have adopted a jaundiced attitude toward Italy's difficulties if he hadn't been involved in the conspiracy. I can give an idea of how deceitful Grandi was by mentioning that even while he was plotting against the Duce, he had no qualms about asking for Benito's support in his bid to obtain the Collar of the Annunziata from the King.

Duke Pietro Acquarone was the head of the royal household, the King's evil surrogate in the sinister conspiracy to remove Mussolini. Acquarone, another wretched victim of self-delusion, foolishly aspired to the heights of glory.

Marshal Pietro Badoglio was a collector of statues—especially of himself. He had always managed to make capital out of a situation, as, in 1935 when he stole the credit for the victory in Ethiopia from Marshal Rodolfo Graziani and, according to some rumors, also stole the treasure of Haile Selassie. Badoglio, who came into his own only when he was the center of attention, pictured himself loaded with honors and invested with the highest offices of responsibility for personal gain. The interests of Italy came second.

There was also Giuseppe Bottai, a Fascist from the early days and minister of education, a man my husband had referred to so fondly in his indictment of the Nazis' massacre of Hitler's former friend Ernst Röhm: "It's as if I were to kill Federzoni, Grandi, Bottai, and the others with my own hands." Luigi Federzoni, president of the Italian Academy, and Giuseppe Bastianini, undersecretary of state at the foreign ministry, were also involved in the conspiracy.

I knew that these unexciting people were not the only ones, but I never expected to hear that the foreign minister, my son-in-law Galeazzo Ciano, was with them—that he was, in

fact, one of the principals in the plot to depose my husband
and betray our alliance with Germany. I couldn't really believe
what I was told about this until I'd had confirmation from
various sources.

Eventually, amazed that I knew so much and yet saw the
police doing nothing, I decided to have a chat with Carmen
Senise, the chief of police. This interview, which I asked that
he keep secret, took place at the Villa Torlonia and was fairly
lively.

"How can the police be ignorant of everything I have
managed to find out without going to a great deal of trouble?"
I asked him. He was skeptical until I produced an impressive
number of documents and photographs. Then he seemed shaken,
but I didn't know if he was being sincere or just playacting.
"Are you a friend or an enemy?" I asked him, in an attempt
to break his resistance.

Naturally he swore he was loyal to the Duce and to fascism,
and that he didn't know any of the details I had told him. This
response provoked an acid comment from me about the effi-
ciency of his forces. "This kind of ignorance is hardly to the
credit of your force or of your professional rating."

In one last attempt to convince him the situation was serious, I added, "I have spoken to you as an Italian woman who
has given a son to the country, not as a Fascist or as Mussolini's wife. Just think of it, the fall of the Duce in the present
situation can only lead to total collapse for Italy."

It was pointless to go on. From the moment I started,
Senise had avoided my eyes and had been looking for loop-
holes. He was familiar with everything I had told him, and,
what is more, he was one of the conspirators.

While the conspirators were planning their great betrayal
both of my husband and of our war effort, the people were
showing evidence not only of courage and patience but also
of self-sacrifice, accepting their ordeals and suffering without
protesting. There was never any mass demonstration against
the regime in Italy before July 25, 1943, the day of my hus-

band's arrest, and even afterward there were no mass movements, but rather localized and skillfully organized outbursts.

Altogether the foundations of the society held better than the leaders, as was also the case in the army. The people could not agree to shilly-shallying when they had to bear the cost while the men in charge lined their pockets. When it came to a choice between war and peace in July, 1943, the ordinary Italian wanted peace. But if he had to go through with the war, he wanted everybody to be in the same predicament.

The Duce knew all this. The daily reports to the Palazzo Venezia didn't tell him everything, but I could fill in the gaps with what I knew. The total picture was not a very happy one.

On February 5, 1943, my husband decided to take action against the evident dissension among these subordinates. He reshuffled the government from top to bottom, taking over various key ministries himself, as he had done before at times of crisis. He called this great upheaval "the changing of the guards."

The Duce formed a ministry of war. Younger, more dynamic men came into it and were a symbol in the eyes of the public that the Duce had decided to stand firm. Several ministers learned of the loss of their portfolios by listening to the radio or opening the newspapers. There was immediate panic. The conspirators, thinking they had been discovered, were expecting the wrath of Mussolini to descend on them and bombarded me with phone calls to assure me of their loyalty. Those who were not plotting were equally scared, for it was dangerous to be caught up in a political whirlwind at that time. These innocent ones also phoned endlessly for reassurances that they wouldn't suffer any repercussions.

One needs to have known Rome in 1943 to understand why anything seemed possible there. The capital was a gigantic laboratory where the most surprising mixtures were being concocted, where everyone was plotting against everyone else. Besides, the climate, the character of the city, and the general atmosphere had a softening effect on the people who were most implicated. It was difficult to see clearly, and even the best bloodhounds in the Gestapo had trouble finding their way around. When they themselves were not in the process of concocting something, they simply assumed that everything could be sorted out. In fact, although the Germans were on the alert for the slightest sign of weakening in the Italian regime, they never realized that fascism was in danger. I remember that on July 16 I had an interview with Colonel Dollmann, Himmler's confidante in Italy, and gave him my honest opinion of the situation. Although he told me he shared my views, I derived the impression that he wasn't as loyal as he made himself out to be; indeed, he hadn't the slightest concern for the fate of either the Duce or the Führer.

Unfortunately, Benito's changing of the guard couldn't save the day. In April, 1943—and even more so after the loss of Tunisia in May—the number of conspiracies simply increased. Each one had its own answer. The only point all the *combinazione* had in common was the commitment to remove Mussolini. More and more Fascist leaders were beginning to think, in all good faith, that they should invite the Duce to resign, surrendering his powers to the King so that Victor Emmanuel could try to bring Italy out of the dead-end situation of alliance with Germany without Mussolini's suffering loss of dignity. These Fascists were victims, poor things, of the propaganda of Radio London and the Voice of America, which stressed continually that the Allies were making war not on Italy but on Mussolini and fascism. These officials thought that peace would be within their grasp if Mussolini were willing to go.

It is important to clarify this point, because it has since been suggested that the attitude of all the Fascist leaders who contributed to the fall of Mussolini was hostility directed at the Duce himself. To a large extent that impression is inaccurate. Pietro Acquarone, Dino Grandi, and Pietro Badoglio, the archconspirators who sought to eliminate Mussolini for personal aggrandizement, played on this ambiguity and misled most of the other Fascist dignitaries.

Whatever were my husband's faults, he was no fool, and he realized quite well that everything revolved around himself. Perhaps contrary to general belief, he was not particularly in love with power. If his departure would have enabled Italy to steer clear of chaos, he would have resigned of his own accord. He even said once in private that when weapons could no longer determine the outcome of the war, the next step should be diplomacy. But he also knew that nobody other than himself could negotiate with the Allies.

"These gentlemen are in a hurry to talk about peace," he said, thinking of the conspirators, "but they don't know that the British and Americans want unconditional surrender. What Italy must do, even now, is stop the Allied advance, win a victory; and then I know I am the only man capable of negotiating with them. If Mussolini goes there will be chaos, for one way or another, whether the war carries on or grinds to a halt, there'll be disaster. If war persists, the people who clamor for peace will see that Mussolini's going has changed very little. If Italy leaves the war, what will the Germans do? They'll just trample Italy underfoot. Nearly everything I've done so far has aimed to prevent that happening."

The Duce had not overlooked the threat of General Kesselring and his Nazi troops. Besides, there were the 600,000 Italians scattered all over the territory controlled by the Germans. These Italians had gone out trusting in the word of Mussolini, who was sending them to Axis areas. If their government yielded, they would suffer and become prisoners; which is precisely what happened after September 8, 1943, when the Germans began to retaliate against Badoglio's betrayal of the Axis agreement.

Conscious that hundreds of thousands of human lives depended on what he did, the Duce remained determined to stem the Allied advance, achieving this with as many reinforcements as the Führer could provide by withdrawing German units from the Russian front and arranging a possible truce with the Soviet Union.

Against this policy, there were the conspirators, the men who saw themselves as the saviors of Italy but who in fact were only paving the way for the final tragedy. The Badoglio-Acquarone-Grandi triumvirate waited for the strategic moment to act, having been joined by Giuseppe Bottai, Luigi Federzoni, Ciano, Emilio de Bono, and Vittorio Ambrosio, who had himself collaborated with the Court in search of a "military solution."

Meanwhile the King, lurking in the gloom of his palace like a cat stalking its prey, bided his time for a surefire opportunity. He delayed until June 15, but the next day, once he knew that the Grand Council would be meeting, he gave the conspirators the signal to go ahead. Like Pontius Pilate, he could then wash his hands and say that he had only adhered to the wishes of the Fascist Grand Council, which Mussolini himself had convened. Let me explain. I have already said that one of the quarrels between Victor Emmanuel III and my husband arose from the assignment of constitutional prerogatives to the Fascist Grand Council. The King of Italy, who was very down to earth, remembered these prerogatives at just the right moment. By using the Fascist Grand Council, the conspirators could betray Mussolini without violating constitutional requirements. They would simply vote him out of office. Ironically, just as he had taken power through the most lawful means, the Duce would lose it in the same way.

A range of events, a convergence of varied interests, and mistaken sincerity in some quarters all meant that the Duce was in a particularly solitary position in July, 1943. He knew that these people were conspiring against him, but there was one person in whom he placed consummate trust, believing he could count on him in the final resort. That person was the King. I think that if Benito Mussolini had known for certain that he could not rely on Victor Emmanuel III, history would have followed a different course on July 25, 1943.

As it was, Mussolini played into the conspirators' hands. When, early in July, various officials asked him to convene the Grand Council, he immediately agreed and even fixed the date of the meeting for the evening of July 24. For the plotters this was too early. Grandi asked the Duce to change the date, but Benito refused.

The incident raised a few suspicions in his mind. As if he had come to some conclusion after debating with himself, he commented to me on Grandi's attempts to delay the meeting of the Grand Council. "They want this meeting of the Grand Council. Well, they'll have it. Now everyone has got to recognize his responsibilities. This Grand Council business is some idea of Grandi and Federzoni. If there's any disagreement they're always at the head of it, those two. But they're satisfied with words."

On July 18, less than a week before the scheduled meeting, chance dealt the conspirators a setback. Hitler told the Duce that he wished to talk to him immediately, and that the rendezvous should be at Feltre, near Venice. There could be dangers in this meeting for those intriguing against my husband, for if Benito gave Hitler the slightest hint of his suspicion of disloyalty, the Führer would take measures for his friend's security, thus frustrating the conspirators' scheme. And if the Duce persuaded Hitler to provide him with further resources he would be less vulnerable when the Grand Council met.

Thus for one week the conspirators had a single overriding aim: by whatever means to prevent Hitler and Mussolini from talking at length when they got together at Feltre on July 20. Therefore the conspirators sabotaged the discussion between the Führer and the Duce, and by the easiest and least controversial method: because the security of the two men called for special measures, it was arranged that they were to travel by train and then by car to the villa where the meeting was to take place. These unexpected delays nibbled away a major part of the schedule before the meeting had even begun.

Nobody thought to wonder why at such a critical moment Mussolini and Hitler were frittering away their time in planes, trains, and cars when for the journey home they traveled direct to the Trevise airport. Indeed, they could have held their talks quite easily at Trevise.

All these complications were intentional, as—probably—was the air raid on Rome that was reported to the Duce at about midday on July 20, hardly an hour after the meeting had begun. Altogether the two men spent a maximum of four hours together, while Hitler was prepared to stay indefinitely to settle the question of Italy's defense. That day, by keeping Hitler and Mussolini from earnest conversation, the conspirators ensured the success of their own venture, and also made way for Italy's later tragic days.

Incidentally, I would add that my husband phoned from Feltre to Rome, checking that relief work was well under way. He was assured that this was the case, but when he returned to the capital the truth stared him starkly in the face: none of the things he had been promised had taken place.

That evening the Duce and I quarreled at the Villa Torlonia. He was dressing, and Irma was buttoning his collar, when I tried to pass on the news I'd received that day about the evil machinations of Badoglio, Grandi, and company. My information was clear and explicit: they would stop at nothing, not even murder. I knew, for example, that because I was an embarrassment, they would dispose of me before they dealt with my husband; that they would hand Benito over to the Allies or kill him if he tried to resist or escape; that the meeting of the Grand Council was to be the constitutional excuse the King was waiting for.

I had also learned that from then on our telephone lines were to be tapped by the army's general staff, which was also embroiled in the plot through its chief, Vittorio Ambrosio. Finally, I had indisputable evidence that Giuseppe Bastianini had delivered eleven passports to men implicated in a lesser plot. The implications of this discovery were serious, because

Bastianini was undersecretary at the foreign office, which my husband had just taken over, in February. It was evident that Bastianini was not to be trusted either.

I had already told my husband about the matter of the passports. He had asked Bastianini for an explanation, only to be given a vigorous denial.

When that evening I brought up the subject once more, the Duce brushed me off with the words "Rachele, I'm telling you again, it's the American tanks I'm worried about, not Badoglio's activities or other people's intrigues." Then, when I reminded him of the case of Bastianini, he cut me short with the terse comment that I was the one who was plotting.

Angrily I grabbed the telephone and promptly phoned Bastianini himself, telling him of all my suspicions, giving him the names of the people for whom he'd obtained passports, and adding that I had told Mussolini about the conspiracy myself. My husband was beside himself, cutting the line because he had heard enough of my telling Bastianini a few home truths.

It was just four days before the meeting of the Grand Council. I knew that that would be the day of judgment, but I couldn't persuade the Duce to take prompt action, because he had won a last reprieve by upsetting the conspiracy when he arranged for the Grand Council to meet on July 24. Originally the officials involved had planned everything for August 7, thinking that the meeting would be held on that day. If Benito had gone all out to destroy them, by making use of this snag, later events might have been very different.

But he declined to listen. Having reached his decision, he stubbornly refused to budge an inch. Indeed, in his view, the meeting of the Grand Council could only clarify the situation, since everyone would have to face up to his responsibilities. Besides, my husband believed that, should the King's intervention prove necessary, it would doubtless swing in his favor. I was confident that the very opposite would be the case, but Benito didn't want to know. He had put implicit trust in the monarchy because he could see nothing on his own side to warrant betrayal, and he wouldn't give the matter another moment's thought.

My daughter, Edda, tried in vain to warn her father about Grandi; and Carlo Scorza, the new Fascist Party secretary, hinted of possible surprises, but neither they nor I could make him change his mind. It was maddening. I wasn't counting days any longer, but hours.

On the morning of the twenty-fourth, I rose earlier than usual, not having slept that night. I couldn't even express my anxiety to my children, because Vittorio was on a mission and Romano and Anna-Maria were with my grandchildren at Riccione.

I pushed open the door of Benito's room. He, too, was already up. "Is this evening's convocation really necessary?" I asked point-blank.

He looked at me in surprise. "And why not? It'll only be a discussion among comrades—at least I think so. I don't see why it shouldn't take place."

At the mention of "comrades," I burst out, "Comrades? Is that what you call that bunch of traitors who are deceiving you? There's Grandi, for a start. Do you know that nobody has been able to find Grandi for the past few days?"

At Grandi's name he looked uncertain, as if he'd suddenly remembered something. Then he calmly tried to explain that he wasn't expecting anything serious.

We said good-bye to each other that morning without having made any concessions to one another, but I was distraught. I knew that in a matter of hours the final curtain would fall and that my husband had only been looking on the bright side to allay my fears.

I was also sure that the men who had sworn to ruin my husband wouldn't make it easy for him, because they couldn't. I had received a detailed report a few days before the Feltre talks about various secret meetings between Ciano and other members of the Grand Council. Benito had phoned Ciano, asking if he had really met these people, and Ciano had admitted as much—saying that it was for private reasons. Afterward my son-in-law had come to see the Duce and declared his loyalty once again, but the harm had been done and the masks were down; the conspirators now knew that Mussolini had knowledge of the treachery.

Several times during the morning I was surprised to find myself thinking about what my husband was doing at that particular moment. "Now he is holding such and such a meeting," I thought. I felt as if I were living out a nightmare and that the following day Benito would say, as he had before, "You see! You were wrong!" I hoped with all my heart that this would happen, but deep down I was sure of the opposite.

At lunch he wasn't visibly nervous, but from his pale face and the way he kept putting his hand to his back I knew that his ulcer was giving pain. It was hardly surprising after the life he had led during the previous year.

While the Grand Council usually opened its proceedings at ten in the evening, on July 24 the session was due to start at five, since the debate was expected to be long. At twenty minutes to five Benito left the Villa Torlonia, carrying a brief-case full of the papers he had gathered in his office.

I went out on to the steps with him, and while he was getting into his car, I couldn't help saying, "Have them all arrested, Benito. Do that before you even start." He made a gesture that could have meant that he would, or that it was too late. Irma had asked him if she should send the usual Thermos of milk, and he told her not to do anything unless he phoned himself.

I should mention that the Duce himself decided to give leave to the militia that day and not to reinforce the guard at the Palazzo Venezia. Once again, the man was overriding the dictator; Mussolini didn't want to force anyone's hand.

21/Mussolini Dismissed

Is there any point in my describing the meeting of the Grand Council yet again? I doubt it. It has already found its niche in history, and virtually everyone who was present has given his own version—each varying the nuances as best suits his personal situation. What's more, I wasn't there myself, and my account of the facts would not be very enlightening since it would be based on what I have heard or read.

I can say, however, that Mussolini's own person was never under attack. Though criticism was leveled at the political system, the alliance with Hitler, and the course of recent events, most of the nineteen councillors (of whom fourteen were Freemasons) who supported Dino Grandi's motion to restore the constitutional monarchy of Victor Emmanuel aimed merely to relieve the Duce of some of his responsibilities, thus enabling him to devote more time to straightforward political activity.

The men who aimed to destroy Mussolini—Grandi, Bastianini, Bottai, Ciano, and Federzoni—spent the whole eight hours of the meeting casting blame on my husband. But even when the vote went against him, Mussolini continued to command respect. In fact, the Duce's democratic attitude actually led one councillor to vote with Grandi. This was Luciano Gottardi, who was sitting on the Grand Council for the first time. He had understood almost none of the debate, and had assumed that Mussolini must have agreed with Grandi once he allowed the motion to be put to the vote.

There was another factor in the course of the Grand Council meeting: two hours before the meeting began, while Benito was working in his office at the Villa Torlonia, he had suffered acute stomach pains. He'd remained silent about them, not wishing to give me any additional worry, but through the debate, he later confided to me, he had been floating in a kind of mist.

Even if he'd been in perfect health, Benito would have acted as he did, for he wanted to clear the field once and for all. Moreover, he was sure the King would support him through this new time of trial—though for that matter, I am sure that, even if he had known that Victor Emmanuel was to desert him, he would have done nothing to militate against the wishes of the Grand Council. It may have been only a consultative body, but the Duce had no wish to minimize its importance, for all that.

As I write about it now, it occurs to me that Benito may well have thought there was no way out; that once something gets off to a bad start it cannot be recovered. By midnight that evening, I was in a terrible state of suspense. I called De Cesare, the Duce's secretary, who told me that the meeting was still in progress.

I phoned the Palazzo Venezia again at one in the morning, at half past one, and at two. The meeting still had not ended. I knew just how much was at stake, and I hadn't expected to see Benito home after only an hour or two, but I couldn't control my anxiety. I became the prey of bizarre thoughts, as always happens in moments of crisis—and I even became nostalgic for our early and exacting years together. I wondered whether, all things considered, they hadn't been happier. In the silence of that house, as if to forestall disaster, I determined that once it was all over I would drag Benito away—forcibly if necessary. I would make him forsake politics. It came graphically to my mind that ordinary, unim-

portant people can be really happy. They may not climb as
high as the great men, but they don't fall so low either. We
are like that; we always seek more, and we are ready to fling
everything overboard when the game is over. During those
twenty years in power, our effort and sacrifices had outweighed
the glory, and it seemed a sad irony that Mussolini should be
accused of self-seeking. He'd had one immovable aim: to make
Italy a great, strong, and respected country, and it looked as
this prospect might be swept away in one snap of the fingers
by people who put self-interest before Italy.

Paradoxically, while I was thinking about my husband's
future and ours, my thoughts turned increasingly to the future
of my country, which was to be tossed in the wind of personal
ambitions and shady dealings. The men who were to die as
the result of others' egoism would be sacrificed for nothing.
All the crosses that stood as a sign of our children's sacrifices,
over marked or unmarked graves in Italy and elsewhere in the
world, would have lost their purpose. I was afraid that Italian
parents would be denied even the consolation of having lost
their children for the honor of their country.

At about three-thirty, a message from the Palazzo Venezia
informed me that the Duce was on his way home. It was about
four when I heard the sound of the car. I ran down to meet
Benito on the stairs. He was with Carlo Scorza, the Fascist
Party secretary. I could see from the signs of fatigue and tension on his face how the meeting had gone. Before he could
say a word, I exclaimed, "You've had them all arrested, I
hope."

Scorza looked at me in surprise. My husband murmured
tiredly, "No, I haven't yet, but I will tomorrow morning."

"Tomorrow morning will be too late," I said despairingly.
"Grandi must have covered some distance already."

He shrugged, released Scorza, and handed me his brief-
case. We went up to his study, and there, utterly exhausted,
he fell into an armchair. With his head in his hands, he sat
staring at me in silence for a long while, as if my presence

were proof that he was not dreaming. Then, holding the telephone out, he said, "Call the general headquarters for me, please. I want to know if there have been any alerts and air raids."

I knew already of the incidents that evening, because while waiting for Benito, I'd phoned several people in various towns and learned that there had been raids and alerts in Bologna, Milan, and other centers. However, I now called the general headquarters and, expecting to hear the same reports, passed my husband the receiver. I overheard the answer—"All quiet, Duce; there's nothing to report anywhere on the home front"—and my patience snapped.

I snatched the telephone out of Benito's hands and shouted, "Liar! Practically the whole of Italy is on the alert. Bologna has been bombed. Do you have to lie to the Duce about that too? Even now?" Benito replaced the receiver and said, "Calm down, Rachele. There's nothing you can do; not now. There's nothing to be done at all. They want a showdown whatever it costs. I'm afraid even my own wishes count for nothing now."

Then he began to tell me how the meeting of the Grand Council had gone. I realized he needed to get it off his mind, so I let him talk for about twenty minutes without interrupting. I broke in only once, when he told me that our son-in-law, Galeazzo Ciano, had voted against him.

"Even him," I exclaimed unhappily.

We always feel that life has caused us enough suffering, but it seems as if fate, in its cruelty, keeps one blow in store to test us when we are least able to withstand it. Ciano's vote was that kind of blow. I remembered the day when I'd entertained Ciano for the first time and had told him that I wanted him to be completely aware of Edda's true nature. I had placed my cards on the table.

It was nearly five o'clock in the morning when we said good-night, though the words were meaningless, for I knew all too well that neither of us would be able to sleep. Before going to bed, I watched the dawn breaking over the garden—ushering in a day that could have been like any other. And, once in bed, I found myself looking round my room as if I'd never seen it before. I wondered how many more nights we would spend there; then I fell into a few minutes' restless sleep.

When I got up I found Benito already dressed. Dr. Pozzi soon arrived to administer the daily injection, but Benito would have none of it, explaining, "My blood's boiling over today." In fact, he was in a hurry to go and was in his office by nine.

Carlo Scorza phoned quite early, telling him that Tullio Cianetti, who had voted for Grandi's motion, was retracting his vote. He had even written a letter, which he'd given to Scorza to forward to my husband, begging the Duce's forgiveness.

Then Benito sent for Grandi, who was not to be found. At the time my husband thought that the conspirator was too ashamed of the previous day's dealings to face him.

Next Benito phoned his private secretary, De Cesare, asking him to obtain an audience with the King. Surprisingly, there was no immediate reply. Only later did I learn that Benito's request had upset the conspirators' plot. The Duce usually visited the King on Mondays and Thursdays, but, today was Sunday, and Victor Emmanuel was not at the royal palace but at the Villa Savoia, his private residence. Before agreeing to the meeting, the King had to change the nefarious plans for Mussolini's arrest and abduction, which the conspirators had planned to carry out at the royal palace on Monday. The Queen was also faced with a moral problem, for according to the modified plan the Duce would be arrested under their own roof, which was contrary to any code of honor.

But my husband was totally ignorant of all this. In due course an answer came from the King granting the Duce an audience at five that afternoon. Rather oddly, the head of protocol asked that the Duce should attend in civilian dress; this point surprised Benito, but with so much else on his mind, he forgot about it.

At eleven, Albini, undersecretary of state at the Ministry of the Interior, went to the Duce's office for the daily report.

Albini, by the way, had voted against the Duce the night before and could easily have tendered his resignation because of
political differences with both his prime minister and the minister of the interior. (My husband had retained this portfolio
and that of foreign affairs.) But without any qualms and as if
nothing had happened, Albini continued with his duties.

Benito asked, sarcastically, if Albini thought he'd made
good use of his first vote in the Grand Council—"seeing that
you are a guest in the Grand Council, thanks to the position I
have given you; you're not a titular member."

Blushing with shame, Albini answered that if he had made
an error of judgment in voting for Grandi's motion, nobody
could doubt his devotion to the Duce. When Benito told me
about the conversation over lunch, he summed Albini up with
the words "When he left, he had the face of the self-confessed
traitor."

I knew Albini and had taken his measure from the moment he'd been appointed to his post some months before. He
had asked to see me, having heard of my opinion of him and
knowing, besides, that I was well aware of various irregularities he'd committed while he was prefect of Naples. His appointment had been followed by adverse reactions in several
quarters. I had discussed the appointment with my husband,
but he'd replied, "Men are like apples, I buy them by the
box. There may be several good ones and one rotten. I am
hoping his new duties will give him a chance to make amends
and clear his reputation."

So Albini had come to see me and had spent the entire
interview repeating the stereotyped flatteries of the well-trained
official. "But, Excellency, for us the Duce is everything. Excellency, I am ready to give my life for him." I had no illusions
about Albini, any more than I had about the others, but my
awareness was little help by then.

About eleven o'clock on the morning of July 25, I received
a phone call from Guido Buffarini, Albini's predecessor at the
Ministry of the Interior, who asked to see me without ex-

plaining why. We arranged a meeting for five that afternoon.

At midday, as if nothing had happened, the Duce welcomed the new Japanese ambassador, who asked on his government's behalf for information about the military situation in Europe. My husband gave him a clear picture of events, emphasizing the point that his government should impress upon Hitler the need for a settlement with Russia. "When arms no longer afford a sufficient means for tackling a situation, a political solution must be sought," he said.

These words, which came to my ears only later, were Mussolini's last pronouncement on the war as head of government. They demonstrate that he was completely lucid and conversant with the situation. If the Japanese diplomat is still alive to read these words (I understand that this book is to appear in Japan), he will surely remember that my husband gave no impression that he was a marked man, living his last hours of freedom, but that he was as clearheaded as ever.

At about two, I learned that Benito was leaving the Palazzo Venezia. When he had not arrived at the Villa Torlonia half an hour later, I began to grow anxious. He finally arrived at three, after driving around Rome with Gen. Enzo Galbiati to see the extent of the bomb damage. He had distributed money to the unhappy people who had lost everything, giving all that Galbiati and his police escort had with them. Even then he was more concerned about the sufferings of his fellow countrymen than concerned about his own safety.

All this time Marshal Badoglio was celebrating with champagne, for he had been named head of the Italian government by royal decree at the end of the morning. The crowds cheering my husband at San Lorenzo had not the faintest idea that he no longer counted for anything. For that matter, Benito had no idea either. And thus it was that for a few hours Italy had two heads of government. Only in Rome could such things happen.

For the sake of history, I would like to add that, some days before, Victor Emmanuel had visited the same quarters in Rome as Benito visited that afternoon, and had been given quite a different reception. And when I say "different," I am being extremely kind.

I still remember nothing of that fateful afternoon except that Benito told me he was going to see the King at five. I sprang to my feet as if I'd been bitten, and pleaded, "Don't go, I beg you not to go." We were sitting at the lunch table, though in fact we had sat down quite mechanically, for Benito would not eat anything; he took only a few mouthfuls of soup.

"I must go and see the King," he replied. "For we have a treaty with Germany and we must honor it. The King signed it, as I did, and we must discuss the whole business. If necessary, I shall stay in command to keep our side of the agreement. Otherwise I shall resign on condition that he gives me the means to arrest the traitors. We're going through a difficult time, as we did at Caporetto, but we'll survive this one too."

Benito was not thinking of himself or talking about his predicament. His whole concern was for Italy. I, on the other hand, was increasingly certain that Victor Emmanuel would not want to tackle the moral problem raised by arresting the commander-in-chief of the Italian forces to whom he—the King—had delegated his powers because of the war.

After lunch I went to join Benito, who was dressing in his room. As I entered, he asked, "Which suit shall I wear?"

I didn't even answer. Wringing my hands, I tried desperately to dissuade him from going. I began by reminding him of something that he had once told me himself and that he had found amusing. One of the keepers at the royal hunting lodge at Castel Porziano, where the conspirators had met, had written Benito a letter warning him to beware of the King. "He is not to be trusted," the keeper wrote; after various graphic phrases about the sovereign, the letter ended, "His Majesty is afraid you are becoming too powerful, because the people love you."

Benito had forgotten this warning. I had not, however, since I had also received a corroborating report from one of the ladies of the Court on May 8—just over two months before. She'd given specific details about the development of the conspiracy and the part each of its members was to play. Acquarone was the heart of the treason, Ambrosio was to arrest my husband in due course, and so on. As my husband dressed, I reminded him of this report, but he said nothing.

I added that I had every reason to suppose that the whole royal family, apart from the Queen, was hostile to him. True, Princess Maria-José had written Benito two cordial letters after meeting him at Castel Porziano when the Empire was declared. And Crown Prince Umberto had reason to thank the Duce for having hushed up some minor personal scandal in which he'd been involved. But were they grateful? Rather to the contrary.

As for the King, he'd never forgotten the various "attempts" on his rights made by the Duce's measures. He also remembered that my husband had chosen to ignore the transfer abroad of royal capital and securities at the very time when Italy was struggling against the League of Nations in Ethiopia and in Geneva.

Poor Benito assumed that these factors could not outweigh twenty years of loyal collaboration with the House of Savoy. "If you think about it, Rachele," he concluded, "the King can't possibly act against me, because by doing so he'd destroy not only me, but the monarchy and Italy itself."

When he was ready to leave he took from his desk a bundle of documents, including that section of the constitution that laid down the prerogatives of the Grand Council. He also drew out the letter from Tullio Cianetti that Scorza had sent him that morning. He asked me to take care of it, and that is how Cianetti emerged from the Verona trials, where the Salò Republic pronounced sentence on the traitors of the Grand Council, with his life.

It was nearly four-thirty when De Cesare arrived, since as the Duce's private secretary he was to go with Benito to the King's residence at Villa Savoia. As I greeted him, I said, "I'm very afraid you may not be going home this evening." But like my husband, De Cesare thought I was being over-anxious.

When Benito was about to leave, Scorza phoned, advising

that Marshal Rodolfo Graziani offered his services as chief of staff if they were needed. Benito answered that he would see Graziani after his discussion with the King. I add this detail to illustrate that not once had it occurred to my husband that by going to the Villa Savoia he was putting his head into a noose. However important this meeting might turn out to be, he never thought it would end in disaster.

It was just before five when, in a blue suit and his bowler hat, Benito Mussolini got into his car. Ercole Borratto was driving. I cannot convey my emotions as I watched the car disappearing down the drive. It was not until he'd gone that I realized we hadn't even said good-bye.

Guido Buffarini arrived at five as arranged, still stunned by the session of the Grand Council. As he told me his version of what had happened the previous night, he handed me a sheet of paper which my husband had covered with the kinds of doodle one makes when one is bored.

We were talking about Scorza when the telephone rang. I literally leaped toward it, and heard a breathless, almost inaudible murmur from the other end of the line: "They have just this moment arrested the Duce."

I stood frozen, still holding the receiver but no longer listening to the repeated hellos from the other end. Buffarini came over, took the telephone, and asked, "Who are you? Tell me who you are."

The voice, distorted with emotion, could only mutter, "There is nothing else I can tell you. That's all I know. Be quick and warn the children at Riccione." Then the line went dead.

Less than half an hour had passed since I had begged my husband not to go and see the King, fearing he'd be arrested. And now I had proof that I had been right. Mussolini was a prisoner.

22/Ten Minutes to Wipe Out Twenty Years in Power

It was July 25, 1943. I had to wait until September 13 to hear from my husband's own lips the precise circumstances of his arrest. But on July 25, the thought that I would some day see him again was far from my mind. It took me a few minutes after I had heard the telephone message to grasp what had happened.

I had told Benito so often that he was going to be arrested that, logically, the knowledge that it had finally happened shouldn't have upset me. But now I was standing there in the drawing room looking at Buffarini, Irma, and the caretaker without really seeing them. I had one thought throbbing my head—that Benito was no longer with me. I didn't even know where they had taken him.

In Forlì and Milan I had always known if Benito was in prison, for someone always came to tell me and bring some hastily scribbled message. This time the rules of the game were different. The treachery came from the top; there was nobody to whom I could appeal.

And like a complete idiot, I concentrated my whole mind on a single idea: if Benito was alive, where would he get his medicine? Would they think to cook him fat-free meals?

Having overcome the initial panic, I began to fight back. I called the headquarters of the militia, the German embassy, the Palazzo Venezia, and the home of General Galbiati, who had left my husband at three o'clock. But everywhere I got the same reply: "They've lied to you, Donna Rachele. Nothing's happened."

I was almost beginning to wonder whether the whole thing hadn't been some tasteless joke when I heard the sound of running engines. Going to the window, I saw some trucks stopping in front of the door and Carabiniere getting out of them. I immediately grabbed the telephone, but the line was dead. I couldn't even get through to the caretaker any longer.

Any last doubts I may have had were dispelled when I saw the Carabiniere sending our security police away. Some of the police looked as though they wanted to come toward the house, presumably to say good-bye to me, but I saw the Carabiniere officer barring their way.

In the end everyone went, leaving the Villa Torlonia in the care of two agents and a telephone operator, none of whom was armed. I would have been at the mercy of the first maniac who wanted to use me for his own ends. Worn out, I went into the garden and sank onto a bench. Buffarini, who was beside me, had been following me around because I was his last and only hope. He was drinking cognac after cognac to keep his spirits up.

It was then that I realized how strange the pattern of history can be. Less than an hour after Benito's arrest, I myself had informed everyone who might have been able to free him by taking prompt action, even if it was only the German embassy. Everyone had thought the news so absurd that nobody had made a move.

Suddenly I thought of Vittorio, who had been flying the previous night and was now sleeping peacefully in the villa he used to stay in at the other end of the grounds of the Villa Torlonia. I sent a message summoning him; he arrived, his eyes puffy with sleep, whistling in an offhand way, and asked, "What's the matter, Mamma? Is the house on fire?"

"They've arrested your father. You must find refuge quickly."

Vittorio didn't waste time. Leaping into his car, he left the Villa Torlonia without difficulty, through a gate opening onto the Via Spallanzani which he invariably used.

The telephone rang some moments later. It was Romano calling from Riccione to ask my permission to go to the cinema. My daughter-in-law Gina, Bruno's widow, who was with both Romano and Anna-Maria, had told him he couldn't go, because she was afraid of air raids. I knew that our line was tapped, and I couldn't warn him about what had happened. Besides, I didn't want to alarm the children. When I was non-committal in my reply, Romano thought I was refusing to let him go. So, as he always did when I wouldn't agree to something, he told me to ask Benito for him, because he was sure he could force agreement out of his father.

How could I shout down the line that his father had been kidnapped and was a prisoner? I wasn't even with my son to comfort him. Therefore I chose to say nothing, but it was a terrible strain.

After Romano, it was Vittorio's turn; he called me several times to find out how I was. These calls were the only link I had with the outside world.

Vittorio admitted later that he was convinced his father was already dead. It wasn't until about ten that I managed to talk to the quaestor Agnesina and the prefect Stracca, who had been responsible for the Duce's security right up to that day. But I extracted little news except that, according to Agnesina, the Duce had arrived at the Villa Savoia at five o'clock and had been arrested soon afterward. Because his car had remained in the grounds until the evening, the quaestor had supposed that Benito was still at the Villa Savoia. Soon after the two officials left, I listened to the news bulletin, hearing for the first time the announcement that Badoglio had succeeded Mussolini.

That night I had a guest. Terrified by the thought of what might happen to him if he fell into the hands of the mob, Buffarini asked me to put him up. I had never valued Buffarini very highly and was to show him so later, but at that time we were both in the same boat, and it would have been churlish of me to show him the door when he had come to try and cheer me up.

As if one ordeal a day wasn't enough, fate dealt me another blow on July 25. It was then that Irma, whose nerves were in a terrible state, told me about Benito's relationship of several years with Clara Petacci. The special editions of the newspapers announcing the Duce's dismissal were already talking about the affair. Poor Irma, who had looked after us so kindly, suffered the consequences of her admission there and then, for her husband slapped her in my presence.

In the street, groups of people were gathering in front of the main gate and shouting, "The war is over." Unhappily, they had to retract their words very soon. Meanwhile, there was also the chanting of anti-Mussolini slogans. An anti-Fascist—and who wasn't one that evening?—who had once been told by a guard not to sound his horn in the vicinity of the Villa Torlonia took his personal revenge by parking his car near the entrance and jamming his horn.

Two days later, on the morning of July 27, the caretaker informed me that someone wanted to speak to me. It was the maid of Princess Mafalda of Savoy. She had brought me a letter from her mistress assuring me that the Duce was alive and in no danger. "God be praised," I murmured, closing my eyes for a few moments so that I could concentrate all my heart and soul into these few words of gratitude.

According to Princess Mafalda, her maid told me, a lively tension existed between Victor Emmanuel and his wife. The Queen had refused to allow the Duce to be arrested under her roof, since for her such an action would have been both treacherous and a breach of the most elementary rules of hospitality.

At any other time I would have taken violent exception

to their villainous behavior, but that day I didn't care what anybody said about the King, the Queen, or anyone else. The earth could have stopped turning on its axis and I wouldn't have minded, because now I knew that Benito was alive.

Of all my experiences during that harassing time, only a few are still as vivid in my mind as if they had happened only yesterday. My husband's first letter was one. A certain General Polito brought it to me at the Villa Torlonia, ceremoniously escorted by two high-ranking Carabinere officers. When he held it out to me I read it diagonally at first, jumping from the first line to the last, trying to take in the whole contents at once.

"Dear Rachele," he wrote. "The bearer of this letter will tell you what has happened to me. You know what my state of health allows me to eat, but don't send me very much, just a few clothes, because I haven't any, and some books. I can't tell you where I am, but I can assure you that I'm well. Keep calm and kiss the children for me. Benito."

General Polito also gave me another letter to read, this one signed by Marshal Badoglio. But he took it back once I read it through. Roughly speaking, Badoglio was asking me to send my husband some clothes and money. Otherwise— he had the audacity to tell me—he couldn't provide for food. I was incensed. "For twenty years," I flung at him, "Mussolini has disclaimed every title, even his salary. All the presents that he received from Italians and from abroad, he gave away. That Badoglio, with his pockets full of the millions he earned through my husband's regime, should now dare to refuse a crust of bread to a prisoner like Mussolini is an outrage."

To hear me, nobody would have thought I was the wife of a man in hostile hands. But grief and anger lower the gates of caution, and I could see myself showing Polito the door.

The officers with him could appreciate my sentiments, and one of them, a colonel, took me a little to one side and said, "Madam, you are perfectly right. Unfortunately I can't do very much to help you, but you can rely on my loyalty. However, you must keep cool because these people are prepared to do anything." And with these last words, he pulled back his tunic to show me the Fascist badge pinned to the inside.

For that reason, I put on a bold face and packed a parcel with some presents for Benito's birthday (it was now July 29), some handkerchiefs, a pair of socks, and a tie. Then I put in the items I'd always sent him in prison, from the days when we were living in Forlì: a chicken, some really fresh tomatoes, fruit, and tagliatelle. I also slipped in a bottle of oil, because the doctors had forbidden him to eat anything cooked in butter (I later found out that this bottle never reached him), and a book that I found open on his bedside table with some notes in the margin, entitled *The Life of Jesus* by Giuseppe Ricciotti.

Polito took his leave, and I couldn't help letting fly with a final barb when I saw the brand-new general's star on his cap. "My congratulations," I said. "I see that July twenty-fifth has helped more than one person."

From the hate in his eyes I realized that I had made myself an enemy. I couldn't have cared less, because I had just recalled another encounter with this brilliant General Polito. I had met him in Bologna in the days when my husband was in power. As a quaestor, he had never missed a chance to proclaim his admiration for Mussolini and his fervent faith as a Fascist who was ready to go through fire for the Duce. At that time he'd been waiting to make his way in the world and glad to have the honor of carrying Donna Rachele's suitcase. It was less risky than going through fire.

On August 2, I left the Villa Torlonia forever. Polito again came to fetch me and drove me to Rocca delle Caminate, where, he told me, I would find my children. I wanted to pack my bag in his presence to show him that I wasn't taking anything of value. Giving away everything except Benito's little chest and decorations, I gritted my teeth to keep from showing how flustered I was. But when it came to making a quick round of the house, I couldn't hold back the tears, though nobody saw them. I had the impression that the furniture took on human form and that everything looked fondly at me, as if to say, "Go in peace, we'll protect what you have entrusted to us." As I passed, my hand brushed over the back of a chair, a table, and they seemed warm to the touch. In a few minutes I took my leave of what I had built over fourteen years. Even the animals, suddenly quiet, seemed to be murmuring, "And what's to become of us?"

I scolded myself: "You mustn't give way; you, after all, are still free, while Benito is a prisoner."

It was about eleven at night when I got into the car. Through the open window, I shook hands with the few people who had served us over the years. We didn't say anything, but I could feel the emotion.

If I had any doubts about Polito's hostility, our journey to Rocca delle Caminate removed them. The trip was torture, both physically and mentally—physically, because the journey, which we could have completed quite easily in six or seven hours, lasted more than twelve. The Carabiniere colonel was sitting beside the driver, and in the back Polito sprawled beside me. He had closed the windows and doors, making the atmosphere already polluted by the cigars he chain-smoked even more unbearable. Even when we stopped, he locked me in the car as if I had the plague. When I pointed out that the detours he made the driver take were only wasting gasoline, he burst into smug and mocking laughter. "Don't worry about that," he jeered, "we have enough gas. We've always had enough, for us."

Utterly hateful, after nauseating me with his very presence, he went on to the mental torture of humiliation. There were no more tremulously respectful murmurs of "Donna Rachele." He was very familiar now, that cardboard soldier. Taking advantage of the situation, he even dared to suggest that my husband's fate depended on him alone and that my attitude would decide his treatment of Benito. He actually ventured to put his hand on my knee, but the way I looked at him even in the gloom stopped him short. If he'd gone any further I think I would have killed him. I don't know how, but I would have.

In the end he thought it prudent to give me his visiting card so that I'd know where to find him, for he was sure that I'd rush to throw myself at his feet.

It was eleven in the morning when I saw the tower of Rocca delle Caminate standing out in the distance. I breathed a sigh of relief; at last I was going to be rid of my odious companion. In spite of everything I'd had to bear, my journey had given me one satisfaction: the ever conceited Polito had disclosed all the police conspiracies in minute detail. If he hadn't done so, some of them would never have come to light.

When the car stopped I heard the voices of my children. They were the sweetest sounds I had heard for nine days.

23/The Rescue of Mussolini

"When I drove into the grounds of the Villa Savoia, I saw an ambulance parked not far from the door and naïvely imagined that some member of the royal family must be ill. I told myself that I hoped it was nothing serious."

Only Benito Mussolini could have entertained such thoughts while the King, who was waiting for him on the threshold, corseted in his impeccable uniform, made ready to play out the final scene of a cruel conspiracy.

I heard this story on September 13, 1943. At about two o'clock that afternoon I saw my husband for the first time since July 25. He'd just arrived at Munich after his rescue by the Nazis, and when I saw him emerge from the plane—in a broad-brimmed Romagnole hat, his face pale and wasted, and so thin that his black overcoat seemed to swamp him completely—I felt my heart miss a beat.

As he kissed me, he said, "I thought I'd never see you again." But no words could have said more than the few moments' silence while we gazed at each other.

For the time being, we went to my hotel room in the Karls Palast. My husband had intended to continue his journey to Rastenberg, where he was to meet Hitler, but unexpected bad weather had forced him to spend the night in Munich. I took the opportunity to run him a much-needed bath.

His socks were full of holes and sticking to his feet, his shirt was dirty and creased, and his underpants—which were much too big for him and fastened with a big black button—took me completely aback.

"Who gave you those?" I asked.

"A sailor on board the corvette *Persephone*. The Germans were looking for me, so they dodged about from port to port. While we were sailing toward the island of Ponza, some sailors came up to me and asked if I needed anything. One of them offered me four hundred lire and the other these pants. I took the lot, seeing that I had nothing of my own."

Although we had separate rooms, Benito decided to sleep in mine. "I'll sleep with you," he said. "My room's too big and I've had enough of being alone." We were both happy with this arrangement, and my husband took the opportunity to tell me what had been happening to him.

"The King greeted me in an extremely agitated state," he explained, going back to the day of his arrest. "His speech was very clipped and he could not keep still. As soon as we had entered his office, he said, 'My dear Duce, there's no point in going on. Italy is on her knees, the army has been completely defeated, and the soldiers no longer want to fight for you. The Alpine infantry even have a song which says as much.'

"And with total disregard for the seriousness of the situation," my husband went on, "the King began to hum a few words of the song in Piedmontese dialect. Then, chewing nervously at his nails, he reminded me of the meeting of the Grand Council. 'At this moment you are the most hated man in Italy. You haven't a single friend left, Duce. There's only one man who is still your friend, and that is me. So you needn't worry about your safety. I have decided to ask Marshal Badoglio to take over as head of government. He will pick his own officials to administer the country and continue the war. We shall have to see how it goes.' "

"And what about you, what did you say?" I asked.

"Very little. I tried to remain calm and dignified, but it was a hard knock to take. I suppose there are bound to be repercussions after twenty years in office and going to war. I wished my successor good luck, but added, 'Your Majesty, you are making a very serious decision, which is going to have disastrous consequences. You are going to excite a crisis that will mislead the people and may even cause a tragedy. For they will suppose that if you've dismissed the man who led the country into war, it is because peace is in sight. If you deceive the people there will be terrible aftereffects. Army morale will feel it. If the soldiers don't want to fight for Mussolini any longer, then that's that. But will they agree to go into action for you? Your Majesty, the crisis you are about to cause will simply mean victory for Churchill and Stalin.'

"All this took no more than some twenty minutes, at the most. We then walked toward the front door, and as we crossed the hall the King said in a matter-of-fact way, 'It's hot today.'

" 'Yes,' I answered, 'it's more close than usual.'

"In the doorway, De Cesare was presented to the King for the first and only time. Then, when it came to shaking my hand, the King asked, 'Where would you like to go now, Duce?'

" 'I've only one house, Majesty, Rocca delle Caminate, and I'd like to retire there.' "

Events followed thick and fast. When my husband went to get back into his car, after the King had gone inside, a Carabiniere officer, Captain Vigheri, came up to him and said, "His Majesty has ordered me to see to your protection, since we've learned that you may be in danger. I'm to escort you."

"I don't need an escort. I have my own," Benito replied.

"No, it is essential that I escort you myself."

"In that case, get into my car."

"That's out of the question. We have provided an ambulance for better security."

"You must be joking! What is all this? You must be exaggerating, anyway."

"I'm sorry, Duce, but it's the King's order."

To put an end to this absurd conversation, and out of respect for the royal command, the Duce went over to the ambulance.

"I was surrounded by armed men," he went on. "De Cesare was in front beside the driver. At the time I really thought that the ambulance was a security measure, and I didn't worry. The streets were quiet, as on any Sunday. There were bands playing, people strolling about, going in and out of the cinemas. The ambulance was going so fast and rolling about so much that I couldn't help saying to the officer, 'If this is how you always handle your patients, you must make the doctors' work easier.' As soon as I said it, the driver slowed down."

Even a night spent in the school of Carabiniere did not suggest to Benito that he was a prisoner. It was not until the following morning, when he saw sentries in the corridor outside his room, that he began to suspect he'd been tricked, and that he wasn't bound for Rocca delle Caminate at all.

Now that I had him with me, what concerned me most was his health.

"And your stomach? Who looked after you?" I asked.

"The evening we reached the school of Carabiniere, Major Santillo of the medical corps came to see me. I wouldn't let him examine me, and refused to eat." Remembering one point, Benito interrupted the story to say, "Ah, Rachele! I've just thought. I owe the price of a shave to the barber who came in for me. I couldn't give him anything, because I hadn't any money on me. But I must find out his name so I can thank him." Then, returning to the story, Benito told me what had happened that first night in captivity.

"At about one in the morning I had a visit from General Ferone, who brought a letter from Marshal Badoglio. While I was opening the green envelope, stamped from the war ministry, General Ferone, whom I'd already met in Albania, smiled contentedly as if he were enjoying the sight. In Badoglio's own hand, the letter ran: 'The undersigned head of government wishes to bring to your Excellency's attention that the measures taken concerning you are due only to the interest taken in your personal safety. We have precise information gathered from various sources to show that there is a serious conspiracy against your person. I regret all this, but I wish to inform you that I shall be glad to arrange for you to be driven, in total security and with the consideration you deserve, to a place of residence of your choice.' And it was signed 'Head of Government, Marshal Badoglio.' "

"And you believed what that traitor wrote?" I burst out.

"Why shouldn't I? On the one hand, I'd heard about the King's proclamation—and about another from Badoglio—that fighting was to continue. On the other hand, as far as the whole world knew—and that meant the Fascists as well as our enemies—Badoglio was one of the most prominent Fascists in the public eye, a registered party member, and his family too."

"But a registered Freemason as well," I added. "He's even one of their leaders."

"You know, he's not the only one. But I couldn't believe that a man who'd acquired so much glory, so many titles, and so much wealth through fascism could betray me in such a despicable way. He had even agreed to become president of the National Research Council. Do you remember, Rachele? Admittedly he only set foot in the building occasionally, to read his newspaper. But at that time, I'm telling you, I really thought Badoglio—although he was restructuring the government—had decided not to change Italy's general political position. And more than that, I thought he was carrying out the King's instructions for my safety. If I'd thought there was anything else, I would never have dictated a letter for Badoglio to General Ferone, saying that I was ready to go to Rocca delle Caminate. And if I'd thought for one moment that he was discontinuing the war on the side of the Germans, I, Mussolini, would never have written assuring Badoglio of my support and good wishes. I assumed he was acting out of respect for our commitments—to keep Italy's honor bright."

The following day, despite Major Santillo's entreaties, my husband refused to eat. In the end, he accepted a hard-boiled egg, a little bread, and some fruit.

On the evening of July 27, all further doubts about his situation were removed, when General Polito—that man seemed to be everywhere at once—arrived to take Benito, so he said, to Rocca delle Caminate.

"Through a gap in the car's curtains I saw that we weren't traveling north at all, but south. 'So we're not going to Rocca delle Caminate?' I asked General Polito.

"He merely answered: 'No, there's been a change of plan.' "

The first stop was Gaeta, where Benito commented, "You are doing me too great an honor. This is where Giuseppe Mazzini, the famous patriot, spent his exile. I am overwhelmed." But it was only a stage in the journey. "I embarked on the corvette *Persephone*, which sailed to Ponza, where I spent ten days or so in total isolation. I used the time to translate Carducci's *Odi Barbara* and to finish the life of Jesus you sent me."

During this time, Benito was surprised and comforted by the obvious sympathy and respect he encountered everywhere. On the *Persephone* the sailors asked him if he needed anything—a gesture that compensated to some extent for the order to stay in his cabin. It was the same in the garrison at Ponza and at La Maddalena, where he spent about three weeks.

"When I arrived," he told me, "two Carabiniere came forward and gave their names—Avallone and Marini. Their eyes were full of tears. Marini dared to give me the Fascist salute, saying that he wished he had met me much earlier so that he could have told me everything he'd seen and heard. 'You've achieved your ambition now,' I answered, 'but in the oddest circumstances.' "

For some moments my husband was silent, staring at a point on the wall. Then he went on as if he were talking to himself. "The amazing thing is that the people who were supposed to hate me, according to Badoglio, Polito, and their colleagues, couldn't have been kinder to me. When we docked at La Maddalena, for example, the admirals and generals went off to dine without giving me a thought, leaving me in a room where the furniture consisted of a dirty, rickety table, a chair, and a metal box bed with no mattress or covers. I rolled up my jacket for a pillow—as I used to in 1909, when I came back tired from some meeting in Romagna and lay down in a ditch by the roadside to rest—and fell asleep. The islanders and the Carabiniere woke me. Some of them had brought fish, others fruit, and the soldiers had got their wives to cook soup and eggs. And these were the people who were anxious for revenge! On August first I finally heard from you, receiving the ten thousand lire you sent and the parcel of clothes with Bruno's plate, Edda's letter, and yours. Then I began to feel I wasn't alone."

On August 28, leaving La Maddalena in a seaplane, Benito alighted on Lake Bracciano, about forty miles from Rome. Again in an ambulance (before this ordeal he hadn't been in one since World War I), he was taken to a little village called Assergi, near L'Aquila, spending three days there in a specially requisitioned villa. His jailers were in a quandary, not knowing what to do next to prevent the Germans—who were acting under Hitler's personal order of July 26 to rescue Mussolini— from finding a clue as to his whereabouts.

Finally, on August 31, he reached the last stage of his travels, at the Gran Sasso, in resort hotel atop the highest mountain in the Apennines. "You can imagine how well Badoglio organized things," said my husband, with a touch of sarcasm. "The only place he could be sure to keep me was in the highest prison in the world, nearly two miles up."

If our "cousin" Badoglio had organized things well, he had been equally liberal with the security measures. Both my

husband's guards and the men watching us at Rocca delle
Caminate had orders to shoot if one of us tried to leave.

"Just once," said Benito, "I managed to leave the hotel
at the Gran Sasso. There was a guard with me, but he was
having a struggle holding four wolfhounds that strained at the
leash. They'd been detailed to watch the prisoner too. At one
point the guard was dragged a few steps away from me, and
it was then that I saw an old shepherd coming toward me. He
cut a proud figure in that imposing landscape, with his fur
waistcoat, velvet trousers, and a long beard.

" 'So it's true you're here, Duce,' he whispered. 'The
Germans are looking for you everywhere to free you. I'll go
and tell them, don't you worry. When I tell my wife I've seen
you, she won't believe me.' Before he went, he took my hand
and kissed it."

I can now confirm one point: Benito Mussolini would
never have allowed Badoglio to deliver him into Allied hands.
When he heard on the radio—on September 10, I think—that
one of the clauses of the armistice Italy had signed specified
that he would be surrendered to the Anglo-American forces,
Benito decided to kill himself.

"In spite of this solemn promise, the commander of the
place, Lieutenant Faiola, swore he would never hand me over
to the English," Benito added. "Faiola told me in tears that
he had been a prisoner of the English himself, that he knew
what it meant, and that he would never give up a fellow Italian.
I think that if Hitler's man Skorzeny had not arrived to rescue
me on September twelfth, I would have killed myself."

There seems no point in relating the details of Mussolini's
rescue yet again. It was one of the great exploits of the latter
half of World War II.

It might be interesting to mention, however, that as he
watched his own rescue from the window of his room in the
Gran Sasso hotel, Benito was more concerned about the Italian
soldiers who would have to try to prevent his escape than he
was about his own safety; he was afraid the Italian Carabiniere

would fall under the fire of his rescuer Otto Skorzeny's commandos. As the Carabiniere were about to shoot, he shouted from his window to them, "Don't open fire. There's an Italian general with them. It must be in order."

It was no trick. The Germans had taken an Italian general, Soleti, as a hostage, though I think he would have gone with them of his own accord.

"I've had some adventures in my time," Benito said, "but nothing to equal taking off from the Gran Sasso in that Fieseler Stork. Just imagine an overloaded plane tipping from side to side and lumbering forward to the edge of the precipice. Suction seemed to keep us there. We nose-dived, but the pilot managed to regain control. He's an ace, that Gherlao. Skorzeny was with us. He thought it better to risk being killed with me than to appear before the Führer without me."

"And what are you going to do now?" I asked, no longer able to hide my anguish.

After a pause, he replied with a note of bitterness in his voice, "Start again from nothing."

"There's nothing left, Benito. In the last six weeks everything you built has been destroyed."

I didn't know if I should hide the truth from him too; if I should omit to tell him that once Badoglio had signed an armistice with the Allies, on September 8, all Benito's former supporters had joined the rush to forget him, to trample him underfoot after raising him to the skies. Had I the right to blurt it out all at once? I decided to lie by omission and merely gave him to understand that he'd find Italy remarkably changed.

Then, as if he'd guessed what I was thinking, Benito said, "I know I may die for it, but whatever the cost, I must honor our agreement with Germany. It's the only way to keep the Italians from paying for the armistice of September eighth. If I don't stay with them to deaden the blow, the Germans will take terrible vengeance. In any case, I must have talks with Hitler, and then we'll see."

Once again, on September 13, 1943, Benito had sealed

his destiny. He could not hope to gain by his attitude. The Allies were bound to win sooner or later, as everyone now agreed. Mussolini had his family with him in safety. He could have gone to some neutral country, and the Allies themselves would have welcomed that decision. But there were still Italians in Germany and Italians in Italy, caught between the Allies invading from the south and the Germans invading from the north.

As in 1936 and 1937, several paths were open to him, and my husband chose the hardest. Who could suggest that he was aiming at anything other than the safety of hundreds of thousands of human lives? The members of Badoglio's Liberation Committee in Rome? What a grotesque joke!

24/My Husband's Secret Dream

"You were right, Rachele. There's nothing left. It's as if a hurricane had destroyed everything in its path."

This was Benito's first comment to me when he returned to Italy, at the end of September. He'd decided to come back to set up a government in opposition to Badoglio's as soon as he heard that the Badoglio government had declared war against Germany. "What Badoglio has just done is absurd," he said. "It's going to cause a confrontation between the Italians and the Germans."

My husband would have liked to settle in Rome again, but the proposal failed to rouse German enthusiasm, mainly because the capital had been declared an open city and might therefore be difficult to defend. Besides, geographically Rome was too far from that part of Italy, the north, that was still governed by Benito's Social Republic.

Milan was also out of the question as a seat of Benito's government, for the Milanese might have had to suffer the problem of additional bombing, especially as the air raids had never seemed so heavy as in August—that is, while Badoglio was in power.

It was finally decided to set up the various ministries of the newly declared Italian Social Republic in any of the small towns around Lake Garda where buildings were available. The

Italian Social Republic later became better known as the Salò Republic, since the foreign ministry was situated in the village of Salò.

It was no easy task to form the new government, for my husband wanted men who were new, trustworthy—at least so we hoped—and trained in affairs of state. He finally managed to build such a staff and was glad to have Marshal Graziani as minister of war. This was the same Graziani who had assured the Duce some minutes before he left for the Villa Savoia on July 25, 1943, that he was ready to serve him. It was he, too, who had been truly responsible for victory in the Ethiopian campaign, as I've already mentioned. That he should be a member of government in the Italian Social Republic gave it considerable weight.

To keep in touch with Hitler, the Duce had the services of Rudolf Rahn, the German ambassador for political affairs, of General Wolff, commander of the SS in northern Italy for security matters, and of General Kesselring, who was to prove a worthy marshal for military operations.

One sunny afternoon in November, 1943, I arrived at Gargnano, on the shores of Lake Garda, where my husband was already staying. The countryside had something grand about it. At a bend in the road I suddenly glimpsed the lake with its shimmering surface and snowy Mount Baldo overlooking it.

We were to live in the Villa Feltrinelli, which belonged to the family of Giacomo Feltrinelli, the extremely Left-wing publisher. There was a fixed rent of eight thousand lire a month to pay, because the Duce wasn't treating the house as captured territory but was respecting other people's property. Altogether it was an attractive house, with slender colonnades and a floor of pink marble inside, surrounded by olive trees in the grounds. Yet it looked cold and sad, and I was anxious to give it more warmth and welcome just as I had for the Villa Torlonia. With the help of some faithful Romagnole friends who would have stayed with me at the gates of hell, we transformed the Villa Feltrinelli into a real home, which was just what Benito needed to keep his sanity.

While it wasn't hard to do the decorating and rearrange the interior, it was quite another matter to persuade the officials and soldiers to decamp. I should say, in their defense, that the Villa Feltrinelli had originally been intended to house both the private residence of the Duce and the offices of the head of government and chief of state, since Mussolini held both these positions in the Italian Social Republic. And after the Duce's arrest on July 25, 1943, Hitler's orders were extremely strict: there was to be no chance of the Duce's being kidnapped or facing an assassination attempt. This meant that the Villa Feltrinelli was less like a home and more like a barracks and a ministry, with all the military and official comings and goings.

I went straight to work on the task of freeing our domestic life from official interference too. My husband helped me a great deal, for he didn't particularly like all the measures taken for his security. In less than a month we got the offices moved to another building, the Villa Orsolina. Then the officers and men of the SS went elsewhere. Soon the Duce's guard was reduced to about thirty men, some of the best fighters in Romagna and a small unit of SS. The Germans also had to leave because Benito considered it a point of honor that only Italians should protect him. The only people I couldn't get rid of at once were some SS officers who were under orders to protect the actual person of the Duce. Admittedly, they were faultless in their behavior toward my family, but they were so suspicious. More than once our maid, Maria, had the fright of her life, when she realized there was someone behind her. It was one of the SS who, following her like a shadow, left her only when she went into our private apartments or into the kitchen. Finally, I appealed to the Duce, and before this surveillance came to a halt, he had to tell General Wolff that he trusted our staff completely and wanted them left alone.

And so our daily life at Gargnano gradually fell into shape.

My husband resumed the precise and organized work patterns that he'd followed in Rome, and his daily schedule was still equally full. He divided his day among the Villa Feltrinelli, where we were living, the Villa Torlonia in Gargnano, and the Villa Orsolina, where he housed all the offices of the presidency of the Italian Social Republic, a state that he had to piece together himself.

Without going into great detail, I can say that my husband had first to put together all the machinery of this state, obviously on a smaller scale than when he was ruling the whole of Italy except Rome. Yet the Italian Social Republic was possibly even more important, seeing that it included the largest industrial plants and most of the economic activity vital for the whole country.

But the Italian Social Republic had no flag, no uniforms, no constitutional structure. Everything had to be started from scratch. Designed by Vittorio and some friends, the new flag used the green, white, and red of the traditional Italian flag but replaced the arms of the House of Savoy with an eagle holding the fasces in its claws. During the first few months the soldiers chose their uniform themselves—a practice that gave the army of the Italian Social Republic both color and a whimsical effect. This diversity was also brought into line, however, and before long there was a uniform common to all.

Some tidying up was imperative on the political side. From the beginning, everyone agreed on the need for a constituent assembly, but my husband postponed any meeting, claiming that the Italian Social Republic ought first to take its place in the theater of military operations. "What we need are fewer words and more action, and we ought to be doing more fighting than parleying," he once declared.

An army of 500,000 men was assembled, and by September, 1944, the Italian war effort on the German side amounted to 786,000, including men-at-arms and paramilitary workers serving with the Todt organization for defense engineering. In addition, there were several squadrons of fighter and bomber planes, and the submarine base of Bordeaux, which the Italian navy had retained. Small, fast, and efficient boats for chase and surprise operations completed our arsenal. Finally, there was the Decima MAS, famous for its sabotage activities under the command of Valerio Borghese, which was a constant source of anxiety to the Allied general staffs. I should also mention that factories like Fiat, which were making trucks, continued to supply vehicles that the Germans used to great advantage.

All this meant that the Italian Social Republic was not the puppet state that enemy propaganda took such delight in ridiculing. If that had been the case, the Italian front would never have held for six hundred days.

My husband was particularly keen to reform the army into an efficient fighting machine, because he had not forgotten a hurtful comment of Marshal Keitel: "The only Italian army that can't fail the Reich is one that doesn't exist." But in 1943 the Duce found himself in a paradoxical situation. Up to that year he'd had to battle with the royalist Italian generals to force through his ideas for modernizing the army, but now that he no longer had this problem, he had to contend with the German general staff. After the betrayal of July, 1943, they were reluctant to have anything to do with an Italian army of some size, making no attempt to conceal their suspicion and their desire to act in isolation, without any concern for Italian sovereignty. More than once the Duce had to intervene personally so that the Italians would not have to tolerate the ignominy of the presence of German forces in their midst.

From September, 1943, until 1945, Benito Mussolini took a solitary stand against the generals, the diplomats, and the Führer's closest advisers; he was determined to drive home his viewpoint and prevent what would otherwise have been an inevitable clash between the Italian forces of the Social Republic and the Germans. Luckily, Hitler's friendship and esteem and the German generals' trust enabled Benito to avoid this calamity.

The Duce had to heal the wounds inflicted by the sense-
less armistice that the King and Badoglio, shirking their responsibilities and feeling no concern for those who hadn't
sheltered with them behind Eisenhower's guns, had handed to
the Allies. I'm proud to say that because of my husband's skill,
the territories controlled by the Social Republic never had to
use the "mark of occupation," whereas the Americans distributed large amounts of "Am-lire," or American lire, in the
Italian zones that they occupied. Furthermore, there was no
inflation in the Salò Republic; goods were cheaper in the north
than in the "liberated" areas; and the government of the Italian
Social Republic repaid a huge loan contracted before July, 1943.
Faithful to his principles, my husband paid off his debts even
when they no longer concerned him. Anyone who doubts my
words has merely to consult the archives—that is, if they
haven't been hidden away by people trying to disprove that
Mussolini served some purpose to the end.

Meanwhile, there was our ordinary family life. That, too,
returned to a normal routine, less frenetic and more intimate
than in Rome, if only because we were geographically and
spiritually closer to each other. As at the Villa Torlonia in Rome,
I set up my farmyard and my rabbit hutch, and even bought
a cow that supplied milk to others as well as my family. Our
children and grandchildren soon joined us—to the great delight of Benito, who needed this family circle more than ever.

My husband had changed psychologically, chiefly as a
result of the shock of his arrest and abduction. It was not so
much his dismissal that distressed him as the vindictive treatment he'd received from generals who owed their careers to
him. When they were dragging him from one place to another,
between July and September, 1943, he had asked one of them,
"Why are you behaving like this? I've been a man who respected even his own enemies. I've turned them into senators or
found some way to show my regard for them. I've never scorned
or reviled them."

Most important of all, after July, 1943, Benito Mussolini,

my husband, thought that his star had completely faded; from that time he spoke of himself solely as *"Mussolini defunto,"* or the late Mussolini. He greatly feared German intentions for the future of Italy and was conscious that as head of the Italian Social Republic he was merely protecting the Italians from German revenge. He had accepted this buffer role—an act of sacrifice so that he could at least leave something positive to his successors after he had gone.

Generally speaking, surely he—and no one else—drafted the birth certificate for the present Italian republic. On November 15, 1943, when my husband drew up an eighteen-point manifesto with social measures that were later christened the "social storehouse," nobody could accuse him of acting in his personal interest. As in the early days when he expressed his Socialist beliefs, he dreamed of founding a popular state that was truly Socialist but of a socialism different from the chameleon one sees today.

He sold his newspaper, which had given him impetus along the road to power, doing so because he could never have tolerated his own creation's being published under German control. Just as Mussolini felt that he had reached the end of his journey, so the *Popolo d'Italia* had to close its doors. I didn't hear about the sale until it was accomplished, for Benito, aware that I, too, would be sad, didn't wish to talk about it beforehand. In the main, the money that he realized was shared among the children and the family, but part of it was used to defray his debts to people who had worked on the *Popolo d'Italia.*

That completed, Benito began to write *Storia di un anno,* a historical account of one year from November, 1942, to November, 1943, as well as articles for various newspapers; briefly, toward the end of his life, my husband returned to his first love: journalism.

At home his favorite recreations were cycling and reading and playing with the children. Even the noise that they made, which had once annoyed him, was now a source of amusement.

The great change that came over my husband left him indifferent to the material things of this world, more sociable,
more human than before, more kind in his relations with the
people he saw.

25/The Moment of Sacrifice

Though neither Benito nor I suspected it, the Christmas of 1944 was to be our last Christmas together. Benito was now particularly relaxed—perhaps because of his pending meeting in Milan about a proposed transfer of the Salò Republic to the Italian Socialist Party in that city.

Four months later the inevitable happened. I don't know why, but when my husband left for Milan on April 17, 1945, I felt that this separation would be unlike the rest. I had urged him to stay at Gargnano, and so had an SS officer, but he refused to go back on the decision he'd reached.

To calm me, he said, "I'll be back in two or three days," adding that he had to make some very important decisions in Milan; he mentioned Cardinal Schuster.

I still recall his departure on that April day. It was early evening. We were standing by his car, which he was about to enter, when suddenly he turned around, stared at me for a while, then walked back to the house. From the top of the steps he looked out over the garden and the calm blue waters of Lake Garda, then raised his head toward the window of his room and listened for some moments to Romano playing the piano in the drawing room.

Then, as if he regretted having yielded to a moment of weakness, he strode toward the car, banged the door, and said to the driver, "Let's be off, we're late." Behind him two escort cars revved up.

That was the last time I saw my husband alive.

For me the end of Benito Mussolini's life consisted of a short letter, a whirl of events which lasted four days, and, the day before his death, a voice full of emotion—his voice— saying, "I must follow my destiny, Rachele. You must start your life again."

After he left, on April 17, I received no news until the twenty-third, when he phoned, explaining that he would be back at about seven that evening. Some hours later he phoned again, saying that he couldn't come home because the road from Milan to Gargnano was blocked, the Allies having occupied Mantua.

"It's not true," I shouted into the telephone. "They're lying to you again, Benito. A military truck has just arrived from Milan. I've been chatting with the soldiers myself. They didn't encounter a single obstacle on their route." Then he cut in, ordering me to leave at once for Monza, where arrangements had been made to help us.

At Monza I found Luigi Gatti, Benito's secretary, who hadn't eaten for two days, so I gave him a little chicken and a bowl of soup. Benito called me twice: first to ask me how we were, then to tell me that he couldn't join us and that we must leave for Como. It was April 24. That was the last time I heard his voice before the final telephone conversation of our life together.

I spent the twenty-fifth and twenty-six trying to reach him without ever managing to do so. I was alone with Romano and Anna-Maria, listening for the slightest noise behind the door or leaping to the window whenever the sirens began to whine.

During the night of April 26–27, I heard someone knocking on the door of the villa where we had taken refuge. It was a soldier. "I have a letter for you from the Duce," he said.

I opened the door quickly and took the envelope. I recognized his writing. "Who gave it to you?" I asked.

"His Excellency Buffarini."

Buffarini? What could he be up to now? He was no longer a minister, and since my visit to Clara Petacci I had stubbornly refused to see him. I wondered how the letter could have got into his hands.

I woke the children and we began to read the few lines he had written; from his first words an icy feeling swept over me.

"Dear Rachele," he wrote. "We may never see each other again. That is why I am sending you this letter. I ask your forgiveness for all the harm I have unwittingly done you. But you know that you have always been the only woman I have really loved. I swear it before God and our Bruno in this supreme moment. You know that I must go to make a last military stand against the partisans at Valtellina. You must try to reach the Swiss border with the children. You can make a new life for yourself there. I don't think they'll refuse to let you through, because I have always helped them, whatever the circumstances, and because you have never been involved in politics. If it isn't possible, give yourself up to the Allies. They may be more generous than the Italians. Look after Anna and Romano for me, especially Anna, who has so much need of affection. You know how I love her. Bruno will help you from heaven. Kisses to you and the children. Your Benito."

I wasn't able to keep this letter, but I remember every word, every comma. It was written in blue crayon, the signature in red. So the end had come. In less than two minutes, thirty-five years of life together had drawn to a close. No one could understand what I was feeling, and I couldn't begin to explain.

I wanted to hear his voice again—just one last time. It was too stupid to say good-bye forever in that way, both so close and so far from each other. Hoping for a miracle, I lifted the telephone, which had been dead for two days. To my joy, we had a line again. I spent half an hour trying to reach Benito, and finally I heard his voice.

"Do what I wrote to you, Rachele. It'll be much better

if you don't follow me into Valtellina. Save yourself and save the children." I felt the tears coming to my eyes, and I couldn't speak, and so I handed the receiver to Romano.

"You must be organizing some defense for yourself, at least?" Romano said. "Who is with you?"

"There's nobody any longer, Romano. I'm alone. Everything is lost."

"But where are the soldiers—your personal guard?"

"I don't know, I haven't seen anybody. Even Cesarotti the chauffeur has abandoned me. Tell Mamma that she was right not to trust him."

With the sudden realization that he would never see his father again, Romano began to sob. I therefore took the receiver from him. I would have liked to go on talking for hours, hoping that I could cheat fate of something.

"You must start a new life, Rachele. I must follow my destiny," he murmured in a muted voice. "Go, leave quickly." With that he broke off.

There is no point in dwelling on how he died. The whole world knows that the partisans shot both Benito and Clara Petacci, and then hung them both by their heels, along with other executed Fascists, in the Piazza Loreto in Milan. Hardly a month has passed over the last twenty-nine years without some fresh revelation that kills him all over again. All that remains of Mussolini is a skeleton wrapped in a cloth and crammed into a white-wood box, with the kind thoughts of numerous people all over the world to watch over his last sleep.

Some years elapsed before I was able to pray by Benito's grave, because his corpse had vanished; when it was finally returned, I discovered to my horror that the Americans had taken away half of his brain. Presumably they wanted to know what makes a dictator. I had to ask the American ambassador in Rome before I could recover this part of my husband, who had not been able to find peace even in death.

I never worry whether or not Mussolini will ever be commemorated by a statue in his own country. Such a memorial would serve no purpose, and there is something much more encouraging than a statue; that is, the memorial one leaves in men's minds. If I ever feared that all the people—however famous or insignificant—who visit the little cemetery of San Cassiano at Predappio do so out of curiosity, something that happened a few years ago would assure me that the opposite is true.

It happened in 1969. One Sunday I went to lunch with some friends in a restaurant in Milano-Maritimo, a small resort on the Adriatic. At the next table a group of men were celebrating, noisily singing songs that left no doubt as to their political ideas: they were Communists. Aware of my ready temper, my companions began to look for a place elsewhere, but I told them not to bother; it was a lovely day, I was relaxed, and I had no wish to make a scene.

We were eating the hors d'oeuvres when one of the nearby men said in a loud voice, "Even with all the ones who were killed, there are still just as many Fascists. You'll see statues going up to the glory of Mussolini before long. All things considered, we were the idiots."

I stiffened at these words. Did he know who I was? Was he trying to start a scene? In 1946, that would have been feasible; in 1969, the remark was just a stupid and unwarranted piece of provocation. Embarrassed, the waiter went over to my noisy neighbors, explaining tactfully who I was. Silence fell on the room, and while every eye was turned in my direction, a man left the table and came over to us.

"Are you Signora Mussolini?" he asked.

"Yes. Why?"

"Because I'm a former partisan."

"Well? Should that make any difference to me? Don't you know that the war is over?"

"I know, but I wanted to meet Benito Mussolini's wife."

"Well, you have. Now would you please let me eat my lunch with my friends?"

"I haven't come to annoy you, signora. On the contrary,

I want to ask your forgiveness. I was one of the Fifty-second Garibaldi Brigade."

"Ah, you were with the men who used the purge as a cover to kill women and children. Aren't you ashamed of what you did? And you have the nerve to stand here before me, Mussolini's wife!"

Trembling with suppressed rage, I nearly shouted these last words in spite of myself. I was reliving the appalling scenes I had witnessed in 1945, after my husband's death. Vivid in my mind was a young man, wounded and fleeing, shouting something about a hospital, whom I'd seen slaughtered like a beast. In normal circumstances I would never have willingly thought about that period again.

Leaning toward me, the man gently took my hand, raising it to his lips; looking me straight in the eyes, he said, "Signora, in the resistance they called me Bill. I was the one who recognized your husband in the German truck at Dongo on the way to Veltellina. It was I who made him get out, who searched him and arrested him."

My heart beat wildly. There in front of me, holding my hand, was the man who had made my husband take the first steps toward his terrible death. What a strange turn of fate to meet this man twenty-four years later! He must have been very young in 1945.

Clearly Bill wished to ease his conscience. As if he had guessed my thought, he went on, "I asked Mussolini if he had any money on him. Then he looked me straight in the face and replied in a strangely calm voice, 'You can search me, I have nothing. In the truck I've a briefcase. There isn't any money in that either, but something that may save Italy—some documents.' Signora, I went to check and it was true. Your husband was arrested. Since 1945, I haven't had any peace of mind. I can still hear his voice and see the way he looked at me. Signora Mussolini, I was eighteen. Now I'm a man, but I can't go on living until you've forgiven me. Chance has brought us together. Perhaps it's a sign of fate. Please, signora."

So in the silence of that restaurant room in Milano-

Maritimo, twenty-four years after the tragic event, I made the sign of the cross over his forehead as he leaned toward me, and forgave the man who arrested Benito Mussolini the day before his execution. What use is there in keeping hate alive? He had been eighteen. Later, I learned that the Communist Party had sent Urbano Lazzaro, called Bill, to Argentina. Victims can forgive, the victors must not forget.

Now I am eighty-three and peace prevails in my heart and soul. I have gathered my family around me, and those whose work prevents them from living under my roof come often to see me. I am a contented mother, grandmother, and great-grandmother. But at my age I expect the inevitable to happen any day. If someone asks to meet me, I answer that I can accept only for that day, since I don't know whether I shall still be here tomorrow.

That is not the opinion of my good Dr. Gentile, however. He finds me sound in wind and limb and still the same by nature. May God grant that it is so for a long while yet— not for my sake, but because every day that passes brings fresh proof that my husband was not entirely wrong.

His work still stands, whether in stone or in men's minds, and an increasing number of people are discovering that, basically, Mussolini did more for his country than all his successors. This is some comfort to lighten my old age.

I am certainly not commenting as a Fascist, for even when Benito was at the height of his glory I always thought of myself as an Italian first, and then as a Fascist. And today my position remains the same; I am Italian first and foremost.

So what can an Italian hope for? To live as long as possible to see her country strong, happy, and peaceful.

I would have been so glad if the Italians and their leaders had said to themselves after the war, "Well, all that is over now. Let us respect the dead, but let us ensure that the living may benefit from their good and generous example." Instead, the political parties saw fit to continue widening the gap that was already dividing the Italians. Rather than make roads, build houses, and put the economy back onto its feet, they allowed the situation to deteriorate; a bid for popularity ruined everything. It is so bad that now, in 1974, Italians have to resort to a medieval system of private messengers to send a letter, rather than entrust it to the postal service. Do otherwise, and the letter has one chance in a hundred of reaching its destination if a strike breaks out.

So to everyone of whatever age who comes to see me, or writes to me, or seeks advice, or complains about the present situation, I say, "Think first of your country. You must love Italy as if she were your own mother. We're always ready to run down our country, but when we're far away we miss her and think her the loveliest in the world."

To all of them, to the young people who are inspired by generous and impetuous ideals, I, Mussolini's wife, say, "Don't forget that everything you do, you must do for your country, because your country is your family—is yourself."

To the rulers of Italy, whoever they are—Leone, Andreotti, Fanfani, and so on, all of whom I knew in their youth—I say, "Be generous, be ready to forgive. Bring unity to the Italians and don't let them tear each other to pieces. The Italian is a great, big, well-meaning baby, but he doesn't like to be made a fool of."

Of the leaders of the political parties—Left wing, extreme Left wing, Right wing, or Center—I ask that they should give a little more thought to Italy, which needs all its energies to confront a world that has lost all sense of morality and respect for the human being.

I beg the parents not to stand aside. They are the foundations of society, for they support the first steps of their children. If children are never given this guidance, they will grow twisted, like untended trees.

If I want to live a little longer, it is because I can see the gradual realization of this marvelous dream. It was also the dream of Benito Mussolini, my husband.

That is why I do not regret the life I lived by his side.

Chronology

July 29, 1883	Benito Mussolini born in the district of Dovia, commune of Predappio, province of Forlì, Italy.
1901	Received normal school diploma.
February, 1902	Went to teach elementary school in Gualtieri, Emilia.
July, 1902–April, 1904	Emigrated to Switzerland. Began career as Socialist agitator. In March, 1904, played a leading role at the Zürich conference of Italian Socialists in Switzerland. In April, 1904, expelled from Geneva for traveling on false passport.
1905–1906	Performed compulsory military service in Italy.
1906–1907	Taught elementary school at Tolmezzo.
March–June, 1908	Taught high school at Oreglia.
November, 1908	Served short prison sentence for Socialist agitation in Forlì.
1909	Spent eight months in Trent, in Austria-Hungary, as a Socialist journalist and agitator. Expelled from Trent in September. Returned to Forlì.
January, 1910	Appointed secretary of Forlì section of the Italian Socialist Party. Founded and became

	editor of a party weekly, *Lotta di Classe*. Began living with Rachele Guidi.
September 1, 1910	Daughter Edda born to Mussolini and Rachele Guidi.
1911–1912	Served five months in prison for agitating against Italo-Turkish war.
July, 1912	Made member of the executive committee of the Italian Socialist Party.
December 1, 1912	Appointed editor of *Avanti!*, daily paper of the Italian Socialist Party, published at Milan.
October, 1913	Defeated as Socialist candidate for Parliament.
July–October, 1914	Exhorted Socialist Party to adopt policy of "relative" neutrality of Italy in the Great War.
October 19–20, 1914	Executive committee of Socialist Party—predominantly pacifist—refused to accept "relative" neutrality formula. Mussolini fired by *Avanti!*
November 15, 1914	Founded *Popolo d'Italia*, a daily paper published in Milan, advocating Italy's intervention in the Great War on the side of the Allies, against Germany and Austria.
November 29, 1914	Expelled from Socialist Party.
April, 1915	Dueled with pacifist Socialist Party deputy Claudio Treves.
May, 1915	Italy declared war on Austria-Hungary.
September, 1915	Mussolini called up and sent to the front. Private in the Bersaglieri.
November, 1915	Son Benito Albino born to Mussolini and Ida Dalser.
December, 1915	Civil marriage to Rachele Guidi.
August, 1916	Italy declared war on Germany.
September, 1916	Son Vittorio born to Benito and Rachele Mussolini.
February 23, 1917	Severely wounded during trench mortar practice. After hospitalization returned to editing *Popolo d'Italia*.
April 22, 1918	Son Bruno born to Benito and Rachele Mussolini.

March 23, 1919	Created Fascist movement in Milan, the Fasci di combattimento. Called for a constituent assembly, the abolition of the senate, and workers' control of factories.
September, 1919–1920	Supported D'Annunzio's occupation of Fiume.
November, 1919	Defeated as a Fascist candidate for parliamentary seat representing Milan.
May 15, 1921	Elected deputy (*onorevole*) of Parliament. Thirty-five other Fascists also elected to Parliament.
August 2, 1921	Signed truce between Socialists and Fascists.
November 21, 1921	Congress of Rome: organization of Fascist movement into a political party called Partito Nazionale Fascista.
February 6, 1922	Election of Pope Pius XI
August, 1922	General strike staged in Italy by the trade-union council, the Socialist Party, and the railwaymen's union. Strike broken by Fascist armed guards.
October 24, 1922	Fascist convention at Naples. Threatened Fascist March on Rome to signify Fascist intention to take over government and restore order to society.
October 27, 1922	The cabinet led by Luigi Facta resigned. Beginning of Fascist mobilization for March on Rome.
October 28, 1922	March on Rome.
October 30, 1922	Mussolini received by King Victor Emmanuel III.
October 31, 1922	Mussolini formed cabinet. Became prime minister as well as minister of interior and minister of foreign affairs.
November 25, 1922	Chamber of Deputies granted vast powers to Mussolini ministry.
January 12, 1923	Fascist Grand Council created.
August, 1923	Ordered occupation and then evacuation of Greek island of Corfu.

January, 1924	Italy annexed Fiume by treaty with Yugoslavia.
June 10, 1924	Fascists murdered Socialist deputy Giacomo Matteotti.
January 3, 1925	Established full dictatorship.
December 29, 1925	Religious marriage to Rachele.
1926	Three attempts to assassinate Mussolini.
November 6, 1926	All opposition to Fascist rule prohibited.
April 7, 1927	Established protectorate over Albania.
September 26, 1927	Son Romano born to Benito and Rachele Mussolini.
1928	Fascist Grand Council made a constitutional organ. Parliamentary government ended.
February 11, 1929	Signed Lateran Treaties signifying conciliation between Italy and the Holy See.
September 3, 1929	Daughter Anna-Maria born to Rachele.
April 24, 1930	Daughter Edda married to Galeazzo Ciano.
June, 1934	Mussolini met Hitler in Venice. Nazis assassinated Ernst Röhm.
July 25, 1934	Germans assassinated Austrian Chancellor Engelbert Dollfuss. Mussolini sent troops to the Austrian border to express his opposition to the Anschluss, Germany's intention to annex Austria.
1935–1936	Ethiopian War: Italy's conquest of Ethiopia in defiance of League of Nations sanctions.
May 2, 1936	Creation of Empire after Ethiopian War. Victor Emmanuel III named emperor of Ethiopia.
1936–1939	Hitler and Mussolini gave military aid to Franco in Spanish Civil War. Commitment to halt the advance of communism.
September, 1937	Visited Hitler in Vienna.
March, 1938	Abandoned stance against the Anschluss. Allowed Hitler to annex Austria.

May, 1938	Hitler visited Mussolini in Italy. Two leaders agreed on aggressive policy.
July, 1938	Laws against Jews in Italy.
September, 1938	Hitler (Germany), Mussolini (Italy), Chamberlain (England), and Daladier (France) signed Munich Pact, giving Czechoslovakia to Germany as of October 10, in an attempt to forestall major war.
December 6, 1938	France and Germany signed nonaggression pact.
January 11, 1939	Received Neville Chamberlain and Lord Halifax, who thus endorsed the British government's recognition of the Italian Empire. Last public show of peace.
March 23, 1939	Inaugurated the Chamber of Fasci and Corporations, replacing Parliament.
April, 1939	Italy occupied Albania.
May 22, 1939	Pact of Steel. Mussolini signed aggressive military alliance with Germany.
August 23, 1939	Nazi-Soviet nonaggression pact.
September, 1939	German invasion of Poland. Britain and France declared war on Germany. Italy declared policy of nonbelligerence.
November, 1939	Soviet army attacked Finland.
February, 1940	Received Sumner Welles, envoy from President Roosevelt.
March 18, 1940	Hitler and Mussolini met at the Brenner Pass.
June 10, 1940	Italy entered war on German side. Declared war against France and Britain. Mussolini took over supreme command of Italian forces and launched invasion of France.
June 18, 1940	Met Hitler in Munich.
June 24, 1940	France signed armistice.
Autumn, 1940	Italy attacked Greece and suffered defeat.
October 4, 1940	Galeazzo Ciano and Mussolini met Hitler on the Brenner Pass.
October 28, 1940	Hitler met Mussolini in Florence.
January 19–20, 1941	Summoned by Hitler to the Berghof.

June 22, 1941	Germany declared war on Russia.
1941	Italian east African empire overrun by Britain, and Italy's influence in Balkans replaced by Germany's.
July 22, 1942	Spent month on north African front.
February 5, 1943	Reshuffled Italian government in response to evident dissension.
April 7, 1943	Met Hitler at Salzburg.
July 10, 1943	Anglo-American landings on Sicily.
July 19, 1943	Met Hitler at Feltre.
July 23–24, 1943	Fascist Grand Council repudiated Mussolini's leadership. Marshal Pietro Badoglio named head of government.
July 25, 1943	Arrested by supporters of the King and the Badoglio government.
September 3, 1943	Allied troops landed in "boot" of southern Italy. National Liberation Committee formed in Rome.
September 8, 1943	Badoglio announced armistice with Allies and declared war against Germany.
September 12–13, 1943	Rescued from Gran Sasso by Germans. Returned to northern Italy.
September 15, 1943	Proclaimed Italian Social Republic (Salò Republic).
January, 1944	Had his son-in-law Galeazzo Ciano and other Fascist rebels executed after a mock trial at Verona.
July 20, 1944	In Berlin for last meeting with Hitler.
April 25, 1945	Mussolini negotiated with the National Liberation Committee in Milan to turn Salò Republic over to Italian Socialist Party. Germany completed separate agreement to turn Italy over to Allies. Victory for partisans.
April 26, 1945	Mussolini and Clara Petacci arrested by partisans.
April 28, 1945	Mussolini and Clara Petacci executed by partisans.

Index